How to Build
FORD RESTOMOD
Street Machines

Classic Looks with Modern Performance!

TONY E. HUNTIMER

CarTech®
Auto Books & Manuals

Edited By Travis Thompson

ISBN-13 978-1-932494-03-7
ISBN-10 1-932494-03-0

Order No. SA101

Printed in China

CarTech®, Inc.,
39966 Grand Avenue
North Branch, MN 55056
Telephone (651) 277-1200 • (800) 551-4754 • Fax: (651) 277-1203
www.cartechbooks.com

OVERSEAS DISTRIBUTION BY:

Brooklands Books Ltd.
P.O. Box 146, Cobham, Surrey, KT11 1LG, England
Telephone 01932 865051 • Fax 01932 868803
www.brooklands-books.com

Brooklands Books Aus.
3/37-39 Green Street, Banksmeadow, NSW 2109, Australia
Telephone 2 9695 7055 • Fax 2 9695 7355

Front Cover: Tate Walthalls Mustang isn't your average fastback. It features a built 351W, a Viper 6-speed, and big Baer brakes all around. Some of the modifications are subtle, but this car really stands out in a crowd.

Inset Left: This Torino sees street time, as well as frequent track time at open-track road-course events. The owner is a member of the Norcal Shelby Club. The red Torino feels right at home with the Cobras and Shelby Mustangs.

Inset Middle: The healthy 351W was already in place. The owner added A TCP Tower Brace kit to strengthen the front unibody structure. The modified Shelby hood scoop feeds directly into the top of the K&N air filter.

Inset Right: Derrick Yee is a big fan of the Ford Maverick. As you can see, his passion for them is shown by this great example of an out of ordinary Restomod. The lack of bumper guards and the prominent carbon-fiber hood give this Maverick a powerful look. (Photo Courtesy Phil Royle)

Title Page: Martin Pond taking the line in turn 11 at Infineon Raceway with his '71 Torino GT. For more details on this street and track driven Restomod, turn to page 124.

Back Cover, Upper Right: This front suspension is a mix of off-the-shelf stock-car racing parts and custom fabricated and machined parts. Suspension analysis software and experience were combined to pull off this feat. Even the frame is completely fabricated. (Photo Courtesy John Parsons, Photography by John Ulaszek)

Back Cover, Lower Left: Just because a car didn't come from the factory with a certain engine as an option, doesn't mean you can't make the swap. Probably the most labor-intensive engine swap is putting a 4.6- or 5.4-liter Modular engine into a shock-tower-equipped Restomod, because the shock towers have to be modified. (Photo Courtesy The Mustang Shop)

Back Cover, Lower Right: Your Restomod can hold its fuel in a small, stock fuel tank, or for more mileage you can install a larger aftermarket fuel tank or fuel cell. Rock Valley makes stainless fuel tanks for Restomods. The fuel cell in this Year One-built Mustang is from Fuel Safe.

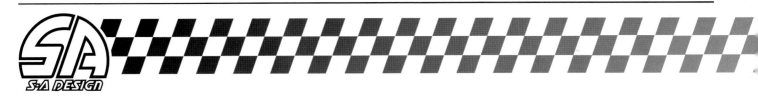

Introduction: **Restomod: The Term** 5

Chapter 1: **General Suspension, Brakes, Tires, and Wheels** **12**
Shock Absorbers .12
Sway Bars .13
Bushings .15
Handling – Understeer and Oversteer . .16
Why Upgrade Brakes? 17
Brake Parts .18
Factory Interchange 18
Aftermarket Brake Upgrades 22
Brake Cooling 23
Boosting Brakes 24
Balancing a Braking System 24
Tires 26
Wheels 26
Fitting Tires and Wheels 27

Chapter 2: **Front Suspension and Steering . . .28**
Alignment 28
Bumpsteer .32
Control Arms and Front
Suspension Kits 34
Springs 39
Ball Joints 40
Steering 41
Power Steering Pumps 44
Rack-and-Pinion Steering 46

Chapter 3: **Rear Suspension** **50**
Pinion Angle 50
Universal Joints 54
Leaf Springs 54
Coil Springs 58
Link/Bar Suspensions 59
Independent Rear Suspension 63

Chapter 4: **Frames** **65**
Frame Types 65
Body Bushings 66
Subframe Connectors 66
Front Support Systems 69

Full-Frame Modifications 70
Rear Frame Rail Tricks 71
Roll Bars and Roll Cages 74
Tubbing 78

Chapter 5: **Engines** **79**
Engine Swaps 79
2.0 and 2.3-Liter 4-Cylinder Engine . . .79
Ford V-8s 81
Engine Swapping Parts 84
Engine Parts 85
Cooling System 87
Oiling System 94
Induction and Fuel Systems 97

Chapter 6: **Drivetrain** **104**
Manual Transmissions 104
Automatic Transmissions 110
Transmission Coolers 112
Rear Ends .112
Differentials 112
Gear Ratios 113

Chapter 7: **Body and Electrical** **114**
Stock Body 114
Custom Bodywork 114
Fiberglass .116
Spoilers, Air Dams, and Body Mods . .118
Aerodynamics 120
Safety Upgrades 122
Charging System 127
Basic Electrical and Wiring 128
Interior 130
Air Conditioning 133

Chapter 8: **Buying Parts and Finding
Information** **135**
Purchasing Parts 135
Purchasing Cars 137
Getting Information 140

Appendix A: **Source Guide** **143**

Acknowledgements

For some extra technical help, I enlisted a few professionals (and friends) as contributors. Vince Asaro is a professional builder, fabricator, and racer. Paul Caselas is a fuel system specialist, engine specialist/builder, and racer. Kevin Long is a builder, tire and wheel specialist, and racer. Matthew Pankau, a designer, builder, and racer, helped with his vast knowledge of Fords and suspension systems. Kyle Tucker is an ex-GM suspension engineer, builder/fabricator, designer, racer, and holds a mechanical engineering degree from University of Missouri-Rolla. Thanks guys!

Special thanks (in no particular order) goes out to my wife, Vikki Huntimer for the support and sticking by me, Travis Thompson, Steve Hendrickson, Maureen and Robert Cera, Randy Oldham, Steve D'Aurora, Mark Schwartz, Kyle and Stacy Tucker, Mark Deshetler, Mark Stielow, Lindsay Jones, Vic DeLeon, Kevin Stearns, Ray Barney, Nick Kikes, Joe Pettitt, John Parsons, Larry Callahan, Ken Sink, Lee Grimes, Cam Douglass, Rick Love, David Barker, Andrew Borodin, Steve Chryssos, Johnny Hunkins, Preston Peterson, Kevin Sittner, Derrick Yee, Larry Erickson, Kevin Doyle, Angela and Matthew Pankau, Jim Smart, Jeff Ford, Ron Bramlett, Slim and Yetta Huntimer, John and Rebecca Litteral, and Elliot Franklin.

About the Author

Tony Huntimer has been into hot-rodding since he was old enough to build model cars. In high school, his friends, Chris Mead, Ed Matthews, and Chris Fogarty, were driving hot-rodded American iron while he was interested in VWs. Finally, at the age of 19, he purchased his first V-8 muscle car and has been sold on them ever since.

After graduating high school, Tony earned his living as a mechanic. For five years he was able to gain first-hand knowledge of how Detroit designed and engineered their chassis, bodies, and interiors. This was a huge influence on how he builds his own cars, as you will see in this book.

In 1999, Tony began navigating for Karl Chicca and his 1969 Camaro in the Pony Express open road race. The following year, Karl and Tony took first place in the Pony Express 140-mph class, with an average speed of 139.985 mph. Tony became interested in what it takes to modify a car for speed and handling. It wasn't long before he was racing his own car in open-track events alongside Chicca.

Tony's writing career really got started in 2004 when his first technical book, *How to Build and Modify GM Pro-Touring Street Machines*, was published by CarTech Books. Since then, he has written for *Popular Hot Rodding* and *Drive* magazine.

INTRODUCTION
RESTOMOD: THE TERM

If there was a single Hollywood car that created a generation of die-hard Ford enthusiasts, it was Steve McQueen's Mustang in Bullitt. Eleanor, the fastback Mustang from the recent remake of the 1974 film, Gone in 60 Seconds, has really helped fuel the Restomod fire.

When and where did the term Restomod come to exist? Jim Smart, Senior Editor of *Mustangs & Fords Magazine* (along with many other job titles), came up with the term. He wrote, "The term 'Restomod' kind of fell out of my head and into the computer back in 1995. Ron Bramlett of Mustangs Plus and I were trying to come up with a term for the renewed modification movement with classic Mustangs. The term 'restification' just didn't do it for me. Restomod seemed to embody both modified and stock—keeping the classic lines while making these cars better and safer." It's "restoration" and "modification" combined as one word. Jim also stated, "The classic Mustang movement had been about concours restored cars through the 1980s. When the early 1990s rolled around, people were burning out on the 'restored to stock' routine. Peo-ple were bored. The hobby needed a shot in the arm." In the beginning, Restomod was used for restored cars with bolt-on parts. That way, the cars could easily be returned to stock form if and when the owner wished. Since then, Restomod cars have taken a turn toward even higher levels of performance and safety; it was a turn that required more serious modifications. For all intents and purposes, this book is geared

Building a high-powered Ford that's good at more than going in a straight line isn't a new idea. Some say this 1965 Galaxie is one of the Holman & Moody stock cars with a chassis that was so well-engineered, aspects of its design were the industry standard for about 15 years. This wasn't the first or last car to tear up straight and curvy tracks.

Some Restomods meld track-proven parts and theory from modern-day stock cars. These particular cars are racing on the Infineon (previously named Sears Point) Raceway road course, so they are built for right and left turns, unlike their twins that only turn one direction on high-speed ovals.

toward that higher level of performance, so many of the parts and modifications are a little more invasive than simple bolt-ons.

The definition of a Restomod is open to quite a bit of interpretation. Many enthusiasts have their own ideas about what it actually is, and the level of performance that coincides with it. Restomod is one of the many labels given to Ford enthusiasts for their road/rally-styled street vehicles. Other terms that aren't as popular with the Ford enthusiasts, but describe the same kind of build-style, are Pro-Touring, G-Machine, Turn-n-Burn, Retro Mod, etc. Each term is subjective and can be interpreted differently, but in the end they all mean the same thing: updating your ride so it can accelerate faster, handle better, and be more drivable than the factory engineers ever imagined.

History

When did Fords start getting turned into Restomods? Well, this kind of car existed before the term did. Ford enthusiasts have been leaning toward this build style for a long time. It all started with hot rodding, which has been around since the invention of the automobile. Probably the most influential muscle car-era Ford hot rod was the Highland Green 1968 Mustang driven by Steve McQueen in the 1968 film *Bullitt*. That car gets people's hearts pumping, and it has been called the catalyst for keeping the Mustang so popular after 40 years. Of course, Ford's effort to dominate every facet of motorsports in the 1960s and 1970s helped, too. Ford fanatics are also influenced by the entire line of testosterone-dripping Shelbys. Most recently, Restomodding has been fueled by the fictitious Eleanor, a 1967 Mustang Fastback made famous for its role in *Gone in 60 Seconds* (a remake of the 1974 movie by the same title). Since then, Troy Trapanier and EBay hooked up to build a '67 Mustang Fastback, named *Fastforward Fastback*. These cars and others have helped fuel the Restomod fire and bring it to where it is today.

Racing Roots

When it comes to the racing roots of Restomod, you'll need to look at many different types of motorsports. You will find influences of Trans-Am, dry lakes racing, high-speed open-road racing, NASCAR (and early stock car racing), Formula-1, drag racing, and rally racing, to name a few. Automotive manufacturers have been influencing Restomods for quite some time, too. American manufacturers were turning out some serious perfomers in the mid to late 1960s and early 1970s. Due to the oil crisis, manufacturers took a break from "real" performance beginning around 1973. Detroit started building performance-minded cars again in the mid 1980s. The 1985 Mustang GT came equipped with a V-8 that finally broke the 200-horsepower mark. It took a few more years for some serious performance numbers to come from factory Mustangs and Thunderbirds.

For years, Europeans have been building performance cars that handle extremely well, but putting a Ferrari or Lamborghini drivetrain and suspension in your Falcon or Torino might be outside the average budget. Since Restomods are supposed to get up and go, as well as handle like late-model performance cars, look high and low for engineering and design ideas on late-model Fords and other vehicles. Late-model American cars have powertrains and suspension systems far superior to those engineered for 1960s and 1970s Fords, so they're a great place to get ideas and parts for Restomod build-ups. Performance has many faces, so you never know when or where a new idea will be presented to you. Keep your eyes and your mind open.

Restomods are heavily influenced by early Trans Am and SCCA racecars. This original Hertz SCCA B-Production Mustang is owned by Chad Raynal, and it still commands respect on the track, just as it did back in the 1960s. (Photo Courtesy John Hansen)

What is a Restomod?

Patrick Schatz wrote, "Restomod is simply that, a restored classic refinished back to or above that of its original luster, with a modified chassis, drivetrain, and interior thus bringing your classic up to or near today's handling, power and comfort demands, and standards of today's contemporary sport/touring car or truck."

This book bends the rules on the term Restomod. It takes Restomods to the next level… well, actually, it takes it to many new levels. Be warned: Read this book with an open mind; you shall be rewarded with new drive and ambition to build your Restomod to be more powerful and capable than you had ever imagined.

To further enforce these statements on Restomods, I compiled the following question-and-answer section. These answers are compiled from the collective views of people close to the Restomod build style, in one form or another. Of course, this doesn't set strict guidelines in stone. The answers are basically the popular opinion at the time this book was written.

Q. Is there a cut-off year that a car must fall before or after to be considered a Restomod?

A. This is a controversial issue with Restomod folks. Take a car that handled like a candy bar in a punch bowl and make it handle like it's on rails – that's what makes a Restomod. A car like Eric Pogue's street/autocross 5.0 Mustang Notch would be considered a Restomod. It was originally equipped with better suspension geometry than other

Don't forget to look for styling and engineering ideas from modern super cars like this Ferrari Enzo. It drives and rides like a slightly tamed racecar. Don't overlook building materials and aerodynamics, either.

Drag cars don't handle well on corners, but they definitely have chassis stiffening and some power parts that can be worked into your Restomod. (Photo courtesy Aeromotive and Steve Matusek)

This chopped and slammed Starliner built by Andre's Customs for Kevin Grani shows that pre-muscle-car-era cars can also be Restomods. It's equipped with big Baer disc brakes, Wurth-it rack-and-pinion steering, and other modifications. (Photo Courtesy Kevin Grani)

Late-model Mustang handling is on a completely different level than the handling of a '65 Mustang. With the extensive modifications done to improve this Mustang's performance, it could be considered a Restomod. (Photo courtesy of Eric Progue)

Trever Cornwell's '79 Ford Fairmont fits the Restomod bill, but it wasn't exactly a canyon carver when it rolled off the dealer lot. Suspension and brake upgrades modernize the handling characteristics, and boosted 4.6-liter power is the next step. (Photo courtesy Trever Cornwell)

production cars of its time, but the tire and wheel combo is better than the original rolling stock. It's equipped with upgraded Baer brakes, larger sway bars, weld-in subframe connectors, a roll cage, upgraded shocks and struts, and a strut-tower brace. Although the Mustang was factory equipped with a decent suspension, it has been highly modified to improve the all-around driving experience. That's what makes it a Restomod.

Scott Chamberlain's '85 LTD is a late-model car that didn't handle or brake well when it left the factory. It's definitely considered a Restomod, with its upgraded engine, front and rear suspension, brakes, transmission, tires, and wheels. Of course, Restomodding also applies to cars built much earlier, due to the relatively inferior engineering (compared to nowadays) that went into cars like '71 Mavericks, '68 Galaxie 500s, and '63 Falcons. Even cars like Kevin Grani's '60 Starliner and Summit Racing's small-block-Chevy-powered '32 Ford Quadra Duece are considered Restomods. So, no, there isn't really a limit by year.

Q. Can an import car be considered Restomod?

A. Yes. Australian Fords are great candidates. I've also seen some early 1970s Datsun 240Zs that are Restomod/Pro-Touring cars. Cars like Lamborghini and Ferrari would be hard to improve to Restomod status, since they have been advanced in their designs for so long. For the most part, Restomodding is limited to American auto manufacturers. However, like most trends, the Restomod build style will bleed over into other markets.

Q. Does the car need to be lowered?

A. Part of the Restomod look is the lowered stance. Stance is everything! Besides, lowering your car usually gives you a lower center of gravity and helps your car handle better. In most cases, if you made a bunch of improvements to your car but left it stock height, the higher center of gravity would decrease the effectiveness of the other modifica-tions. However, you don't have to be scraping on every dip in the road or speed bump. A car that is too low is defeating one of the main purposes of building a Restomod: They are meant to be driven on the street, and hopefully on a road course. A car with an extremely low stance may look great, but it's not always practical, safe, or better for handling. A car can be so low that its suspension geometry is adversely affected.

Q. Is there a minimum wheel and tire size?

Here are some different examples of brakes. The photo on the left shows a front drum brake. Drum brakes are ineffective for stopping a car with added horsepower. They fade fast when used on a road course, especially on the front wheels. Front drum brakes are considered outdated technology. The middle photo is of a stock disc brake. This is more than adequate for most Restomod applications. The photo on the right shows a Brembo caliper and slotted rotor. Aftermarket parts like these are necessary on aggressive cars that have extreme power-to-weight ratios. The faster a car can go from zero to 100 mph, the faster it should go back down from 100 mph to zero.

Even imports can be Restomods, but this isn't your average import. It's a mid-1970s XB 351GT, shipped to the U.S. by California Image U.S.A. The company ships Australian cars to America and vice-versa.

A. Like all the other aspects of building a Restomod, you need a complete package, not just big wheels and tires. Restomodding is about appearance *and* the pursuit of better handling. Most people would think it is necessary to have at least a 16-inch wheel-and-tire combination, but for some cars, 15-inch wheels are an upgrade. Technology has come so far in the last 15 years. Tire and wheel manufacturers are focusing on large-diameter tires and the growing market for them. As of the writing of this book, 22-inch wheels and tires are readily available, and 26-inch wheels and tires are starting to show up for SUVs. Who knows if they will start showing up on Restomods? A large-diameter wheel-and-tire package not only gives the illusion of a smaller car, but it also allows for the lowered look without drastically

When achieving the perfect stance, make sure you don't go lower than the highest speed bump in your town. You want to be able to drive your Restomod. This slammed 1969 Mustang was built by David McMillan and driven in Hot Rod Magazine's 2004 Power Tour. It was just right for the type of driving David was doing.

Fuel injection like this set-up on Jim Sheren's supercharged 460-powered Fairmont is nice, but it's not necessary for a Restomod to have an elaborate fuel injection set-up. Jim hand-built the awesome and effective aluminum intake manifold. A mild, carbureted performance engine is just as acceptable as a fancy, fuel-injected big-block. (Photo courtesy www.toohighpsi.com via Jim Sheren)

lowering the car past the effectiveness of the suspension geometry. Small-diameter wheels will not fit over the calipers of larger than stock disk-brake packages, so large-diameter wheels are necessary when 12-inch (or larger) rotors are installed on older cars.

Q. Is there a braking system requirement?

A. Yes. Disc brakes are part of the Restomod image. Front drum brakes are outdated. For your Restomod to brake well consistently, you need at least front disc brakes. If you have four-wheel disc brakes, it's even better. Drum brakes are not as safe or effective on cars that are built to travel at high speeds around a road course. If you are going to have a lot of power under the hood, you need

Restomods can even have four-cylinder engines. This Fox-body has an intercooled, turbocharged SVO 2.3-liter. It handles extremely well, with very little weight over the front wheels. These engines fit in Pintos, too.

to invest in some stopping power, too. You can use aftermarket brake packages, or upgrade to factory disc brakes.

Q. *Is the car required to have electronic fuel injection?*

A. No. Fuel injection is nice, but it isn't a requirement. Carburetors are relatively simple, work well, and are very affordable, but in most cases they will not give you the fuel efficiency and power that fuel injection can.

Q. *Does the car need to have a 6-speed or an overdrive transmission?*

A. No. It's more than acceptable to have a 4-speed behind your engine, but it's common for Restomods to have 5- or 6-speed manual transmissions. Some of them have automatic overdrive transmissions. Having an overdrive or extra gears to row through will give you better driveability and fuel mileage out of your car, but it's not a requirement.

Q. *Does it need to be a streetable car?*

A. Yes. There are different opinions on what "streetable" means. Some people have full roll cages with large, obtrusive door bars. Some people have their car so low that the exhaust scrapes on every little bump. These features make the cars less streetable. For the most part, if the car has a license plate and current registration, it is still legally considered a street car.

Q. *Do you have to modify the suspension?*

A. Yes. Restomods should have some of the following upgrades: larger sway bars, upgraded control arms, performance shocks, and high-rate springs. The original suspension installed on production cars is designed to have a fairly docile ride. Upgrading these items is necessary to get better handling out of your car.

Q. *Is there a minimum engine size or performance requirement?*

A. No. Some guys are running stock engines in their cars. Most cars have V-8s in them. Some cars are running Turbocharged or Supercharged V-6s or high-output Cosworth or Esslinger 4-cylinder engines. Upgrading the performance of

Some Restomods push the envelope. This Mustang was built for road-course racing, so class rules make the door bars necessary. They look cool and make the car fun to enter and exit **Dukes of Hazzard** *style. Hopping over these bars in a street car would get old really fast. A less obtrusive four- or six-point roll bar would be more practical for the street, but not all Restomods need a cage.*

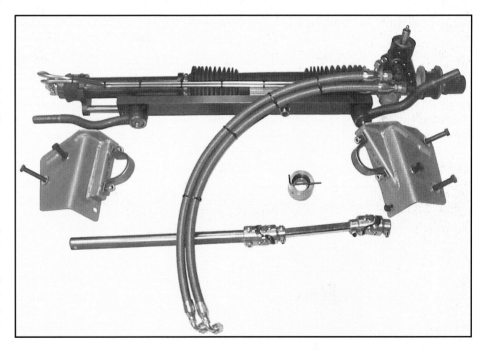

Restomods have upgraded suspension to help the cars navigate tight corners better than they did with factory equipment. Steering systems can be upgraded and should not be overlooked. This rack-and-pinion kit from Revelation Racing Supplies eliminates the sluggish original steering system. (Photo courtesy Revelation Racing Supplies)

your engine is a positive move, but stock engines are not frowned upon.

That should answer some of your questions about what makes a Resto-mod. Read the rest of the book for more information on how to build these cars and what makes building a Restomod practical, and most of all – fun!

GENERAL SUSPENSION, BRAKES, TIRES, AND WHEELS

Shock Absorbers

The basic job of the shock absorber is to control or dampen the movement of the springs. A shock absorber that is too soft will have a hard time controlling the suspension, causing the ride to be bouncy and inefficient while cornering. If the shock is too stiff, the ride will be harsh and cause the vehicle to slide too easily.

Inside the body of mono-tube shock there is a piston with a valve on the tip (shown here). This valve controls the rate of the shock. The small stack of discs partially blocking the flow passages limits the speed of the fluid flowing through the valve. The discs are swapped to change bump and rebound.

Shocks have two functions: compression and rebound. Compression is defined as the collapsing of the shock absorber. This occurs when the car hits a bump and the suspension moves upward, pushing the piston rod into the shock body. Rebound is when the shock extends. Most people associate this with their car hitting a dip in the road, causing the suspension to drop and the shock to extend, but rebound does much more than that. When you drive your car into a hard left turn, the right front (outside) shock compresses, the left front (inside) shock extends. If you have the right shock valving, the inside shock will resist extending (rebound) and the outside shock will resist compression. In this way, the shocks assist the springs and sway bar to limit body roll and increase cornering (lateral) traction.

Most factory replacement shocks do not have adjustable compression or rebound. Some aftermarket performance shocks are available with internal valves that allow you to adjust them for preferred compression and rebound. Those two settings are different for each application, due to many factors, including vehicle weight, tires, and spring rates. In

the past, drag car front shock absorbers were marketed as 90/10 shocks. This generally meant that they were valved for 90 percent compression and 10 percent rebound. Shock experts say that 90/10 shocks are more of a marketing term and a pair of actual 90/10 shocks would be very dangerous. Marketing shocks based on percentages is an old trick that won't seem to go away. They are better measured in terms of how much force it takes to compress or extend the shock. Drag shocks are set up to allow the front of the car to lift easily during the launch (the shock has very little resistance to extension), but come down slow (more resistance on the compression), which transfers more weight to the rear wheels for off-the-line traction. While this type of set-up is great for drag racing, it is not safe for the street. A Restomod would be better with a shock valved with the compression and rebound resistance much closer to equal.

Most conventional shocks are not rebuildable. The more expensive race shocks are rebuildable and can also be revalved for fine-tuning your suspension. These shocks are usually adjustable in some way. Some shocks

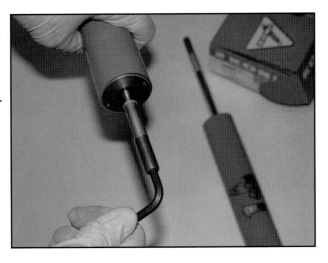

To adjust the firmness of a Koni Classic, you compress to engage the valve inside. Turn it clockwise to increase firmness, and counterclockwise for a softer ride. You are never stuck with a setting; if you don't like the ride – adjust it.

have a knob at the bottom or top to adjust them from soft to firm. Other shocks have to be compressed in order to adjust the firmness.

Mono-Tube Shocks

A mono-tube shock has a single chamber inside the shock body. A single valve at the end of the piston modulates dampening. Mono-tube shocks are typically of high-pressure gas design, ranging from 250 to 400 psi. The pressure inhibits cavitation caused by foaming or aeration if air gets drawn through the valve. Since they only have a single chamber, mono-tube shocks dissipate heat faster than twin-tube designs. They can be mounted upright or upside down.

Twin-Tube Shocks

A twin-tube shock has two chambers inside the shock body: an inner and outer chamber. The inner chamber contains the piston and the oil. On the end of the piston is a valve. There is also a valve at the bottom of the inner chamber, which modulates the amount of fluid forced into the outer chamber.

There are two different ways to build twin-tube shocks. The more expensive way is to use a cellular bag (also known as a "gas bag"). The bag is typically filled with Freon gas to 10 to 20 psi. Other designs also include a foam material inside the gas bag. Some sources say non-gas bag designs are more efficient. Unlike high-pressure twin-tube shocks, twin-tube gas-bag shocks don't rely on gravity. They can be mounted upright, upside down, or even sideways.

Coil-Over Shocks

Coil-over shocks are similar to conventional shocks, except for the threaded body or threaded adapter collar. A coil-over shock replaces the factory shock and spring. The spring rate is determined by the vehicle weight and intended ride quality. The coil is placed on the shock and allows vehicle height adjustment. Both mono- and twin-tube shocks are available as coil-over shocks.

Sway Bars

A sway bar or anti-roll bar is one of many parts that play a role in reducing body roll. The body-roll elements are: spring rate, wheel center rate, tire rate, ride rate, and roll rate. The springs, shocks, bushings, wheels, tires, chassis, and sway bars are all key parts in the car's ability to corner well. Obviously, a car would operate without a sway bar, but it would not be very safe or fun to drive.

The typical front sway bar ends attach to the left and right lower control arms. The main center section of the bar is mounted to the frame rail on the left and right side of the front of the car. The typical (non-IRS equipped car) rear sway bar ends mount to the left and right rear frame rails, and the main center section of the sway bar mounts to the differential housing.

The main center section of the sway bar is horizontally attached to the right and left frame rail, and it is able to pivot on a single axis. If the right end of the sway bar acts, the left end of the sway bar reacts, and vice versa. This means if the right end of the bar moves upward, the left end of the sway bar also wants to move upward. The same is true for downward motion.

In really basic terms, when a car is driven into a left-hand turn, the right (outside) control arm wants to push the right end of the sway bar upward, which in turn makes the left end of the sway bar want to lift the left (inside) control arm. At that same time, the left (inside) control arm is pulling the left end of the sway bar downward, which in turn makes the right (outside) end of the sway bar force the outside control arm downward. The action of the forces of both of the ends of the sway bar counteract each other and are coupled to the

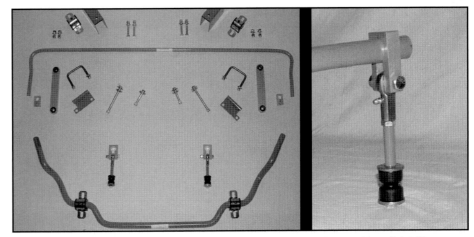

Since 1975 Stam-Bar Stabilizers has been making sway bars for '65 through '73 Mustangs. These sway bars incorporate sliding end links that allow the bars to be fully adjustable for the ultimate suspension tuning. You can adjust the bar when you get to the track and move it back when before driving home. (Photo courtesy StamBar Stabilizers)

frame, which causes the frame to attempt to stay level to the ground, reducing body roll. A sway bar with a bigger diameter reduces more body roll. Body roll affects lateral (cornering) traction of the tires by planting or forcing the tire down onto the asphalt. Some body roll is necessary to increase the traction of the outside tire. If the suspension does not have any body roll, the tires will tend to slide instead of biting for traction with the outside tire.

The front and rear (if your car has one) sway bars can work together or against each other. A rule of thumb: If your car has understeer, you can decrease the diameter of the front bar and increase the diameter of the rear bar. If your car suffers from oversteer, you should increase the size of the front bar and decrease or remove the rear bar.

Aftermarket Sway Bars and Accessories

There are two types of aftermarket sway bars – conventional and racing. Conventional aftermarket bars typically resemble the shape of a stock bar, with the exception of the increased diameter. They even usually bolt into the stock bar locations. Conventional aftermarket sway bars were only offered as solid units until 2000. In 2000, Hotchkis Performance started processing hollow bars. These units are hollow, large-diameter bars that are as strong as their solid counterparts, but only a fraction of the weight. As of the original release of this book, Hotchkis only offers hollow bars for the late-1990 Ford models.

Quickor Suspensions and Addco offer a full line of solid sway bars for Ford and Mercury cars. Stam-Bar Stabilizers offer adjustable front and rear sway bars strictly for the 1965 through 1973 Mustangs. The custom sliding adjustable end link system was derived from racing car technology and it works great for tuning the suspension on your Mustang. Easy adjustments can be made at the track or in your garage. If you are going to race on a track that has 85 percent right turns and 15 percent left turns, the Stam-Bar can be adjusted to increase bias and get more traction from the outside tires.

Stock-car-style splined sway bars typically require a moderate level of fabrication to mount them. Since the arms on these sway bars are mounted at 90 degrees to the shaft, tire clearance is greatly increased. Rod-end end-links (not shown) mount the bar to the lower control arm.

Gun-drilled racing sway bars are completely different from conventional sway bars in appearance, but they do the same job. Typically, this type of sway bar consists of a straight-splined solid or gun-drilled (hollow) bar with adjustable aluminum or steel arms. They are mounted with solid bearings or Delrin inserts. The aluminum or steel arms are available in many lengths, and they are usually straight. The installer can then bend them to the desired shape, so that they clear the tires and suspension pieces. These bars are used on circle- and dirt-track racing cars, but they also have been showing up on full-tilt Restomods. At the time of this book's publication, these types of bars were only available from Griggs Racing for their 1965 through 1970 Mustang GR-350 custom front suspension systems.

You can also engineer your own racing-style sway bars. You can pick up different width, diameter, and wall thickness bars; different length and shaped arms; and the necessary hardware from Speedway Engineering.

Sway bar bushings and end-links come in a few different types. The bushings are available in rubber and polyurethane. The end-links are available in the standard rubber and polyurethane through-bolt type, the solid rod-end type, or with stud-type rod ends.

The standard through-bolt end-links are the most common way to attach your sway bar to the control arms. These end-links come in different lengths. To determine the length you will need for your application, the car will need to be sitting at rest with the sway bar installed (with the exception of the end links). If you pivot the sway bar so the ends are parallel to the ground, there should be a gap between the end of your sway bar and the locating hole in the control arm. Measure that distance; it will be the length of the end-link that you will need.

The solid rod-end style end-links work well on the track because they offer non-binding, fluid motion. On the street, most car builders prefer the longer life of bolt-through types over the solid rod-ends. Once the solid rod-ends wear, they will start making noise. As with any rod ends, installing safety washers will ensure the rod ends will not totally separate if the ball wears out. Automotive engineers are constantly coming up with new ways to mount the ends of the sway bars to control arms.

Keep your eyes out on the higher performance cars for new end links and other hardware. Always keep your eyes and your mind open for new designs when you are around racetracks and new car dealerships. You never know when you might see something that would work great on your Restomod. This goes for every aspect of your car, not just the suspension.

Bushings

Sway bar, upper control arm, and lower control arm bushings on most Ford and Mercury front suspensions are made of rubber. Aftermarket companies offer replacement bushings made from polyurethane, which is a stronger compound that offers performance benefits. For even more performance and a more road-ready feel, solid bushings are another option. Solids are either a combination of Delrin and metal, or just metal.

Keep in mind that the stiffer bushing you use, the more precise your suspension geometry will be. Flexible factory bushings distort under load, altering your alignment to the point of reducing the effectiveness of your steering and suspension. Read further to help make your decision on what is best for your application.

These polyurethane end-link bushing kits are available from Prothane and come in different lengths. They are available with 2 to 6 inches between connecting points. Installing an end link that is too short will introduce more bind during suspension articulation.

Rubber

Most stock front suspension bushings are rubber, especially in Ford cars built before the late 1980s. That's when manufacturers started introducing polyurethane in some applications. The rubber bushings create a comfortable ride for the average driver by absorbing shock from imperfections in the road. Unfortunately, rubber bushings do have a drawback—they also flex and distort. When a car is driven hard into a corner, the control arm bushings distort enough to completely change the alignment settings. The changes in geometry can create unpredictable handling.

Urethane

There are benefits of using polyurethane over rubber bushings. Polyurethane has a higher load-bearing capacity, greater tear strength, and supe-rior resistance to oils, depending on the formulation. Polyurethane bushings don't distort like rubber bushings. For instance, when the control arms are under load while cornering, the polyurethane bushings will keep your alignment closer to where it's supposed to be. This is a great advantage to creating a more predictable and controllable Restomod, especially if you take it to the track. Of course, polyurethane bushings also increase road feel in comparison to rubber bushings.

There is a big urban legend about polyurethane. People say it squeaks. Polyurethane does not squeak. The squeak you hear is caused by the lack of proper lubrication between the bushings and the surface of the surrounding part. Not all polyurethane bushings are created equal. Each company has different theories, designs, and compounds to

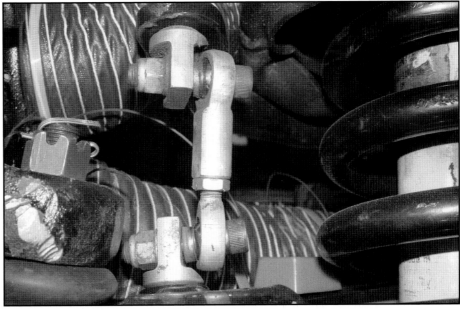

Rod-end-style end-links are available for some street applications. It's more common to see them on racing applications. The rod-ends create less bind and allow length adjustability, but they get hammered on street applications and wear out fast.

The factory inner/lower control-arm bushings are rubber. Replacement bushings are available from polyurethane manufacturers to reduce deflection. Global West makes lower control arms for some applications that have a radial aircraft bearing (inset). These bearings allow for a full range of motion, yet are free of bind and deflection.

achieve its idea of a superior bushing. Each polyurethane manufacturer has its own blend of materials for urethane and lubricant. For best results, use the lubricant supplied by the manufacturer and follow the provided instructions to fully clean the surrounding parts.

Polygraphite

Polygraphite bushings, available from Performance Suspension Technology (PST), are an alternative to the regular rubber and polyurethane bushings. PST's graphite-impregnated Polygraphite bushings offer good road manners, but they do not allow suspension deflection. PST also claims its bushings don't squeak because of the naturally lubricating quality of the graphite.

Solids
Delrin and Aluminum

In some cases, control arm and leaf spring bushings on Fords, Lincolns, and Mercurys can be replaced with Delrin and aluminum bushings. They consist of a steel inner crush sleeve, an outer aluminum housing, and a Delrin bearing sleeve to keep the two different

metals from binding. Since the materials don't flex, they offer precise suspension geometry. They also give the driver a little more road feel than the polyurethane bushings. The bushings you can replace with these types of solid bushings are in upper control arms, lower control arms (in non-strut rod equipped cars), leaf spring eyes, and IRS control arms.

Unfortunately, these bushings are only produced for a select few of these applications, due to popularity or the lack of it in the Ford Restomod hobby. Global West offers Del-A-Lum for 1979 and newer Mustang control arms, 1980 through 1988 T-birds, and in leaf-spring shackle kits on 1964-1973 Mustangs.

Delrin and Steel

Many stock-car racing companies offer Delrin and steel control-arm bushings for custom applications. Stock-car products are heavy-duty, but not always best for street use. I have seen Delrin and steel bushings with extremely loose tolerances, which work well, but they can generate some loud clunking in the front

suspension when loaded and unloaded. It's great for low-buck racers, but not great for a street car.

Metal and Metal — Spherical Too

Stock-car racing companies offer bushings with steel housings and inserts. They are also available in aluminum versions. These bushings are not forgiving. They transfer all road feel to the chassis and steering wheel. If you are building an extreme Restomod and only plan to drive it on the street about 50 miles per year, you could get away with using these. They are equipped with grease fittings, and it is necessary to keep solid bushings lubricated to minimize galling. You have to remember that the only thing preventing the two pieces of metal from binding is that thin layer of grease.

The other type of metal-to-metal bushing is the spherical aircraft bushing. Global West and other companies offer these for specific applications that require the movement offered by these bushings. Global West offers these bushings in its tubular, lower front control arms for many shock-tower-equipped Fords. Where the lower control arm meets the frame, the rubber bushings can be replaced with these inflexible, full-range-of-motion, spherical aircraft bushings. They will increase road feel, but also improve the handling with more precise, consistent suspension geometry.

Handling – Understeer and Oversteer

When I was at a driver meeting for a high-speed open-road racing event, I was given a simple explanation for understeer and oversteer. Understeer is when your front end hits the wall. Oversteer is when your rear end hits the wall. That is about as simple as it gets. Understeer and oversteer can be caused by many things: road conditions, tire compounds, spring rates, shock compression and rebound ratios, sway bar choices, alignment, acceleration, braking too hard, and much more.

Understeer condition is described as a loss of traction in the front tires, which

Why Upgrade Brakes?

A car is made from thousands of different parts. A few of those items have more importance than others, especially when it comes to safety. The highest on this safety list is probably the brakes. Drum brakes and disc brakes are the two brake systems used on cars today. Brakes build up heat every time you use them, and disk brakes disperse heat better than drum brakes. Less efficient drum brake systems slow the car using brake shoes pushing outward against the inside of the brake drum. Disc brake systems are more efficient and have brake pads that work together to pinch the brake rotor. You may ask, "My car came factory-equipped with disc brakes; why should I upgrade them?"

If you plan on driving hard around corners and your engine is pumping out extra horsepower, you are going to need some extra stopping power to be safe. If you are planning on ever driving a road course, you will definitely need to upgrade to bigger rotors and better calipers. The stock drum and disc brakes are fine for stopping a vehicle under normal driving conditions, but on a road course, you are forced to use the brakes more than they were ever designed for. This is especially true if you race the correct way, which is to slow your car down with the brakes, not the engine and transmission.

After a few hard stops, the stock brakes start to lose their effectiveness because of the heat caused by the excessive friction. Stock brakes don't cool off very well, and heat in the stock brake material causes outgassing. Outgassing results in gas pockets forming between the pad and rotor surface. This is even more pronounced with drum brakes, because the brake lining has even more surface area. When the lining doesn't completely contact the rotor surface, it cannot effectively slow or stop the vehicle. This problem is known as brake fade. Installing a brake cooling system (covered later in this chapter) may combat brake fade, but it doesn't eliminate the problem. Aftermarket brake pads made for racing or high-performance driving use newer-technology materials

that minimize or eliminate outgassing problems. Look for pads that advertise with terms like "race ready" and "dynamic surface treatment."

The best improvement you can make to your braking system is to upgrade to large-diameter rotors that have more contact surface area for braking and for cooling, along with more brake torque (increased leverage). Upgrading to performance pads, along with rotors and calipers, will also give you more braking power (or cowbell, if you get my Christopher Walken reference). With a properly balanced system (explained later in this chapter), the upgraded system will shorten your stopping distances and greatly improve the vehicle's ability to make repeated stops on a road course. With better brakes, you'll be able to drive faster around the course. You can drive deeper into a corner without braking, since you can wait longer before applying the brakes. You will leave lesser-equipped cars in the dust.

This is a Baer Brakes Track System rotor and caliper. The 13x1.1-inch rotors are a one-piece cast design that have been upgraded with cross-drilling, slotting, and zinc-washing options. The caliper is a two-piston floating PBR unit. (Photo Courtesy Baer Brakes)

in turn causes the front end to push. That push can be very dangerous since steering ability is usually non-existent. Not being able to control the direction that your car is traveling in can be dangerous and costly.

Oversteer is described as a loss of traction in the rear tires during cornering, which in turn causes the rear end to slide. Many drivers prefer oversteer rather than understeer. In oversteer conditions, the car can at least be corrected by steering into the slide, unless extreme oversteer is experienced. Controlled oversteer can be helpful to get the car around a tight corner more easily, but any loss of traction can be detrimental if you are shooting for fast lap times at the racetrack.

Drifting, or a four-wheel drift, is caused when traction is lost in the front and rear tires. Both understeer and oversteer conditions are present. Experienced, highly skilled drivers pilot their cars in controlled drifting conditions in almost every corner. Track experience and in-depth knowledge regarding your car's set-up are important when pushing your car to the edge.

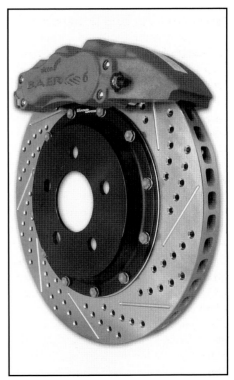

This Extreme Plus System is at the top of Baer's product line. The Plus automatically denotes the directional two-piece rotors with 6061-T6 billet hats and cast rotors. The caliper is a staggered-bore, six-piston unit. (Photo Courtesy Baer Brakes)

If you look closely, behind that nice 17-inch front wheel, there's a stock drum brake. For less than the cost of these wheels, you could upgrade to front disc brakes. Looking good is important, but safety should be high on your list, too.

Brake Parts

I could write a whole book on performance brakes, but I'll just scratch the surface regarding the types of performance brakes, balancing your system, and brake cooling. To make things simple, only four-wheel disc brake systems will be covered in this chapter.

Most of the brakes covered in this chapter are Baer Brakes. Due to experience with brakes and kits from five different brake companies, I have found Baer Brakes kits to have the highest overall quality. They are the most likely to have all the necessary parts included and the parts fit correctly without the need to next-day-air a replacement part. Baer Alcon calipers have a superior internal design that makes them easier to bleed than some other comparable big-name calipers. You might have other experiences, but these are my recommendations.

To save a few bucks, some industrious enthusiasts have found ways to adapt disc brakes to their Restomods from Granadas, Lincoln Versailles, Lincoln Mark VIIs, or other vehicles. These brake conversions can work great when installed with the correct parts, but people don't always get the system balanced (covered later in this chapter) by

installing the correct master cylinder with the correct bore size. There is quite a bit more to upgrading your brakes than bolting on a set of disc brakes from another car.

Factory Interchange

Low-buck Granada 11-inch Brake Upgrade

Adding Granada brakes is one of the most popular and longest-standing front disc brake upgrades for V-8-models of 1965 to 1973 Mustangs and 1963 to 1969 Falcons and Rancheros. If you are working on a non-V-8 car, you will need to upgrade to V-8 steering components when performing the Granada brake upgrade. The V-8-equipped Granada is equipped with 11-inch rotors, while the 6-cylinder Granada is equipped with 10-inch rotors. If you're going to go through the trouble, you might as well go for the 11-inch rotors. You'll need the following parts from the front of a 1976 to 1979 V-8 Granada: spindles, rotors, brake brackets, and brake calipers. These parts can be obtained at your local wrecking yard. You can acquire the other parts needed to complete this job from an auto parts store. These (Granada) parts include: inner and outer wheel bearings and races, wheel seals, rubber

brake hoses, remanufactured calipers, new brake pads, and rotors (if your donor rotors are in rough shape).

Replacing the master cylinder is suggested. Each application is different, so it's impossible to suggest a master cylinder from a certain vehicle. If your car is equipped with a single-reservoir master cylinder, I highly suggest replacing it with a dual-reservoir master cylinder. A single-reservoir unit is unsafe. If brake fluid was to leak out of any portion of a single reservoir system, you would lose all braking pressure. A dual-reservoir master is safer because if the fluid were to leak out of the rear of your brake system, you would still have pressure in the front system, and vice-versa. In the case of replacing your single-reservoir master with a dual-reservoir unit, you should expect to spend some time bending and flaring some brake tubing to plumb in the new set-up. If you're changing master cylinders from a dual to another dual master, you may not need to spend as much time on it, but don't think it will be a simple bolt-in. You will need to do some careful research to help you choose the proper master cylinder for your specific application. It is very probable that you won't find a "brake expert" at your local car parts chain store. Choose your

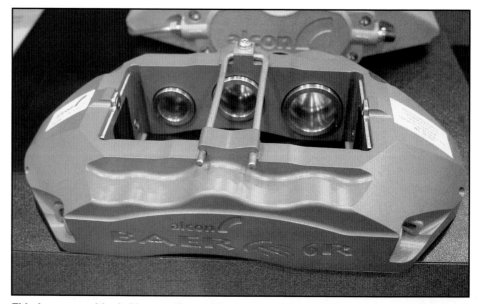

This is a mono-block Alcon caliper with staggered bores. The piston bores are staggered in size for better pad wear. The term mono-block means that the caliper is machined from a single-cast unit, which makes it extremely rigid. The design eliminates the need for an external balance tube.

This is a two-piece, fixed-caliper design. Two separate machined blocks are bolted together. This caliper requires an external balance tube to balance the left and right half of the caliper's fluid pressure.

sources wisely; the ability to safely stop your car is a matter of life or death.

When choosing a master cylinder, also take into consideration which side of the master cylinder the brake lines exit the unit. If they exit toward the engine, you may have clearance problems with the valve covers. Choosing the bore size is the most important aspect of the quest for a new master cylinder. You'll most likely need to install a brake-proportioning valve to balance the brake system.

Once you have all the necessary parts, you can start the brake swap. With the exception of choosing and plumbing the master cylinder and locating the correct tie-rod ends for your application, performing this swap can be fairly easy. For your safety, once you've swapped all the parts, you should have a shop align your front suspension.

There are a couple of items you should be aware of before starting the installation.

1. The snout on the Granada rotors are larger in diameter than the early Mustang drum brakes, which means most early stock wheels will not fit. Even some aftermarket wheels do not fit over the Granada rotor snout.

2. The outer tie-rod ends will not fit either, so you'll need to purchase some specific units to have the correct fit. Manual and power steering set-ups require different tie-rod combinations. These specific parts are available from Mustangs Plus.

3. Granada brake hoses are too short and will require adapter lines to fit the 1964½ through 1967 Mustangs. These are also available from Mustangs Plus.

4. The spindle height is different on the Granada. Sometimes it can raise the vehicle as much as 1 inch.

5. The master cylinder on your car will need to be replaced with a dual master cylinder from a newer car with the proper brake set-up. For instance, if you are upgrading to Granada front disc brakes and you are keeping your stock drum brakes, you will need a ⅞- to 1-inch master cylinder designed for a car with front disc brakes and rear drum brakes. If you are installing four-wheel disc brakes, you'll need a master cylinder designed for a car with four-wheel discs. Read the section in this chapter on balancing your brake system.

6. To help balance the brakes, you'll probably need to install a brake-proportioning valve.

7. Obtain all the correct torque specs from a repair manual so all the parts can be installed to the correct specifications.

8. If you have any doubts about your mechanical skill level, have a shop perform the Granada brake upgrade for you. There is absolutely nothing wrong with having a trained professional work on any part of your car. It's always better to be safe than sorry.

This is a Tilton brake and clutch-pedal assembly. It utilizes dual-master cylinders with a balance bar for brake bias tuning and a hydraulic clutch master cylinder.

BRAD FAGAN'S 1972 PINTO PANGRA

This 1972 Pinto Pangra is owned by Brad Fagan. One of the most obvious ways to differentiate this Pinto is the redesigned front end. The front fenders and hood are made of fiberglass. The pop-up headlights are operated by a lever under the dashboard.

Back in the early 1970s, the small-car market was filled with sporty cars like the 914 Porsche, Opel GT, and Datsun 240Z. Jack Stratton of Huntington Ford in Arcadia, California, had visions of taking a small production car and modifying it to a level in which it could compete with the previously mentioned sports cars. When the Pinto was introduced in 1971, Jack finally had the perfect candidate for his vision.

Jack started tracing the Pinto body lines from photos and modifying them. He first contacted Kustom-car guru Gene Winfield to help implement his ideas, but Gene was bogged down with other projects and didn't have the time. So Jack enlisted Bob Crowe, who had experience with all sorts of fiberglass ventures from boat hulls to camper tops. With Jack's passion and Bob's experience, they came up with a solid design. The whole external package flowed well with the Pinto's original body lines. It's tough not to notice the Pangra's menacing sloped front fenders and pop-up headlights that look unmistakably like the Pantera.

Back in 1972, Jack Stratton of Huntington Ford in Arcadia, California, had a vision of producing a small sports car that could compete with the 914 Porsche, Opel GT, and Datsun 240Z. He modified the Pinto platform to accomplish this goal. Approximately 50 were sold off the showroom floor.

All body changes were applied to the Pinto's front end. The original front fenders, hood, and lower valance were discarded. The completely redesigned front end consisted of extended fiberglass fenders, which housed pop-up headlights, an extended fiberglass hood, and a fiberglass cowl cover to hide the windshield wipers. The original bumper and grill were cleanly incorporated into the design. In rare photographs of the Pangra being test driven by magazines, a sizable spoiler was attached to the body at the top of the rear window.

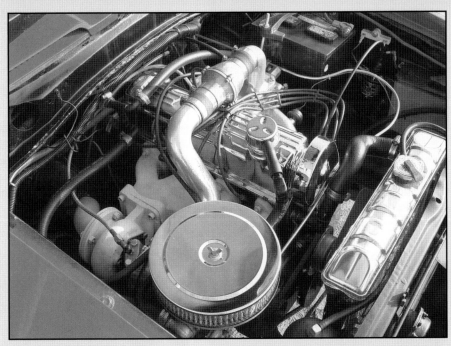

Under the hood, the Pangras were equipped with a turbocharged 2.0-liter and water injection to control detonation at higher boost levels. This combination was stated to produce approximately 175 to 200 hp.

This mostly stock Pangra received suspension upgrades, and the interior was modified too. The car had a custom console and dash, aftermarket gauges, and Recaro seats.

Jack's all-encompassing vision didn't stop at modifying the body. The next step was the suspension, tires, and wheels. The Pangra "Can Am" suspension consisted of lowered front coil springs, front and rear sway bars, lowering blocks for the rear, and Koni shocks on every corner. The Koni shocks weren't off-the-shelf parts. Jack worked closely with Koni to get just the right compression and rebound valving for optimum cornering performance. The tires and wheels were important to the handling, too, so Jack upgraded to 7-inch mag wheels and Continental radial tires. The chosen wheels, tires, suspension parts, and completely different caster, camber, and toe settings resulted in a 0.874 g pull on a 200-ft skid pad. Those skid pad numbers were better than 0.740 g pulled by the expensive sports cars available at that time.

Jack also made upgrades under the hood. The original 122-ci engine needed some added power, so Jack worked with Ak Miller to design the correct power for this project. They came up with a turbocharger, exhaust manifold, header pipe, intake manifold, and water injection (to control detonation). With forged pistons to increase compression, the combination of parts produced approximately 175 to 200 hp. The Pangra's zero-to-60-mph time was 7.5 seconds, the quarter-mile time was 15.4 seconds @ 92 mph, and it had a top speed of 125 mph.

To round out the Pangra package, Jack also changed the interior. He added a custom dashboard, additional gauges, and Recaro front seats. All these changes made a well-rounded car that definitely gave all the early 1970s sports cars a run for their money.

These Pangras were available from the dealer between August 1972 and sometime in 1973. The selling price off the showroom floor was $4,600 (with a stock Pinto selling for about $2,200).

The dealer-assembled Pangra came with a two-year warranty. There were approximately 50 dealer-assembled Pangras sold off the showroom floor. Only four are known to still exist as of 2004—one wagon and three sedans. If you didn't want to purchase a Pinto Pangra (back in 1972 and 1973) as a complete car, you could purchase kits to perform your own Pinto modification the Pangra specs. Kit number one was the Pangra front-body assembly, which retailed for $595. Kit number two was the "Can Am" suspension package, which retailed for $951. Kit number three was the Ak Miller turbocharger kit along, with kits numbers one and two, and it retailed for $1,691.

The 1972 Pangra in the photos belongs to Brad Fagan. He has been a Pinto fanatic since 1976. He's swapped V-8s and 2.3-liter SVO turbo power-plants in the past. The red 1972 Pangra is mostly stock, and he plans to keep it that way. For more information on Pintos and Pangras, go to www.fordpinto.com. The website has stock and modified Pintos, tons of great information on Pinto history, and a community of people who can answer your questions.

Aftermarket Brake Upgrades

Rotors

Performance rotors come in a few different types. They come machined from a single cast piece, a cast outer ring with an aluminum hat, or a carbon fiber outer ring (for racing only) with an aluminum hat.

Different manufacturers offer different options with their rotors. Baer Brakes offers cross-drilling, slotting, and zinc washing. Cross-drilling allows gasses to disperse from the pad surface, so the pad has better contact on the rotor surface. Brake-pad technology has almost eliminated outgassing, so these days cross-drilling and slotting are more for visual appearance. Cross-drilling creates the potential for stress-risers that can lead to cracks in the rotor, so Baer casts its rotors with the cooling vanes in a specific pattern to lower the potential of crack migration. For full-on racing applications, Baer Brakes suggests rotor slotting, but not cross-drilling.

Zinc washing is great for rotor appearance. The zinc coat comes off the rotor surface where the brake pad rides, but the coating stays on the rest of the rotor. If you coat the rotor, it protects all other surfaces from ugly rust that builds up on the part of the rotor surface that is visible through most of the aftermarket wheels used on Restomod vehicles.

Calipers

There are two types of calipers: floating and fixed. The floating caliper relies on pressure applied to the rotor from its single inboard piston to pull the outboard pad into the outside face of the rotor. This design is much more forgiving in production tolerances, and it is used on almost all production vehicles on the market today. Fixed calipers are solidly mounted to the spindle or axle housing with opposing inner and outer pistons. When brake pressure is applied, the pistons squeeze the rotor equally and simultaneously. This creates a better pedal feel, and a much quicker braking response than floating calipers can produce. The tolerances on mounting the fixed caliper over the rotor needs to be

This is a balance bar for the Tilton brake-pedal assembly. A spherical bearing is located in the pedal. The threaded rod moves the bearing from side to side for the correct amount of front and rear master-cylinder actuation. Front and rear brake bias can be adjusted from the driver's seat with a remote-mounted knob.

This is a lever-style Wilwood proportioning valve. It is within the driver's reach when he is strapped in the seat. The driver can adjust the front and rear brake bias on the fly. Other types of proportioning valves have a knob to turn for adjustment. (Photo Courtesy Joe Pettitt)

High-performance engines don't always produce enough vacuum to actuate the diaphragm in the brake booster for good braking power. You can install a canister that stores vacuum for braking when you need it. Switching to manual brakes require more pedal effort and more room in the engine compartment.

precise. In the mid to late 1960s, the big three (Ford, GM, and Chrysler) were heavy into Trans-Am racing. This involvement influenced some of the factory-option, four-piston, fixed-caliper brakes available to the public. When floating calipers were introduced, factories switched to using them on production vehicles to keep assembly lines moving faster and the cost of parts down. Fixed calipers are now only used on racing applications.

Today, aftermarket fixed calipers are available in standard or staggered piston bore configurations. Standard bore calipers have symmetrical bore sizes from side to side and front to rear on each caliper. Staggered bore calipers have a different size of bores coinciding with the turning direction of the rotor. In the direction of rotation, the smaller bore is first in the rotation of the rotor. This applies the pad to the rotor more evenly. With standard bore calipers, the pistons are equally sized, so they push the pad against the rotor face at the same time. The pushing causes the leading edge of the pad to dig in a fraction of a second sooner than the trailing edge of the pad, resulting in increased wear on the leading edge of the pad.

Brake Cooling

The key to running cool brakes is to have cooling ducts running to the center of the rotor, where the air can cool the internal rotor vanes and evenly cool the rotor. If you run the air duct to the inboard face of the rotor, you will be cooling the inboard face, but the outward face will run extremely hot. This will cause the inboard and outboard pads and rotor faces will wear unevenly.

Air intake ducts and hose can be purchased from racing supply stores. The heavy-duty plastic ducts come in different shapes and sizes. The intake duct should be placed in a high-pressure location, such as a front air dam or an opening in the front valance panel. It is a good idea to install wire mesh over the inlet to keep rocks and debris from entering the duct and hose. The brake duct hose comes in different diameters and temperature ranges. Typically, you have to fabricate your own duct/backing-plate to mount to the caliper bracket of spindle. You want to leave very little room for air to escape without going through the rotor vents. This will ensure that you are getting all the cooling possible. Attach the hose to the back of the intake duct, and attach the other end of the hose to the backing plate/duct on your rotor. A few plastic zip ties are good for affixing the duct hose to stationary items in the engine compartment. Be careful not to mount the hose where it will contact a tire, moving engine, or suspension part. A spinning tire can rip the hose out of its position in a split-second, and possibly damage the tire or cause the hose to bind the suspension.

This racing set-up is a reverse-mounted clutch and master-cylinder set-up. The master cylinders are accessible under a dash panel in this racecar. Reverse-mount set-ups allow the builder to balance the front and rear brake bias using different bore sizes in the master cylinders and a balance bar for fine-tuning.

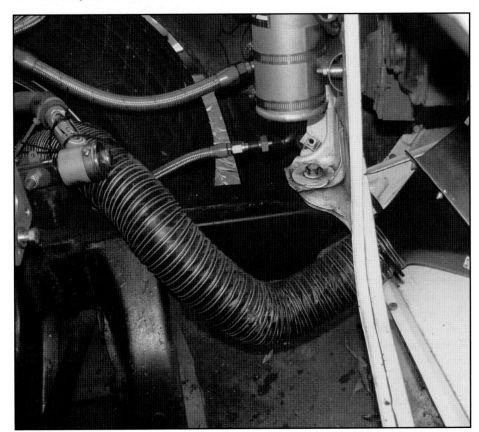

Here's an example of how to route cool air to the brake rotor. There's a plastic brake duct behind the front bumper with a custom aluminum hood to help gulp cool air. The 3-inch racing-duct hose helps direct air to the center of the rotor. The hose is secured to the upper control arm, and the front tire does not come into contact with it.

This rotor is off a Camaro Mustang Challenge racecar. Obviously, it has seen some severe heat during a couple of intense racing sessions. The back side of the rotor had a cooling duct blowing on it, and it was not cracked.

Pushing air into the center of the rotor is the most efficient way to cool the brake rotor and the wheel bearings. The duct is closely fitted to the back-side opening of the rotor, so the cool air flows outward through the rotor's vanes for increased heat dissipation.

Brakes don't like heat. It shortens the life and effectiveness of the pads. In racing and extreme driving conditions, the rotor can warp and/or crack from excessive heat. Most Restomods won't be driven hard enough to require brake ducts, but if you take yours to an open track day, you may want to consider them to protect you and your car. For the most part, brake cooling is for frequent and full-time racers.

Boosting Brakes

If you don't want manual brakes, you will need to boost your brakes in one of two ways. You can choose to install either a vacuum- or hydro-style brake booster. Vacuum-assist brake boosters work great for stock and moderate applications. When increasing your horsepower, you can adversely affect your engine's vacuum output, which can limit your brake boosting to an unsafe level. Large-diameter, vacuum-assist boosters can crowd engine accessories, like valve covers. They can also limit frame bracing. Smaller vacuum boosters might give you more clearance, but they still rely on vacuum that you may not be able to supply. You can try to hook up an electric vacuum pump, but they rarely work as well as the installer hopes.

To increase braking on trucks, manufacturers started offering hydroboost braking systems. The booster bolts between the firewall and the brake master cylinder. The hydrobooster does not rely on vacuum. The boosting comes from fluid pressure that is plumbed in between the power-steering pump and steering box. The pressure operates the brakes during any driving condition. This system is known to work better than any vacuum booster on the market. An aftermarket company named Hydratech Braking Systems offers complete kits that include the booster and hoses.

Balancing a Braking System

Standard brake systems are broken down into two separate systems joined by one link – the master cylinder. The front and rear systems need to be balanced. An average car needs about 70 percent of its braking ability in the front brakes and 30 percent in the rear. If you notice, cars with factory four-wheel disc brakes have smaller brake calipers in the rear than in the front. If the rear system had the same braking power as the front system, the brakes would be unbalanced, and the car would be very dangerous to drive. The rear brakes could lock up before the front brakes have a chance to slow the car down. The same goes for having too much braking in the front.

The correct caliper bore size in both the front and rear is also very important. To explain this, I will give you a detailed account of my own experience balancing a brake system.

I started with a generic 1968 six-cylinder car equipped with four-wheel drum brakes. I converted it to a set of front disc brakes from a newer production car, and put a Ford 9-inch rear end from a '76 Lincoln Mark IV with the stock Mark IV rear disc brakes. I put in a later model master cylinder and brake booster on the firewall. It turns out I was extremely lucky; for my normal street driving, the system was well balanced from front to rear. Then I took the car out on Sears Point road course for a day. After a few laps, the brakes started to fade, so I would let them cool off in the pits and run again. When I upgraded my engine from 350 to 483 hp, I decided it was time to upgrade the brakes. I put money down on a Baer Brakes Track kit for the front. Due to some engine compartment constraint issues with my big-block, I removed the power brakes and converted back to a manual brake system. Against Baer Brakes suggestions, I left the Mark IV disc brakes in the rear. What did they know? Disc brakes are disc brakes. They probably just want me to spend more money on their brakes. I showed them!

The Baer Track kit had some huge 13-inch rotors and two-piston PBR calipers. I installed a master cylinder with a 1-inch bore. The front brakes looked great, but the system didn't work. The system was unbalanced. I had switched the large, single-piston calipers to a pair of Baer PBR calipers that had two pistons much smaller in diameter. Coupled with the large, single-piston Mark IV calipers in the rear, I could not push the brake pedal hard enough to actuate the master cylinder in order to the stop the car in a timely fashion. In fact, I couldn't get the front or rear

Performance Friction sells special stickers that show what temperature your rotor or caliper climbed to during use. If you look closely, you can see the sticker on the rotor has been up to higher temperatures than the caliper.

brakes to lock up even if I put the pedal through the firewall – the amount of fluid it took the master cylinder to move the rear caliper pistons was too much. The front brakes were doing all the work, but they were not doing their job, and the car was unsafe to drive.

To band-aid the system into getting more fluid to the rear brakes, I would have to install a proportioning valve in the front brake system to restrict the fluid and force the rear system to operate sooner. This was not an option I was willing to take. I was already not getting enough braking force in the front, and there was no way I was going to limit it even further. At this point, I tested my stopping distance from 60 to 0 mph. As hard as I tried, I could not lock the brakes. The stopping distance was 177 feet.

I called Baer to find out what to do. They told me to get smaller piston rear calipers. I figured, since I was going to change the brakes, I might as well get the suggested system. I bought a Baer rear Touring kit with 12-inch rotors and single-piston PBR calipers. They were equipped with parking brakes, which was a big plus, since I could never get the parking brake mechanism in the Mark IV calipers to work. I had Vic DeLeon at Speed Merchant install the kit, since the bearings had to be pressed off my axles to remove the Ford backing plates. The

system worked great after that. The new caliper bore sizes were much smaller than the ones from the Mark IV. The front and rear brakes could safely stop my car, and the system was finally balanced. Baer had also suggested switching my master cylinder to a $^{15}\!/_{16}$-inch bore size for even better braking, but I had not done that yet. I tested the braking distance from 60 to 0 mph again. The car stopped in 148 feet; it was a huge improvement over the previous 177.

I had a chance to pick up a used Baer Pro front kit from my friend, Karl Chicca. He was upgrading, and had these left over. I installed the four-piston fixed Alcon calipers onto my Track kit rotors. This further improved the brake feel and the balance of the system. The feel of a fixed caliper over a floating caliper was a night-and-day difference. The fixed calipers actually gave the brakes a power-brake feel at the pedal, since they react so much faster than the floating caliper. I ran one braking test from 60 to 0 mph. The stopping distance was reduced to 137 feet. On that one test, my 137-foot stopping distance was identical to what it took to stop an ABS-equipped '99 SVT Mustang Cobra in the April 1999 issue of Road & Track. Not bad for an iron-headed big-block car. Just imagine what will happen when I change the master cylinder to a different bore size.

Since changing a standard dual-reservoir master cylinder and the bore size affects both the front and rear brake system (except in rare occasions), you can either install a brake-proportioning valve or change to a dual master cylinder set-up.

The proportioning valve is hooked inline between the master cylinder and the rear brakes to help balance the front and rear systems. If the rear brakes are locking before the front brakes, the proportioning valve restricts pressure to the rear brakes, which allows the front brakes to come on stronger before the rear brakes fully activate. Most street cars equipped with proportioning valves have them located in the engine compartment near the master cylinder. Some racing cars prefer to have the proportioning valve located within reach of the driver's seat, so the brake bias can be adjusted

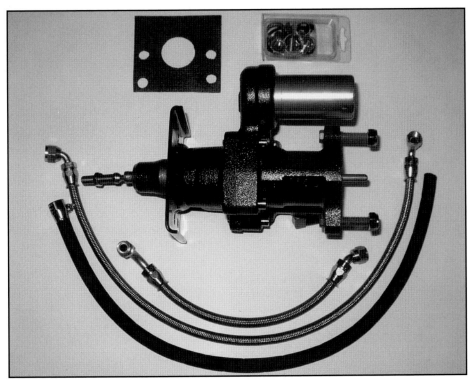

If you want the ultimate in power-assisted brakes, you can install a Hydroboost brake booster. Instead of relying on vacuum for operation, it uses fluid from a power steering pump. This is a kit offered by Hydratech Braking Systems. (Photo Courtesy Hydratech Braking Systems)

while on the track to compensate for tire, chassis, and track conditions.

A more invasive (opposed to using a proportioning valve) balanced system can be achieved using a dual master cylinder set-up with a balance bar. A balance bar system allows you to customize your master cylinder bore size for the front and rear brake circuits separately. The front and rear brake circuits become their own systems. If your front brakes would work best with a ⅞-inch bore master, and the rear brakes would work best with a ¾-inch bore master cylinder, or any different combination, the balance bar system is for you. Once you have installed both master cylinders and the balance bar system, you can make slight adjustments to the balance bar to change the front and rear brake bias. Most brake bias systems are available with an optional knob so you can adjust the bias on the fly. Putting in a balance bar system usually requires installing a new brake pedal assembly. If you go through the trouble of installing the pedal assembly, it only makes sense to install the adjustable bias knob.

Tires

There are a few things to keep in mind when picking your tires. Tire companies measure their tires from sidewall to sidewall, not the width of the tread. Generally, a 275/45ZR17 is 275 mm from sidewall to sidewall. Not all tire manufacturers abide by the same standards of measurement. A 275 tire by one manufacturer may be wider than a 275 by another. A wider tire will increase traction during forward acceleration and cornering. Moving up from a 275/40ZR17 to a 335/30ZR17 can lower your quarter-mile times and increase lateral bite of the rear suspension, which could increase understeer (or decrease oversteer). Wider tires up front can decrease understeer (or increase oversteer). The compound of the rubber used to make a tire plays a big part in the traction of specific tires. A soft compound tire gives your car more traction, but wears it out faster than a harder-compound tire.

Your outer tire diameter changes the final gear ratio. A smaller-diameter tire

This Mustang built by Don Rositch of Mustang Don's looks great with late-model Cobra-style wheels. The factory backspacing can sometimes create difficulty when you are trying to adapt them to early model cars. Sometimes you can get away with using billet wheel adapters to space the wheel correctly. (Photo Courtesy Mustang Don's)

will increase gear ratio and speed up your speedometer, while a larger-diameter tire will react exactly opposite. Large-diameter, ultra low-profile tires can give your Restomod a lifted, four-wheel-drive look. For a good look, Kevin Long, tire specialist from Campbell Auto Restoration, says his general rule is to have about 1.5 to 2 times more tire sidewall than space between the top of the tire and the fender opening. This can keep you from going overboard with wheels that are way too big, or tires that are way too thin.

Your driving habits should be taken into consideration when choosing a tire. Are you: driving strictly on the street, auto-crossing, open tracking, or periodically hitting the drag strip? Kevin Long provides good insight regarding tire choices. For mainly street driving, he suggests ultra-high-performance street tires such as: Michelin Pilot Sports, Goodyear F-1, BFG G-Force KD, Bridgestone S-02/S-03, or Yokohama AVS Sport. For auto-crossing and open track: Yokohama A-032, Michelin Pilot Club Sport, or Hoosier. For drag racing: BFG Drag Radials, Nitto 555R, or Mickey Thompson ET Streets. All these options are DOT street legal. He warns that street-legal racing tires will not last long for street use, and drag radials are not designed to go around corners.

BonSpeed makes a full line of forged wheels with show-quality finish on the front and back side. This one is called Intense. It's available in 16- to 24-inch diameters, with backspace in 1/8-inch increments for an exact fit. (Photo Courtesy Bonspeed)

Wheels

There are many different wheel companies on the market. There are also different types of material used to build wheels. The most common wheels used on Restomods are the cast-center with spun-aluminum outer, cast aluminum, billet aluminum, and forged aluminum.

Forged wheels are the strongest wheels available. Most forged wheels

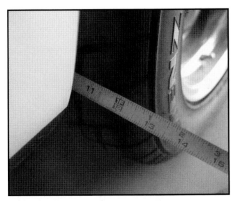

Measuring for proper wheel and tire fitment must be precise. Shops offer services for doing this with the proper experience and equipment. This '68 Galaxie 500XL shows about 12 inches from the frame to the outside of the tire, giving about 11.5 inches of room for a rear tire. Measure yours to be sure.

built today are three-piece designs. The rim is assembled of two pieces, and the center piece is bolted in with high-strength bolts. There are also two-piece forged wheels available. Forged wheels are much stronger and lighter than cast wheels. The strength of the forged wheel offers high durability for street use. I've seen many less expensive, large-diameter wheels bent from hitting potholes and road debris. It's especially easy to damage the large-diameter wheels because guys typically run low-profile tires with them. The tire's sidewall normally takes the road shock, but with a small sidewall, there is nothing to take the shock.

Large-diameter wheels and tires can be much heavier than stock wheels and tires. They increase the rotating mass, which means they require more braking force to slow them down and more power to speed them up.

Wheels are measured between the inner wheel lips, not the outside edges of the wheel lips. An actual 8-inch-wide wheel might be 9 or more inches wide when measured from outside lip to outside lip.

Fitting Tires and Wheels

Going by the basic rule of bigger is better, most people want the widest tire and wheel combination they can cram in the fenderwells. Wider tires help

increase lateral and straight-line traction during dry driving conditions, but typically decrease traction in wet driving conditions. A wider tire tends to hydroplane more easily because the water can't get out from underneath the contact patch of the tire fast enough.

When picking tires and wheels, there are a few more things to take into consideration. Are the tires going to fit within the wheel housing (wheelwell)? Are the wheels going to be the right backspacing (or offset) to clear the suspension components? Measuring for correct fitment is critical.

Too much backspacing can move the wheel and tire inward and cause interference with the control arms, ball joints, outer tie-rod ends, brake hardware, brake calipers, shocks, brackets, inner-wheel housing, frame, and more. Too little backspacing will move the tire and wheel outward, causing the tire to interfere with the fender lip and outer wheel housing. Measuring for proper backspacing is important when you want the biggest tire and wheel package on the front or rear of your car.

The first order of business in getting the correct backspacing is to find the narrowest width of the inner-wheel housing. Measure the wheel housing in many different locations because wheel housings are not always equal widths from front to rear. Keep in mind that the tire needs space to travel upward in the wheel housing during suspension compression. If your car is lowered and the outer wheel housing is shallow and curved inward, like the '67 Mustang wheel housing, you could be limited to a

narrower tire than if you made some modifications to the wheel housing. After measuring the width of the wheel housing, subtract 1 to 1½ inches. This will give you necessary ½ to ¾ inch on the inside and outside of your tire for ample suspension movement. Some extra clearance may be necessary for steering the front wheels. This measurement will be the maximum width of the tire you can run in your wheel housing. Tire manufacturers measure their tires from sidewall to sidewall (when mounted on suggested wheel widths), not tread width.

The next step is to measure backspacing. Safely support your car with jack stands and mock the ride height. With your brake rotors installed, put a straight edge across the mounting face of the brake rotor. With a tape measure or a ruler, measure ½-the distance between the straight edge and the inner wheel housing. Taking the ½-to ¾-inch tire clearance into consideration, the remaining measurement will be your backspacing. Keep in mind that the backspace for a wheel is measured from the back edge of the wheel lip to the back of the mounting surface. Do not measure from the tire bead mounting surface on the inside edges of the wheel. Measure both sides of the car for proper backspacing because auto manufacturers don't build square cars. I've seen cars with as much as a ⅞-inch difference from side to side.

If you don't want to spend the time doing all this work, for a fee, some performance tire shops offer services to test-fit wheels and tires on your car or to measure it for you. This way, you get the correct wheel ordered the first time.

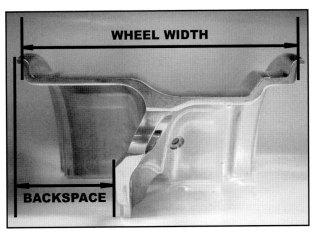

Measure the width of the wheel from the face of wheel lip to the same face on the opposite side of the wheel. Backspacing is measured from the edge of the wheel lip to the wheel mounting surface.

FRONT SUSPENSION AND STEERING

A Restomod has a few key modifications. One of them is the pursuit of better handling, and that makes the front suspension an important focus. This chapter will cover some basics and performance aspects of front suspension alignment, as well as separate components and complete front suspension packages. Getting your car pointed in the right direction is important too, so performance aspects of the steering system are also covered. Front suspension and steering work together to increase performance and drivability, which is why they are matched together in this chapter to help you get your car tuned for your style of driving.

Alignment

There are three main settings of front suspension that affect the performance and drivability of your car: camber, caster, and toe.

If your front suspension bushings and steering components are loose, worn, or broken, you should have them replaced before considering an alignment. An alignment performed on a car with worn-out tie-rod ends or deteriorated control-arm bushings is a waste of time and money. The settings will most likely change before the car gets out of the shop. Worn suspension and steering

This front suspension is a mix of off-the-shelf stock-car racing parts and custom fabricated and machined parts. Suspension analysis software and experience were combined to pull off this feat. Even the frame is completely fabricated. (Photo Courtesy John Parsons, Photography by John Ulaszek)

components are also a safety issue, so take care of these things as a matter of course. A worn steering gear won't affect the alignment between the two front tires, but it will keep the driver from enjoying the benefits of the alignment. The worn gear will cause steering to be sloppy, less responsive, and even dangerous in some cases.

Caster

On a car with upper and lower control arms (as opposed to some strut suspensions that have only a lower control arm), the spindle pivots on the axis determined by the upper and lower ball joints. Caster is the forward or rearward tilt of the spindle on this axis as viewed from the side of the car. On most cars

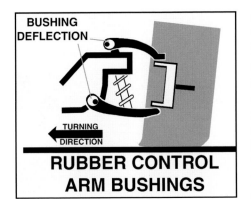

RUBBER CONTROL ARM BUSHINGS

Rubber suspension bushings deflect and distort under hard driving conditions. This distortion helps isolate road shock under normal driving conditions. This movement also allows the suspension geometry to change, hampering handling characteristics. Notice how the spindle is tilted and the tire is barely contacting the ground.

with this type of suspension, caster is changed by adjusting the strut rod or moving the upper control arm on its pivots using shims. A strut front suspension without an upper control arm uses an adjustable upper strut mount known as a camber plate to adjust camber and caster. When viewed from the side, if the upper ball joint is behind (toward the back of the car) the lower ball joint, the

car has positive caster. Negative caster is when the upper ball joint is ahead of the lower. Caster has a tendency to cause the tires to move vertically a small amount as they are steered right or left from the centered position. This vertical movement acts to push the weight of the car off the ground, while gravity tries to pull it back down. The force of gravity, which is trying to pull the car down, pushes up on the tire. This upward force on the tire causes the spindle to rotate about its axis to the point that the forces on both the right and left spindles find equilibrium. This equilibrium is found when both tires are pointing straight ahead, assuming, of course, that the caster is the same on both sides of the car and there is nothing bent or out of alignment on either side. Both negative and positive caster can induce this self-centering action of the wheels and give the car more stability at higher speeds.

The self-centering effect does not come from caster alone. It can also come from steering axis inclination. This is the same basic principle as caster, but in the front view of the suspension. If the axis of the upper and lower ball joints leans inward at the top, as a lot of cars do, there will again be a force trying to push

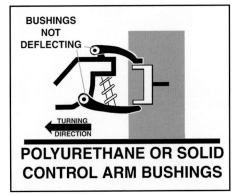

POLYURETHANE OR SOLID CONTROL ARM BUSHINGS

Urethane or solid suspension bushings transfer road feel to the chassis. Solid suspension bushings also help the suspension keep its intended geometry. Notice how the tire is contacting the ground more evenly for better cornering traction.

up on the car. Some cars get this self-centering effect using only steering axis inclination and zero caster.

Camber

Camber is the inward or outward tilt of the top of the tire as viewed from the front of the car. Negative camber is when the top of the tire tilts inward, and positive camber is when the top of the tire tilts outward. Positive camber is not desirable for handling, because it makes the outer edge of the tire dig into the pavement. If only the outside edge of the tire is on the ground, it does not produce as much cornering traction as having the entire width of the tire on the ground. With negative camber, when the top of the tire is tilting inward, the entire width of the tire has a better chance to evenly plant on the road surface for optimum traction. As with anything in life, negative camber is only good in moderation. Too much negative camber will have the inside edge of the tire trying to keep your car from sliding with unwanted understeer.

Camber can be set on your car with an alignment. Camber-curve is something completely separate from the camber adjustment you get with an alignment (except in the case of a race-bred suspension with adjustable control-arm pivot points). The camber-curve is affected by the length of the control

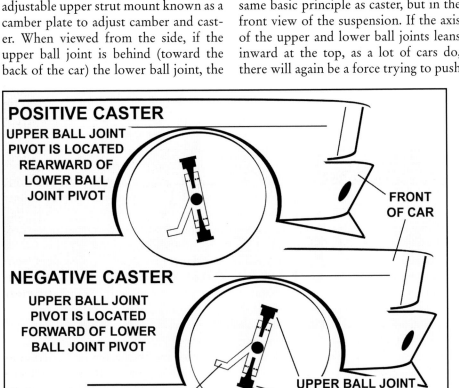

The top of the illustration shows the front spindle in extreme positive-caster position. The bottom of the illustration shows the front spindle in extreme negative caster. Positive caster is preferred over negative caster.

This photo shows a front tire exhibiting positive camber; the top of the tire is pushing out. If you took a hard corner in this car, it would have understeer. Only the outside edge of the tire is biting the ground.

This front tire is exhibiting slight negative camber. The top of the tire is tilted slightly inward. This car corners well. The entire width of the tire tread is able to get traction on the ground. It's possible a little more camber would increase cornering performance.

from above. If, when viewed from above, both tires are parallel, there is zero toe. Toe-in is when the front of the tires are closer together than the rear, and toe-out is when the rear of the tires are closer than the front.

Now that you know what zero toe, toe-in, and toe-out are, you need to know how the settings affect your car. If you aligned the tires with zero toe, the motion of the car moving forward will actually pull the front tires to a toe-out position from the distortion of the rubber suspension bushings and from road friction on the tires. To compensate for the road friction and movement of rubber suspension bushings, most factory cars are designed with a small amount of toe-in. The goal is to have the tires at zero toe for the intended average speed of the car. Factory alignment specifications are intended to minimize premature tire wear and to lower the rolling resistance of the tires. Since factory specs create less rolling resistance, fuel economy is increased. So, if you are planning on driving your Restomod across the United States on the *Hot Rod Magazine's* Power Tour, you may want to have your car aligned to factory specs.

With excessive amounts of toe, whether in or out, your tires will wear out faster and your fuel economy will decrease. Most cars are aligned with around $\frac{1}{16}$-to $\frac{1}{8}$-inch of toe-in. A setting of a $\frac{3}{16}$-inch toe-in is quite a bit, but the small amount of extra toe-in increases high-speed stability. Consider $\frac{1}{2}$-inch over the factory setting as a practical maximum. Toe-out has a tendency to make the car turn in faster. People looking for the fast way around corners will find benefits from careful experimentation with toe-out settings. Too much toe-out will cause the car to wander back and forth on the straights because the two tires are trying to steer in different directions. Wandering will get worse with increased road speed as a result of toe-out. Keep in mind that altering the factory alignment specs should only be done at the track.

A little toe-out will help your car's turn-in around corners and can also help to minimize understeer. What type of driving or racing you plan to do will

determine what toe setting is correct for your application.

Just as a warning, beware of the condition of your front suspension components. Worn or damaged bushings, ball joints, bearings, tie-rod ends, and other suspension components will act to alter your alignment settings. Getting your car aligned will not compensate for broken or worn parts.

Street Alignment

If you want your car to handle predictably on the street and your tires to wear evenly, you should go with the stock alignment settings. However, if you have replaced your rubber control-arm bushings with urethane or solid bushings, you may need less toe-in than the factory's specs. The factory toe-in compensates for the flex and distortion of rubber bushings. Without the flex, you could try changing the toe-in to closer to zero. You may have to look

arms and the control-arm pivot points. A positive camber-curve actually increases the outward tilt of the top of the tire during suspension articulation, which is completely undesirable and intensifies understeer. A negative camber-curve tilts the top of the tire inward during suspension articulation, which is much more desirable for improved handling around corners. I mention articulation because when your car is steered into the corner, the body leans. When the body leans, the outer front tire articulates upward in the fender opening. An extremely aggressive negative camber-curve can be bad, too. The key to a car that handles well is to keep the largest amount of the tire tread on the road surface, if possible. Negative camber settings help compensate for tire distortion under high lateral loads.

Toe

Toe is the relationship between two tires on one end of the car as viewed

The top of the photo shows the front tires in zero (neutral) toe. The car will drive straight and have very little rolling resistance. For demonstration purposes, the middle photo shows the front tires in extreme toe-in, and the lower photo shows the front tires in extreme toe-out.

around for a shop that does performance alignments to get the adjustments you want. A street performance alignment will wear the tires a little more quickly than normal, but the car will grip better on the street. For cars like the early Mustangs, what you're looking for is the most positive caster you can get while keeping the camber between zero and about 1½ to 2 degrees negative. For toe-in, stick with the factory specs unless you have firmer bushings. With polyurethane and similar replacement bushings, you may be able to move the toe closer to zero. You may need to experiment a little to get something that works for you, but these specs should get you in the ballpark.

The caster recommendation above is done to increase high-speed stability and will increase turning resistance at the steering wheel. The camber is to increase cornering potential, but the further away from zero you get, the twitchier the car will be above about 50 mph or so.

Racing Alignment

If you plan to run your car on an open track or at an autocross event, the alignment can be more aggressive. A racing alignment is not good for street use. It will cause the tires to wear very fast, and it will be hard to control in a straight line or over rough roads, which makes it very dangerous on the street. If you are going racing, use common sense and trailer your car to the track.

For tighter tracks, you may want to experiment with a little toe-out, but remember, a little goes a long way. On the longer, faster tracks, you may find that zero toe is a better choice. Again, experiment to see what works. Too much toe-out will increase the drag on the front tires and cause the car to wander at higher speeds. Anything over about 1/16 to 1/8-inch of toe-out is probably too much.

On the street, you will probably not be throwing your car into the corners as hard as you do on the track. The increased cornering speed increases your body roll and suspension articulation, so increasing the camber a little for extreme conditions may benefit your handling and your lap times.

Adding a little bit of negative camber is good for increasing traction to your front tires. You can experiment with a little bit at a time. When driving on the street, negative camber increases your rolling resistance and will wear the inside section of tire tread, so the extra negative camber should be left at the track.

Bumpsteer

Basically, bumpsteer is the toe-in or toe-out caused by upward and downward movement of the suspension. Typical symptoms of bumpsteer include needing a steering correction if one wheel hits a bump; needing steering correction under hard braking; or needing wheel correction when cresting a hill. Bumpsteer comes from inadequacies designed into the suspension. Most cheap, economy cars designed in 2005 have less bumpsteer than sports cars designed in the 1960s. Suspension engineering has come a long way since then.

Before explaining the technical aspects of bumpsteer, you need to learn about instant center. Visualize an imaginary line that travels through the upper control-arm inner pivot point and the upper ball joint, and then visualize another imaginary line that travels through the lower control arm pivot point and lower ball joint. These imaginary lines intersect at a point called the instant center. To have the ultimate front suspension and a steering system with zero bumpsteer, the imaginary line that travels through the inner and outer tie-rod assembly must

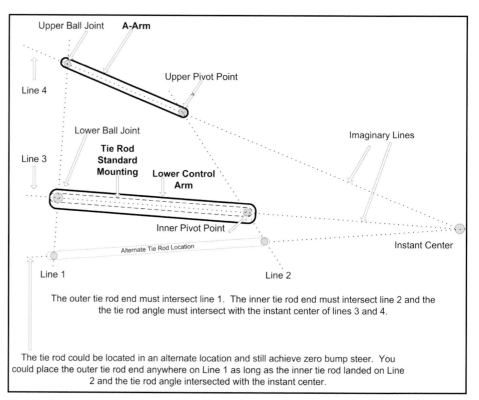

The outer tie rod end must intersect line 1. The inner tie rod end must intersect line 2 and the the tie rod angle must intersect with the instant center of lines 3 and 4.

The tie rod could be located in an alternate location and still achieve zero bump steer. You could place the outer tie rod end anywhere on Line 1 as long as the inner tie rod landed on Line 2 and the tie rod angle intersected with the instant center.

To eliminate bumpsteer, which is almost impossible with stock Restomod suspensions, the suspension parts all need to line up like this illustration shows. Even when the components are lined up, there is still a little tuning necessary from that point. (Photo Courtesy Jeff Butcher and Longacre Racing Products)

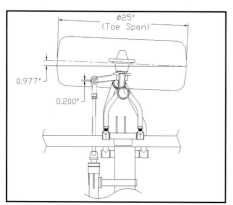

A car with bumpsteer, which is almost every car, will have a change in toe when the tire encounters a bump or a dip in the road. (Illustration Courtesy Art Morrison)

intersect the instant center from the upper and lower control arms. That seems fairly simple, but there's more to it. There are two more imaginary lines. The imaginary line that runs through the upper control-arm pivot point and the lower control-arm inner pivot point must intersect with the pivot point of the inner tie-rod end. The imaginary line that runs through the upper and lower ball joint must intersect the pivot point of the outer tie-rod end. This is all drawn out for you in the illustration supplied by Longacre Racing Products.

Most factory suspension designers for mass-production vehicles have done a good job designing out bumpsteer, but limitations hinder their ability to eliminate it. Racing cars and high-dollar super cars have to perform well and demand a high level of engineering, so engineers go to extraordinary lengths to design steering systems without bumpsteer.

Measuring bumpsteer can be done with some basic tools, but it is much easier with a Longacre Bump Steer Gauge. The gauge makes it easy to measure the amount of toe change during upward or downward travel of the front suspension. Bumpsteer is checked with the car properly aligned, with the wheels steering straight ahead. Start at ride height, and then move the suspension up 3 inches and down 3 inches. If the tie-rod assembly does not intersect the imaginary lines of the pivot points and the instant center, it will cause the spindle to turn inward or outward during suspension travel. This is bumpsteer. If you get your street car down to only hundredths of an inch of bumpsteer during its 6 inches of suspension travel, you're doing awesome work. With stock suspension systems on most production cars, it's almost impossible to attain zero bumpsteer. Most people try to get as close to zero as possible.

Eliminating Bumpsteer

There are several companies that offer bumpsteer checking equipment, as well as other alignment equipment, including Longacre Racing Products and Pole Position Racing Products. You can

Measuring bumpsteer is made easy with this Longacre bumpsteer checking equipment. With the springs removed, the suspension is jacked 3 inches up and 3 inches down from ride height. A dial indicator shows the amount of bumpsteer per inch of travel.

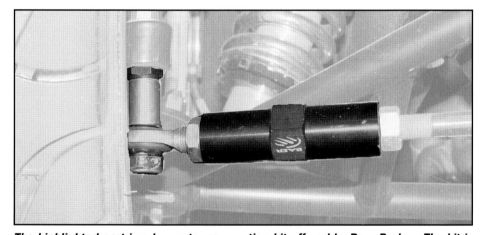

The highlighted part is a bumpsteer correction kit offered by Baer Brakes. The kit is called a Baer Tracker and it replaces your tie-rod end with an adjustable rod end. A special, tapered stud for bolting the steering arm is included.

also build your own low-tech devices. These devices check the amount of fore and aft movement of the tire through the entire range of suspension articulation.

Rod Ends

Bumpsteer can be corrected, or at least minimized, by using spherical rod ends in place of the outer tie-rod ends.

Shims of different thickness are used between the rod end and the steering arm to adjust the rod ends up or down, as desired to correct bumpsteer.

In the past, it was necessary to drill out the taper in the steering arm and use a bolt to attach the rod end to the steering arm. In 2001, Baer Racing Inc. started offering adjustable tie-rod ends called

Baer Trackers, which utilize spherical rod ends. They offer it for rack-and-pinion and reciprocation ball-steering systems. It takes the guesswork out of bumpsteer adjustment because it comes with special tapered bolts, shims, rod ends, and adjustment sleeves. Baer Trackers are available for early to late-model Ford Mustangs, late-model Thunderbirds, Cougars, and more. Baer adds new kits to its Tracker line all the time, so if you don't see your application covered, call and ask about it. Putting together the bumpsteer kit on your own isn't worth the hassle of finding the correct heavy-duty tie-rod ends, custom-length adjusting sleeves, and other adapters. However, if you want to correct or minimize your bumpsteer, and your application isn't covered by Baer, it is possible to make your own system. You could attempt to get the necessary parts by looking at parts offered by stock-car racing parts suppliers. These suppliers offer tapered tie-rod adapters with "bump" spacers and rod ends to dirt track and asphalt racers. Be careful, because if the taper on the adapter is not correct for your steering arms' taper, the adapter could break and cause serious damage to you and your car, or worse. Not all racing parts are appropriate for use on street cars, so proceed with caution.

Bumpsteer Corrector Kits

The bumpsteer can be corrected on some model year Mustangs, Falcons, and Cougars with a Bumpsteer Corrector Kit from Pro Motorsports Engineering and Mustangs Plus. When lowering these cars, the tie-rod angles change to become less than desirable. The kit moves the outer tie-rod pivot point forward and down for an improved angle. This kit changes the Ackerman angle, which quickens steering response, so it is great for handling. On the street, the quick steering and increased steering effort may be too much, so these kits are suggested for track use only.

Rack-and-Pinion

Bumpsteer can be corrected or minimized on cars equipped with rack-and-pinion steering. The steering rack can be adjusted with shims to space it to the

Finding new replacement suspension components, such as steering components and control arms, is a common problem with building up older Fords with less popularity than Mustangs and Cougars. A company called Rare Parts, Inc. offers parts that are not reproduced by any other company. Rare Parts performs manufacturing, destruction, and cycle testing at its facility. Pictured here is a 1970-1971 Gran Torino control arm and a 1965-1968 Galaxy steering arm. (Photo Courtesy Rare Parts, Inc.)

proper position. If shims won't fix the bumpsteer, you may have to modify the steering rack mount, which can be costly and time-consuming. In some cases, the engine or other accessories will limit the amount you can move the steering rack.

The first thing to check is the inner pivot points of the steering rack and outer tie-rod ends. They should intersect the imaginary lines of the front suspension and the instant center. Most likely they don't, so you should attempt to move the rack to a position where they will be as close to those points as possible. Some aftermarket companies offering rack-and-pinion conversion kits for older cars try to adapt rack-and-pinion assemblies from late-model production cars. Some of those racks don't come close to reducing bumpsteer; in fact, they may even make it worse.

Control Arms and Front Suspension Kits

When it comes to handling, upper-front control arms play a large factor. A few Fords are known to benefit from relocating the mount on the frame. Upper control arms can also be shimmed to adjust camber and caster. Many companies offer tubular upper control arms, but not all aftermarket control arms are created equal. Some front suspension kits completely do away with upper control arms for improved geometry and suspension leverage.

Stock Control Arms

Stock upper control arms are great for low-budget Restomod build-ups.

Stock lower control arms can be used by drivers on any size of budget. Vintage racing historians have pointed out that the early Trans Am Mustangs had stock control arms with added bracing. If you are on a budget, you can add some bracing under the upper and lower control arms for added strength.

Control-Arm Relocation – Shelby mod

Probably the most common suspension modification is the Shelby control-arm relocation, also known as the "Shelby mod." According to history books, Ford engineer Klaus Arning came up with the idea and passed it onto Shelby American, which applied it to the Shelby Mustangs. Since then, people have applied this modification to early Ford Mustangs, Falcons, Rancheros, and Cougars. The modification moves the upper control arm down, which lowers the center of gravity, lowers the car approximately ⅝-inch, reduces body roll, and increases negative camber gain. These are all considered positive enhancements to most front suspensions – especially for front suspensions that were adapted from early 1960s-engineered six-cylinder cars. Aftermarket companies and Internet websites offer templates and directions that show where to drill ¹⁷⁄₃₂-inch holes in the shock towers to move the upper control-arm cross-shafts.

The diagrams for performing the Shelby mod on 1964½ to 1970 Mustangs are included in this chapter. These measurements were designed and used back in the 1960s and were also designed for cars using stock upper control arms. Today, aftermarket suspension companies have similar diagrams, but with different measurements. Companies offering after-market control arms and other front sus-

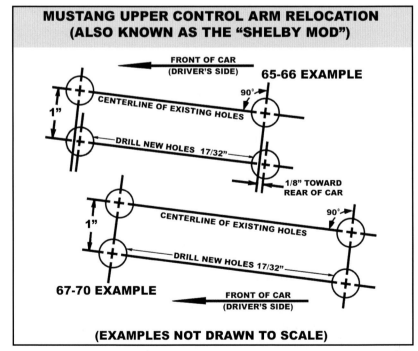

This illustration shows the dimensions for performing the Shelby mod, including lowering the upper control arm to improve the camber curve of the front suspension. These examples are for the driver's side of the car, but the passenger side would use the same dimensions.

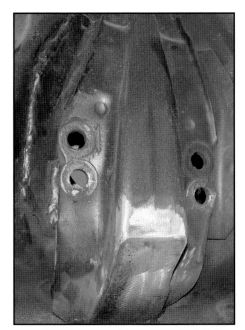

The Shelby control-arm relocation has been performed on this Mustang shock tower. The upper holes are in the stock location, and the lower ones are the Shelby mod holes. The big notch in the lower section of the tower brace was performed by Griggs Racing during serious modifications.

pension parts have found better placement of the control arms to get the ultimate benefits out of their modified geometry. In some cases, the relocation holes interfere with the Shelby mod hole. If you haven't purchased upper control arms yet, but you plan to do so in the future, it might be best to wait on performing the mod.

If you're planning to keep stock upper control arms, and plan on performing the Shelby mod, you should take a few things into consideration. Since the mod lowers the car approximately ⅝-inch, it's enough to cause problems with the tire fit for larger-than-stock tires. It also puts the upper ball joint at a severe angle and increases the unwanted bumpsteer problems already present with the stock suspension's pivot points.

The Shelby mod also requires you to use different alignment specs. You may need to find a reputable shop that specializes in custom alignments because some shops don't like to align vehicles with modified suspension geometry. As long as you follow the

Shelby mod diagram, the Shelby "R" alignment specs will apply. Shelby Mustang specs (with the Shelby mod) are from 2 to 3 degrees (depending on whom you talk to) positive caster, 1 degree negative camber, and ⅛ inch toe-in. If you perform this mod on a vehicle other than a Mustang, you'll need to consult a specialty shop for the correct alignment specs for your application.

The mod lowers the control-arm shaft, which increases the angle of control arm and pivots the upper ball-joint stud close to its limit at full "bump" (the upward movement of the tire and suspension when the tire hits a bump). In some cases, the upper ball-joint stud can bind and break. Pro-Motorsports Engineering and Mustangs Plus offer Negative Wedge Camber Correction Kits, which change the angle of the upper ball-joint and allow for more aggressive control arm relocation for an increased negative camber curve. This mod works best with less shock travel to limit droop because the droop has an adverse effect on steering geometry.

Aftermarket Control Arms and Suspension Kits

Most Restomods are driven harder than the Ford engineers ever intended. The torsional stresses that come from cornering and braking forces can wreak havoc on the stamped-steel stock control arms. You may think, "Why would I need aftermarket control arms on my car? Shelby's racecars worked fine for road racing with stamped steel control

arms." With tire technology and braking force from satellite dish-sized rotors, you will be demanding more from a stamped control arm than Shelby and Bud Moore cars did during good days at the track. Since the 1990s, aftermarket companies have been building control arms designed to handle more stress and include better ball-joint angles. These are great for people who want to drive in a straight line and drive hard through the corners. Be careful, though; there are some aftermarket control arms designed for street rods and air-bag suspension systems that lack integral strength for Restomod applications.

The companies mentioned below are the current companies offering performance control arms for Mustangs, Falcons, Comets, Cougars, Cyclones, Fairlanes, Montegos, Rancheros, Torinos, and Mavericks. Some companies offer control arms that are part of a whole kit, or offer coil-over systems that use their control arms or completely replace the upper arms with the coil-over unit. Those will be mentioned later in this chapter as suspension systems.

Total Control Products

If you have a Restomod or even a slight interest in one, you probably know about Total Control Products. The company started back in 1995 and offered high-quality performance suspension parts designed for street and track use. At that time, the Ford guys were not willing to cut up their cars or modify them in any way that couldn't be

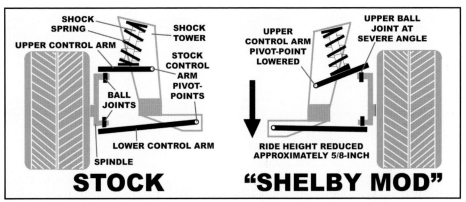

You can see that the Shelby mod relocates the upper control arm, which lowers the car about ⅝ of an inch due to changing the spring-perch position. It also puts the upper ball joint at an extreme angle when using the stock control arm.

Total Control Products offers a fully adjustable coil-over front suspension system with tubular upper and lower control arms, and heavy-duty strut rods. The kit uses Kevlar-injection molded rod ends to achieve movement without the deflection found in original rubber bushings. This kit installs without irreversible modifications.

Global West offers upper and lower tubular control arms with its Category5 coil-over kit (shown here). The kit requires the installer to drill a few holes in the shock tower, so Global West includes quality metal templates and detailed instructions. (Photo courtesy Global West Suspension Systems)

easily reversed. Total Control took this to heart and built top-notch suspension systems with strictly bolt-on parts.

Total Control Products offers tubular upper and lower control arms for muscle car-era Mustangs, Falcons, Comets, Cougars, Cyclones, Fairlanes, Montegos, Rancheros, Torinos, and Mavericks. You get what you pay for with these parts – they don't cut corners. Total Control Products control arms are designed to have less flex than the stock control arms because they're assembled from the best materials and components, and they're TIG welded for strength and durability. The upper control arms have strong mount provisions to use the stock coil-spring set-up (if you choose not to use their coil-over conversion kit). The upper ball-joint angle has been designed to safely operate with the suggested lower cross-shaft location for increased negative camber gain. For strength and durability, the upper and lower control arms are equipped with high-quality injection-molded, Teflon-impregnated Kevlar rod ends. These do not distort like the factory bushings, so your handling will not be erratic. The lower ball joint is a heavy-duty screw-in type

(common in stock-car racing) for easy serviceability and replacement.

Global West

Global West is one of the most diversified aftermarket suspension companies. It makes parts for Fords and GMs, and the performance of its products shows that the company is familiar with both manufacturers. The Ford years span from 1964 to 1973 and 1978 to 2002. Global West calls its suspension systems Negative Roll Systems. This refers to the negative camber gain designed into its systems. Muscle car-era models were plagued with positive camber gain, and the Global West systems are designed to fix that problem.

Global West upper control arms are made from tubular steel, and they improve suspension geometry by not deflecting under heavy cornering loads like stamped stock control arms. The length of the arm is modified from stock, so the front tire will be kept on the pavement over the complete camber curve. Global West suggests lowering the control arm location, similar to the Shelby mod. The upper arms are equipped with billet cross-shafts and Del-a-Lum (Del-

rin and aluminum, pronounced Della-loom) bushings, which allow smooth, deflection-free control arm articulation.

Global West offers two different lower control arm options. One option is a stock lower control arm with welded boxing plates for strength. These control arms also feature spherical aircraft bearings in place of the control-arm bushings for non-binding, full-range motion, and a new standard ball joint. The second option is a full tubular control arm with a spherical aircraft bearing, along with a screw-in ball joint, like the ones used in stock-car racing.

Global West also makes coil-over kits for 1964 through 1973 Mustangs; 1962 through 1967 Falcons and Rancheros; 1967 through 1973 Cougars; 1968 through 1971 Montegos; 1967 through 1971 Fairlanes/Torinos; 1970 through 1977 Comets/Mavericks; and 1975 through 1980 Monarchs/Granadas. Global West calls its coil-over kits Category 5 (or Cat 5) suspension kits. It still requires the use of an upper control arm, but one with a specific design. The extra-long coil-over shock assembly replaces the conventional short shock and coil spring combination. The shock angle was changed for increased performance and leverage. Global West also offers this kit with large-diameter rotors and multiple-piston Wilwood disc brakes for a more complete package.

Revelation Racing Supplies (RRS)

Revelation Racing Supplies (RRS) is an Australian-based company with new distribution in the United States. Don't let its new arrival throw you for a loop; these guys have been around for years. Every product RRS produces is tested by Australia's stringent standards to actually perform and be stronger than the part it is replacing. It would be interesting to see how American products would perform on these tests.

RRS front-suspension kits allow you to ditch old, inferior technology and replace it with a coil-over strut set-up. RRS offers different levels of front strut kits for Mustangs, Falcons, Comets, Cougars, Fairlanes, Rancheros, and Mavericks. The kits all replace the existing upper control arms, coil springs, and shocks. In the place of the old equipment, the kits include coil-over struts that bolt in the stock shock mount location, late-model spindles, disc brakes, calipers, brake hoses, and all necessary hardware for an easy bolt-in application that does not require any fabrication. Slotted disc-brake rotors are available in diameters ranging from 11.3 to 13.2 inches. The brake calipers are available in single- and dual-piston floating calipers, as well as four-piston fixed calipers. As for struts, you can choose between KYB heavy-duty and Koni adjustable units. RRS also offers a strut-rod kit with bearing ends to complement the strut kits.

RRS front suspension kits offer

Revelation Racing Supplies (RRS) offers different levels of front suspension systems for shock-tower-equipped cars. These completely do away with the upper control arm. The kit doesn't require any fabrication and uses serviceable factory tie-rod ends. (Photo Courtesy Revelation Racing Supplies)

improved suspension geometry, reduced (if not eliminated) bumpsteer, adjustable ride height, and up to 5.5 inches of clearance per side with an RRS shock-tower notching kit for big-blocks and Modular engines, all without changing track width. The system works with the stock steering linkage, or it can be used with the RRS performance rack-and-pinion kit.

Fat Man Fabrications

Fat Man Fabrication is probably best known for its Mustang II-type front suspension systems. The company now offers a front strut kit for select shock-tower-equipped Ford models from 1964 to 1973. Fat Man's new set-up is a bolt-on kit, instead of the invasive Mustang II kit that requires moving the engine up

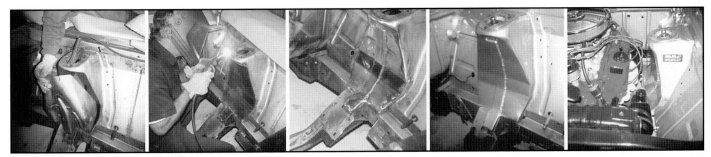

Since the RRS strut front suspension kit totally negates the need for the upper control arms, you can modify the shock tower with an RRS shock-tower notching kit. It creates enough room for the big-block or modular motor you've always wanted to install. (Photo Courtesy Revelation Racing Supplies)

Griggs Racing coil-over front kit totally relocates all suspension pivot points and features weld-in upper-control-arm mounts and a lower K-member. The new steering rack mounts in front of the spindle center-line and uses a racing-style sway bar. (Photo Courtesy Mustang Don's)

and forward, which adversely affects weight distribution and handling. Fat Man claims that this kit allows an adjustable drop of up to 4 inches (with optional parts) and it is designed to operate with zero bumpsteer. That's quite a feat, and a far cry from the undesirable bumpsteer characteristics of the stock Mustang. The kit also allows you to use a stock oil pan and stock sway bar without welding. Since the springs are smaller in diameter than the stock spring, this kit allows the builder to trim the shock towers for wider and larger engines.

The kit includes a tilt steering column, coil-over springs, tubular lower control arms (with new ball joints and bushings), upper strut mounts (with adjustable camber), a steering shaft (with U-joints), special steering arms, a rack-and-pinion mounting bracket, and mounting hardware. You supply a steering wheel with GM splines; a 1981 to 1986 Escort rack-and-pinion system; and 1994 to 2002 Mustang disc brakes, spindles, and struts.

Griggs Racing Products, Inc

Known more for late-model Mustang racing parts, Griggs Racing Products also has a full line of performance suspension parts for the early Mustangs. Griggs Racing sells different kits for different types of racing, including street, autocross/open track, and American Iron (Pro-Road Race). Each version is specifically designed for the intended purpose. Bruce Griggs advises having a good idea of what you are going to do to

a car before purchasing a kit. Changing your mind halfway through or at the end of a project gets very expensive, and this advice applies to all parts of a project. It is especially true with Restomods.

The Griggs packages are more invasive than just bolting on a pair of control arms. These kits take front suspension to a whole new level. The kits completely replace and relocate the front suspension components and pick-up points. In fact, you can completely remove the shock towers if you choose. The suspension pieces are much stronger than the original equipment, so you get precise geometry for predictable handling. Anti-dive, roll-center, and camber-gain problems associated with the stock suspension are

addressed with this kit. If you don't mind breaking out the welder and cutting torch, this kit is a great improvement, and it works best with the rear suspension kit Griggs offers.

The front-suspension kit is called the GR-350 kit. It comes with a tubular K-member, bumpsteer adjustment kit, upper and lower tubular control arms, mini-tower brake kit, coil-over shocks and springs, adjustable racing-style sway bar, spindle and hub assembly, and a rack-and-pinion steering assembly. The kits come in three different levels: Street, Autocross/Open Track, and American Iron (Pro-Road Race). They are designed for the 1965 through 1970 Mustangs.

Martz Chassis

Gary Martz of Martz Chassis builds drag race and road race subframes for all kinds of cars, including a weld-in subframe unit for Mustangs. Martz's Rally and Road Race chassis for the Mustang is the center of attention for this section. The installation is a little more involved, but you might feel the results are worth it. Not only is the Martz set-up a huge leap in suspension geometry engineering, it also has a much stronger and more rigid frame. Martz offers an optional Wide-Track frame, so you can run late-model offset wheels. The frame has extra-long transmission mounting pads,

Martz Chassis saw there was a market for upgrading the front suspension to something other than a Mustang II set-up. This front clip replaces the weaker stamped-steel frame for increased strength. (Photo Courtesy Martz Chassis)

so you can mount just about any available transmission. There are also different mounts for most Ford engines. The customer can choose from production or aftermarket brakes from Baer Racing or Wilwood, and the sway bar is a custom 1-inch stock-car-style unit. The rack-and-pinion is a Mustang unit, and it's available in manual or power versions.

Martz Chassis doesn't use any Mustang II suspension parts; it makes its own spindles using heat-treated 4140 chromemoly. There is no anti-dive built into the subframe, but some feel anti-dive is overrated anyway. The range of caster and camber is unlimited, but typically the suggested caster ranges from +2 degrees to +6 degrees, and the camber range is zero degrees to + or - 4 degrees. Martz tested its subframe for bumpsteer, and found none for 3 inches of travel. The set-up can be ordered with heim joints or with urethane bushing ends. Martz has been in business for 33 years, so replacement parts are readily available and the system has been street- and track-tested.

Springs

Your front coil springs are one of the most important contributors to the handling characteristics of your Restomod. For this reason, it is crucial that you decide on a spring rate that is right for your ride. A spring that is too soft for the weight of the vehicle is great for drag racing, where racers need the weight of the vehicle to transfer from the front suspension to the rear suspension for ultimate traction. Yet, Restomods do more than just drive in a straight line—they rely on the front tires to keep them on track while entering and exiting a corner. A soft front coil spring will also give you excess body roll and cause your inside tire to lose traction in the corners.

Restomods are intended for street use, just as much as the track, if not more. If your front coil springs have a rate that is too high for the weight and set-up of your car, they will give you a harsh ride on the street. Springs that are too stiff may not allow your car to have the body roll it needs to plant the outside tire in a corner. Without traction of the outside tire, the car can push and

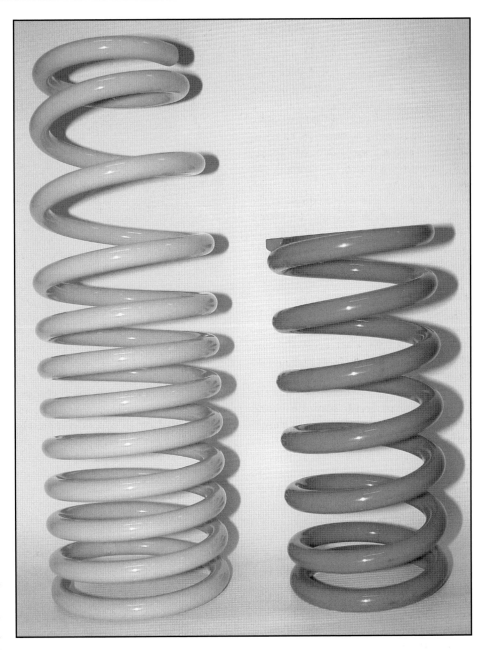

The spring on the right is linear; i.e., its coils are uniform throughout. The spring on the left is progressive; notice the change in winding density. Both types can be used in the front or rear, depending on the suspension type and application.

generate uncontrollable understeer.

Choosing the right spring for your application is not easy. If I told everyone to run a 650-lb front coil spring, I'd be performing a disservice. To make an accurate recommendation, I would need to know your rear spring rate, front and rear shock dampening, bushing types, tire compounds, etc. Every car is different. Sure, you could throw a set of 650-lb front coil springs in your Maverick. You might get lucky and they might be

perfect. In the end, consulting the technical department of your favorite suspension company could help you get the exact spring you need. If your suspension company doesn't have an educated spring recommendation for you, you may want to just get in touch with a reputable spring company.

Coil Spring Basics

There are two different types of coil spring: linear and progressive. They can be identified by looking at the windings. A linear coil spring has equally spaced coils throughout, except at the very end of the spring. The progressive coil spring has coils that are wound tighter on one end of the spring than the other end.

Coil spring rates are identified by how much weight is required to compress the spring 1 inch. A 600-lb spring will require 600 lbs to compress it one inch. A 600-lb linear rate coil spring would require 1,200 lbs to compress the spring 2 inches. A 600-lb progressive rate spring might require 1600 lbs to compress the spring 2 inches. Linear rate coil springs are used on most production cars. Typically, progressive springs are used in racing applications.

Coil springs are available in 400 to 3,200-lb rates. The higher the rate, the harsher the ride will be. Typically, only purpose-built road-racecars need more than 800-lb front coil springs.

When you're trying to increase the performance of your suspension and lower the stance of your car, you should buy some springs designed to perform both tasks at the same time. If you are simply looking to lower your car, you can do it the old-fashioned way by cutting them. Heating your coil springs to lower your car is unsafe and a bad idea. The image of the coil springs in this section shows the ends of the spring are slightly bent to keep the ends fairly flat. The ends fit into pockets in the frame, shock tower, or spring retainer. When cutting coil springs, don't start out cutting two complete coils, because you may end up lowering your car 5 inches by accident. Cut the spring in one-half coil increments. You may need to install the spring a couple of times before you achieve the desired ride height.

Safely remove the springs from your vehicle. Use an acetylene torch to cut half of one coil. Now you need to bend the end of coil so it will seat in the spring pocket. Heat one-half coil leading to the end of the spring where you made your cut and quickly bend that section down toward the rest of the spring. If you can, turn the spring over and push the spring down onto the concrete to bend the coil. Warning: Don't quench your coil spring with water or oil! Let the spring cool

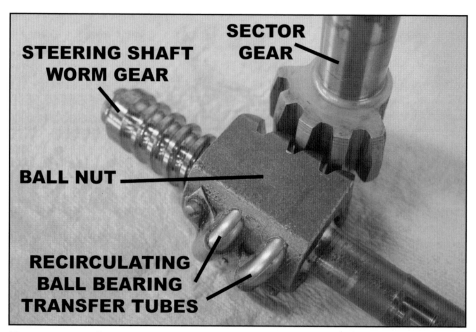

These parts are from a 1965-1966 Mustang steering box. Ball bearings roll around the worm gear and recirculate in and out of the ball nut through the transfer tubes shown. As the steering shaft turns, the ball nut moves up and down the shaft. The teeth on the outside of the ball nut turn the sector gear and steering arm.

slowly in the air. If you quench it, the spring will lose its ability to support the weight of your vehicle. After changing ride height, you will need to have your suspension aligned.

Stock Springs

Stock front coil springs typically deliver a comfortable ride for the majority of the population. For Restomodders, the rate may be too soft or the ride height might be too high.

In the past, it was a cool trick to run "air conditioning" or "big-block" springs for better handling. A stock coil spring for a car equipped with air conditioning and/or a big-block typically has more spring rate to help compensate for the extra weight. Since this is not an exact science, aftermarket springs may be a better choice.

Aftermarket Springs – Available Rates

There are so many companies offering different springs with different weights that it makes sense to tune your suspension with aftermarket springs. Some companies prefer lower-rate springs than others; each company has its own idea of what is best for each application. One company may believe a car should be set up with more oversteer, while another company may believe a car should be set up with more understeer. Since each company has a different idea of what rate is best for each application, you may want to pick a reputable company to ask for help. If you talk with too many companies, you may get too much information for your own good. If you aren't building a full-on competition racecar, you don't need too much information. Keeping it simple is not a bad thing. With the right help, you can get your optimum coil spring rate within 100 lbs, which is more than adequate for most Restomods.

Ball Joints

Serious racers have been replacing stock-style bolt-in ball joints with screw-in ball joints. The welding and machining required to perform this modification should be done by a professional. The screw-in ball joints are stronger and easier to replace in a hurry at the track. Cobra Automotive offers control arms already modified with screw-in ball joints for early Mustangs and Cougars.

Compared to the stock Ford ball joints, the screw-in racing-style ball joint has a larger body and stud. The only way to accomplish this installation is to purchase screw-in ball joints and ball joint adapter rings. You have to weld the screw-in ball joint sleeves into the lower control arms. Since the screw-in ball joint may have a different taper (depending on application and ball joint used) on the stud, the spindle will have to be re-tapered. A reputable machine shop should be able to perform this task, but they might have to buy the special drill-bit to perform the modification.

Keep in mind that the screw-in ball joint has a different pivot point than the stock Ford ball joint. This modification will change the suspension geometry. Installing a suspension part designed for the stock ball joint might not benefit from the changed pivot point, so be aware of this before you do the modification.

Steering

Car builders often overlook the steering system. The stock steering is great for a family cruiser, but if you're going to drive your Restomod on a road course or just want better performance on the street, aftermarket steering systems are available. You may have either a manual or power-assisted steering system on your car. There are two types of steering systems: recirculating-ball gearbox and rack-and-pinion. The power steering system consists of a steering pump, fluid reservoir, hoses, and in some cases there is an add-on power steering cylinder and control valve. Manual steering gearbox systems don't work very well on Restomods, since the Restomod tires are generally wider than stock which makes them more difficult to turn.

Upgrading your recirculating-ball manual system to a power-assisted system requires a power steering box, power steering pump, and in some cases, you'll need to upgrade to power-steering-specific tie rods, center links, idler arms, and pitman arms. You can buy these specific parts from Moog and Rare Parts.

Most Restomod candidates came with the kind of power steering that used a recirculating ball steering box. The steering boxes in 1964 to 1970 Mustangs, Comets, Falcons, and Cougars, and in 1967 to 1968 Fairlanes and Montegos were non-integral units. They all had an add-on assist-type power cylinder and a control valve. The only difference between the actual power and manual steering boxes were the ratios. The fast ratio manual box was the same as the power steering box.

In a recirculating ball steering system, the steering shaft (attached to the steering wheel) turns a worm gear inside the gearbox. Inside the gearbox, there's a nut (a cage that surrounds the worm gear) with teeth on the inside and on the outside. The nut moves forward and backward inside the gearbox. The internal threads on the nut coincide with the external threads of the worm gear. The worm and the nut are separated by a trail of ball bearings that recirculate in and out of the nut, while creating a rolling screw-like thread. The ball bearings allow the worm to turn inside the nut with very little bearing surface area for smooth operation. The teeth on the outside of the nut pivot the sector shaft, which attaches to the steering pitman arm. A power-assisted steering gear puts fluid pressure on the nut to assist its movement inside the steering gearbox. Less effort is needed for applying to the worm gear (meshed with the steering shaft, attached to the steering wheel) to move the nut forward and backward inside the steering gearbox.

Every steering system has a steering ratio. The ratio of the steering box or rack determines how much the wheels turn in conjunction with how much you turn the steering wheel. A wide-ratio (compared to a close-ratio) steering system will require more full steering-wheel revolutions to turn from lock to lock. This could mean as many as six complete revolutions on a 22:1 wide-ratio manual box for a 1967 Fairlane. A typical Ford 16:1 close-ratio steering box will require 3.75 full revolutions of the steering wheel to turn from lock to lock. This might not seem like a big difference, but considering how much less the steering wheel needs to be turned on a road course, a close-ratio box makes driving much less work. Road-course driving can be physically draining, so the less energy spent on turning the steering wheel, the better.

Power-assisted steering systems have a high- and low-pressure circuit. The power steering pump pressurizes the fluid up to 1,350 psi and forces it through the feed line into the steering gearbox. The low-pressure circuit is the return line from the steering gearbox to the fluid reservoir. From the reservoir, the fluid is sucked back into the pump.

The terms "rear-steer" and "front-steer" refer to the location of the steering linkage or rack-and-pinion. The linkage on a rear-steer system is located behind the centerline of the spindles, and the front-steer linkage is located in front of the centerline of the spindles. Before the introduction of rack-and-pinion steering, Ford had been a big proponent of the front-mounted strut rod suspension. Due to space constraints caused by strut rods, most of the early Fords are rear-steer cars. Most newer Ford cars have front-mounted rack-and-pinion steering systems.

Until 1966, most Fords (except full-size Fords) had long-shaft steering boxes, identifiable by their approximately 30-inch-long shafts, when Federal Motor Vehicle Safety Standards required a collapsible steering column. In front-end collisions, the long shaft could be pushed toward the driver with terrible results. In 1967, Ford switched to using very short shafts that used a rag joint to interface with the collapsible steering column.

A power steering gearbox can be set up with custom-tailored efforts. The effort is the resistance you feel in the

If you need a replacement for your worn steering box, check out this offering from Flaming River. The company offers completely new steering boxes—not rebuilt—for 1965-1970 Mustangs. (Photo Courtesy Flaming River)

SCOTT CHAMBERLAIN'S 1985 FORD LTD LX

Scott Chamberlain's 1985 LTD LX is one of 3,260 LXs made from 1984 to 1985. The LTD is built on a Fox-body platform, so many production and aftermarket Mustang parts simply bolt on. In current form, it rivals performance cars of its time, but it has four doors. (Photo courtesy Dave Moore)

When you mention something about a "hot rod," most people don't envision a four-door. To go a little further, most people wouldn't think of an LTD as a "hot rod." Jefferson Morris is a guy who thinks outside of the box. He built most of this LTD before Scott Chamberlain took ownership. Since then, Scott has made this car his daily driver and has taken the performance even further.

This is not your grandma's LTD, or an LTD II, or even a Fairmont – it's a Ford LTD LX. A total of 3,260 were built between 1984 and 1985. Ford took the LTD and dropped in a 5.0 HO engine, AOD transmission, 3.27:1 limited-slip rear end, sport-tuned suspension with larger sway bars, upgraded bucket seats, center console with floor shift, factory tach, special interior trim, and blackened external trim.

That's how the car started. It's been taken further into the performance spectrum since the day Jefferson Morris had the keys in hand. Since the Fox-bodied LX shares many parts with the 5.0 Mustangs, many performance parts simply bolt on. Parts are from the aftermarket as well as Ford. One of the first things to get swapped out was the AOD for a T5 5-speed with a 1987-93 Mustang pedal set,

The LX is subtle. If you didn't know better, you may think it's just an LTD with 17x8-inch Cobra wheels. The car has all the performance angles covered and Scott's not afraid to drive it, so watch out – this may be the only end of the car you will see. (Photo courtesy Dave Moore)

1993 Cobra clutch, Forte's adjustable quadrant, and MAC short shifter.

The car has 140,000 miles on it, so the engine had to be updated sooner or later. The current engine is a 1994 Mustang GT 5.0 with AFR 165 heads stuffed with Crane 1.7 roller rockers.

The intake manifold is a Ford Motorsport Cobra intake with ported lower runners. Feeding the intake is a MAC cold air kit, Pro-M 75-mm MAF sensor, 65-mm Ford Motorsport throttle body, and 24-lb/hr injectors, all handled by a stock 1987-1993 Mustang A9L-calibrated ECM.

This LX is powered by a modified 5.0-liter HO engine from a 1994 Mustang. It knocks down 20 mpg, runs the quarter mile in 13.79 seconds, and glides down canyon roads with speed and confidence. (Photo courtesy Dave Moore)

The exhaust is handled by MAC shorties connected to a stock 1987-1993 Mustang H-pipe to 3-inch single pipe (due to clearance constraints), Dynomax Ultra-flows, and 1999 Cobra dual tips. The cooling is handled by a Mark VIII fan (with a trimmed shroud) hooked to a Delta Current Controls FK-35 unit, which takes the high amp surge out of the Mark fan ramping up. The air conditioning is still intact and works great. The battery has been relocated to the trunk, and gets its juice from a 3G 130-amp 1994 Mustang alternator.

The front suspension was upgraded with 1996+ Mustang spindles, 1996+ Mustang lower control arms, inner and outer tie-rod ends, MAC adjustable caster plates, LX springs (high-rate from the factory), and polyurethane bushings throughout. KYB shocks and struts adorn all four corners. The front sway bar is still the stock unit since it was so stout to start with. The rear suspension consists of a Ford 8.8-inch with 3.73:1 gears and an axle girdle differential cover, box-welded stock control arms, and a 1998 Cobra rear sway bar.

The LTD features 1994+ Mustang Cobra 13-inch front rotors, PBR dual-piston calipers, and late 1980s Lincoln Mark VII 10.5-inch rear discs, all controlled by a Lincoln Mark VII master cylinder and an adjustable proportioning valve. Scott notes that with Lincoln Continental parking-brake cables, the parking brakes actually work. Bolted to the brakes are stock 1999-2001 Mustang Cobra 17x8 wheels wrapped with 245/45R17s all the way around.

The interior currently has most of its stock luster, but it was upgraded with a Momo Monte Carlo steering wheel, 140-mph police speedometer, AutoMeter gauges, CD/tape player combo from a 2000 Ford truck, modified console for new manual shifter, Cobra floor mats, and a dead pedal from 1987-1993 Mustang.

Scott's car sticks out in a crowd because it's not your typical late-model Restomod, but it's subtle enough to avoid attracting undue attention from white-and-black four-door sedans. It's a great mix of luxury, hot rod, and corner carver. It has enough room to transport more than just a driver and one passenger, while knocking out 20 mpg and running a 13.79 in the quarter mile.

steering wheel when you turn it. If the steering box is not built with efforts, you'll be able to turn the steering wheel with one finger, even when the car is sitting still. This might sound good, but it's much better to have a little feedback from your steering so you know how your car is reacting to track conditions.

Contact Flaming River Industries if you want to replace your old, worn Mustang 19.9:1 or Falcon 22:1 ratio steering boxes with a close-ratio 16:1 recirculating-ball steering box. Flaming River saw a void in the 1965 through 1970 Mustang steering market, so they started building gearboxes from brand-new parts. Even the cases are new. They used better materials and re-engineered a few of the areas of the box for better performance.

Power Steering Pumps

Power steering pumps provide the pressurized fluid necessary to drive power-assisted recirculating-ball steering gearboxes and rack-and-pinion steering units. Stock pumps are decent for normal street driving. When you start running your car at track events, you may want to look into upgrading your pump. Upgrading a power steering pump is rarely a simple bolt-in procedure, due to hose and bracket configurations. In some cases, you can utilize factory brackets from a different application.

Thompson Slipper Pump

The Thompson "slipper" pump was offered from 1965 through 1977. It has been called "a bucket-type pump," as well as a few other names I can't print here. The pump worked well for stock applications. The racers who didn't ditch it put up with it because there wasn't a good performance system available. The term "slipper" comes from the eight slipper pistons that are spun around by a rotor inside the internal chamber, somewhat like a vane-style pump. This pump will work fine for most applications, but if you're going to start running 20-minute sessions on track days, where the fluid can reach 250 degrees, you may want to think of upgrading to a later-model pump. Those kinds of temperatures can wreak havoc on the pump's

This is a Thompson "Slipper" power steering pump. The name comes from the design of the internal slipper pistons. If you're planning on periodically running 20-minute sessions at your local road course, you might want to think about upgrading to a new-style pump.

internals. The engineering team probably never envisioned a high-revving 500-hp small-block Maverick running around a road course.

Ford Corporate II (C2) Pump

The Ford Corporate pump used on V-8s from 1978 through 1995 (later on V-6s) is known as the C2 or CII pump. The C2 pump was designed to work better in conjunction with power-assist rack-and-pinion systems. It is known to have problems aerating the power steering fluid, which causes it to groan in some cases. Other than that, it performs great for most Restomods. If one of these fails on you, you might try replacing it with a Saginaw P-series pump (a GM part) with the Ford #F4UZ3C511A pump bracket, the correct pulley, adapter hoses, and some shimming.

If you are sticking with the C2 pump, and you have had problems with fluid blowing out of the vent in the top of the filler cap during racing conditions, you may need to modify the neck of the pump to add a little more expanding room. Cut the top half of the plastic neck off, add a 9-inch heat-resistant 5-ply silicone hose to the neck on the body of the pump, then install the top half of the neck (with the filler cap) to the hose. Use high-quality hose clamps and don't over-tighten them. Basically, you just want to add length to the filler neck to keep the power steering fluid away from the bottom of the vent in the cap. Don't plug the vent hole. That will cause a whole new set of problems—the system needs to breathe.

Saginaw TC Pump

This power steering pump is produced by Saginaw for many auto manufacturers, including Ford and GM. If you plan to race your car on a road course, you might want to take a serious look at upgrading to a Saginaw TC pump (transverse-bearing compact pump). These pumps are well suited for racing and high-performance street applications.

TC pumps are used on most domestic cars produced after 1993 with power-assisted steering. It's easy to find a TC pump to use on your car, but be careful. Saving a few bucks might cause you some headaches. Factory production TC pumps are built specifically for the pressures needed for the steering boxes or rack-and-pinion units they were mated with from the factory, so not all TC pumps are the same. Most have low-drag bearings on both ends of the shaft. One TC pump in particular has a front bushing instead of a bearing. The bushing creates more friction, causing pow-

This is a Ford Corporate II power steering pump. It's also known as a "C2." This pump has been modified by a road racer to prevent fluid from blowing out of the vented cap. The high-temp silicone hose moves the cap further away from the splashing fluid.

The pump on the lower right is a cast-iron Saginaw TC power steering pump built by AGR. The pump held in the hand is an aluminum KRC Racing pump.

er-robbing drag, and wears out faster than a bearing. Luckily, it can be easily identified by its ¾-inch shaft. Using production TC pumps can be challenging since not all of them have the necessary fittings needed to adapt them to your system. Some come with plastic reservoirs mounted directly to the pump, while others use remote-mounted plastic reservoirs.

If you want fewer headaches and better performance from your steering system, spend the extra money to get one of the many available aftermarket TC pumps, which are available in cast-iron and aluminum for weight savings. Aftermarket TC pumps usually come with high-temperature seals and O-rings, as well as low-drag bearings (check with the individual company for specifics). A few companies build TC pumps with different pressures and flow rates that match the performance steering boxes. In that case, get matching components from one manufacturer for best results.

Aftermarket TC pumps are available with all the proper fittings, pulleys, and hardware you will need to hook them up to your steering system. To save you headaches, there are aluminum-mounting brackets available for the 289, 302, 351, and 400 engines. There are even universal brackets if you can't find one

that suits your needs. Not all brackets give you room for the locally mounted reservoir in the position you need, so a little research could pay off, or you could run a remote reservoir.

Some options for aftermarket TC pumps are listed below:

DSE Modified TC Power Steering Pumps

Detroit Speed & Engineering builds brand-new (not rebuilt) pumps for performance applications. DSE has extensive experience with power steering systems and builds each pump by hand, not on an assembly line. DSE offers TC pumps in cast-iron (electroplated for corrosion protection), chromed cast-iron, and aluminum. They are available with and without a custom DSE race-tested integral reservoir. The pumps are built to flow 3.0 to 3.4 gallons per minute at 1,500 rpm. They offer a special pressure valve for use with a Mustang II rack-and-pinion that lowers the flow to 2 gallons per minute, while keeping proper internal system pressure. Without this fitting, your steering may have too much flow, which can make the steering feel too twitchy and over-driven. DSE also offers custom hard-lines, braided lines, fittings, and pulleys for a perfect fit on your custom application.

KRC Power Steering Pumps

KRC Power Steering is a racing power-steering products manufacturer. The company took a good look at the TC pump for racing applications in 1996. KRC could not improve upon the TC design to make it suitable for the grueling abuse of dirt and asphalt racecars, so it designed original aluminum and cast-iron power steering pumps to meet the stringent requirements.

The lightweight aluminum pump weighs just 3.2 pounds with the pulley. It operates up to 70 degrees cooler than other pumps, and it can save up to 3 hp. It features adjustable flow rates with optional flow valves. The cast-iron KRC pump meets the same durability requirements and has the same flow features, but it's less expensive. The KRC pumps have the same mounting pattern as the Saginaw TC pump, so they use the same mounting bracket. The KRC pumps are fitted with the necessary AN fittings.

KRC pumps require the use of an external steering fluid reservoir. Read more about reservoirs later in this chapter. KRC offers aluminum power steering pump brackets for 289, 302, 351, and 400 engines. If KRC cannot locate the pump in the correct location of your engine, it offers a universal bracket you can cut to custom-fit it.

Rack-and-Pinion Steering

A rack-and-pinion unit is also known as a "steering rack." American auto manufacturers have been using rack-and-pinion units in most of their car lines since the 1980s due to the compact, weight-saving design. The aftermarket community saw the performance benefit of the weight-saving, compact design coupled with closer steering ratios, and knew they could be offered as an upgrade for older muscle cars.

Flaming River, Revelation Racing Supplies (RRS), Total Control Products, and Wurth-it Designs offer rack-and-pinion conversion kits for many 1960 through 1970 shock-tower-equipped cars. These kits work for cars originally equipped with and without power steering. The rack is located in the same location as the original steering linkage (and assist ram on power applications), so oil pan clearance remains almost the same.

Flaming River Industries offers a bolt-in rack-and-pinion steering system for 1964 through 1970 Mustangs. It can be installed within hours because it bolts in using original factory holes. The kit replaces the heavy recirculating-ball steering system with a lightweight steering rack. A new steering column and steering shaft is included to further follow the bolt-in features of this kit. They offer a model to be used on 1965 through 1970 Mustangs with Granada spindles.

Total Control Products is another well-known company in the market producing rack-and-pinion steering kits. The company offers kits for 1960 through 1965 Falcons, Rancheros, and Comets as well as 1965 through 1970 Mustangs and Cougars. Kits are available in manual and power-assisted models. The kits are designed to bolt in using as many of the factory bolt locations as possible. Trimming the end of the steering column is necessary on the Mustang kits. There is some cutting and welding to slightly notch the frame when installing the Falcon, Ranchero, and Comet steering-rack kit. The reward of

RRS offers power and manual rack-and-pinion steering systems for many shock-tower-equipped cars. They are well-designed bolt-in kits that install with minimal bumpsteer, if any. They also use factory serviceable tie-rod ends. (Photo courtesy Revelation Racing Supplies)

responsive steering outweighs the work necessary to install these kits.

The RRS rack is a complete bolt-in system that can be fine-tuned to correct bumpsteer. It's also the only system available with a patented linear tracking design to minimize wear, while decreasing deflection. These design features, combined with 2.88 turns lock-to-lock, combine to give you accurate and durable road reel that is comparable with modern sports cars. The RRS kit also has a low roll center, making it possible to eliminate understeer on most applications, including big-blocks. The steering geometry has a complete camber, arc, and steering axis inclination to suit different applications. The kits are available for 1965 through 1970 Mustangs; 1967 through 1970 Cougars; 1962 through 1970 Fairlanes; and 1966 through 1970 Torinos, Rancheros, Falcons, Comets, Montegos, and Cyclones.

Wurth-it Designs offers bolt-in rack-and-pinion kits designed with all-around driving in mind. Kits are offered for 1954 through 1964 full-size cars, wagons, and Galaxies, as well as 1955 through 1960 Thunderbirds. Wurth-it's rack-and-pinion is a true bolt-in kit; it requires no welding or cutting of the stock frame. It doesn't hang down under the crossmember, so it's not a clearance hazard and it doesn't suffer from bumpsteer problems. You can use it with stock spindles or with Granada upgrade spindles. This kit allows you to get rid of

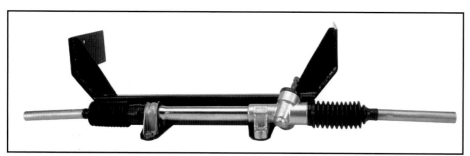

Flaming River offers this bolt-in, front-mount rack-and-pinion conversion kit for your 1965-1970 Mustang. These racks offer a quicker turning ratio; it's only three ¾ turns from lock to lock. (Photo courtesy Flaming River)

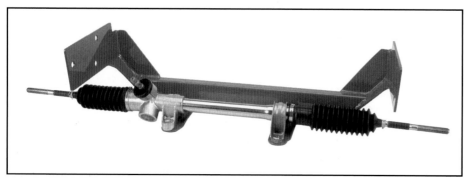

Flaming River also offers this bolt-in, rear-mount rack-and-pinion conversion kit, for 1965-1970 Mustangs. These systems are available with or without steering columns, as well as with a variety of different Header Clearance Kits. The Header Clearance Kits help you avoid fitment problems with different header and engine combos. (Photo courtesy Flaming River)

Wurth-It Designs has answered the prayers of 1955-1956 T-Bird and 1954-1964 full-size Ford owners who want late-model rack-and-pinion steering systems. The Wurth-It bolt-in systems have little to no bumpsteer and they work with stock or Granada spindles. (Photo courtesy Wurth-It Designs)

your sluggish and bulky stock steering system and the leaky steering ram. It updates your car to modern-day steering feel with 3.5 turns lock-to-lock. The kit will fit any engine with a front-sump oil pan. What if you want to use headers on your engine? Wurth-it worked with FPA to build some high-quality headers that will clear the steering rack, Z-bar clutch linkage, frame, and bell housing.

Racing Rack-and-Pinion

Woodward Machine Corporation and Appleton make rack-and-pinion

units for dirt, pavement, and road-racing applications. There is quite a bit of planning and knowledge involved in choosing the right unit for your application. When you get the parts, there's some design and fabrication that needs to be done to correctly mount the rack to your frame and suspension system. There are over 20 different styles of Woodward racks. For help picking the correct rack for your application and installation information, contact either of these manufacturers.

You would find a Woodward or Appleton rack used on an extreme Restomod with fully fabricated suspension, such as the suspension shown in the first photo in this chapter. As seen in that image, a ton of fabrication is required to install it. A bolt-in steering rack was not an option.

Remote Power Steering Reservoir

When running a Saginaw TC pump, it's possible to use a stock plastic late-model-style baffled local or remote reservoir. Remote reservoirs give more options for mounting the pump, since you don't need to mount the pump in a specific position. There are good and bad remote reservoirs on the market, so it is important to be aware of the differences.

The return line and the feed need to be placed in proper locations. If the

All power-steering reservoir tanks are not created equal. The cheap circle-track tank on the right is not fit for street use. The inlet is up too high. The KSE tank on the left has a superior design.

return line is too close to top of the reservoir, the fluid will act as a vacuum and pull air in. This is called aerating. The aerated fluid can cause damage to the steering components. The symptoms will be groaning noises and jerky steering when turning the wheel at low speeds. The return line should be located at the bottom or at least 1½ inches below the surface of the fluid.

Power Steering Hose

There are high- and low-pressure hoses in the power steering system. It's important to use the right power steering hoses in the right places. If you're running stock power steering accessories and brackets, you can use stock replacement hoses. The stock high- and low-pressure hoses will be made to the right lengths and have the correct pressure ratings.

If you're using aftermarket hose on your stock steering system or a custom installation, you'll probably need custom hoses. Whether you're building your hoses, or someone else is doing it for you, make sure they are using the proper hose and fittings for the job. The pressure spikes on the high-pressure side are too much for standard stainless-steel hose and standard anodized aluminum fittings. Using them for custom power-steering hoses is a common mistake, especially on the high-pressure side.

The proper power steering fittings are high-pressure steel, and the hose should be specifically made for a maximum operating pressure of 1,750 psi. A

Woodward Steering and Appleton both make racing power-steering racks. With the right knowledge of steering geometry and moderate fabrication skills, these racks can be adapted to just about anything. They are typically found on racecars and Extreme Restomods.

If the inlet on your power-steering reservoir tank is too high, it can cause the power-er steering fluid to aerate. Air in the steering fluid causes loud groaning and erratic steering-box operation.

performance power steering system can operate upwards of 1,350 psi, but there are spikes in pressure during operation. There are many high-performance hose and fitting companies, like XRP Inc. They offer power steering hose made of elastomeric tube, polyester inner braid, single wire braid reinforcement, and a polyester braid cover. They also offer a full line of steel fittings and hose ends to make just about any power steering hose for your Restomod machine.

Power Steering Coolers

Power steering systems can generate plenty of heat, even on the street. While on the track, the temperatures can soar to over 250 degrees. The heat sources are abundant under the hood. In most cases, the power-steering box is close to the headers, which can reach over 1,000 degrees.

There are ways to cool down the fluid. People have noted a 30-degree drop in steering system fluid with the addition of a remote reservoir. The addition of an inline power-steering cooler is another way to cool the system. There are right and wrong ways to install an inline cooler. Don't install a cooler in the high-pressure side; it puts too much stress on the cooler. Plus, if

This is an extruded aluminum power-steering cooler. Detroit Speed & Engineering offers these to mount between the outlet of the power-steering box and the return port on the steering fluid reservoir. Mount it where air will move around it, but make sure road debris won't rip it off.

the cooler were to get nicked by a rock, there would be 1,300 pounds of pressure pushing fluid out of the system really fast. Just about any lubricating fluid in contact with hot exhaust is a bad idea.

Put the cooler on the low-pressure return side of the system between the power steering box or rack and the reservoir. Coolers can be stacked-plate, extruded-cylinder, or round-tube designs. A stacked-plate cooler is made up of many flat plates (tubes) stacked on top of each other, which looks much like a miniature engine coolant radiator. The extruded aluminum cooler comes in many different forms. They are made of extruded, finned aluminum and are typically at least 8 inches in length with a fitting on both ends. The round-tube cooler is basically a round tube in a straight line, or U-shaped with small cooling fins to help disperse heat. Each design has proven effective in street and track conditions. Be sure the cooler is designed for at least 60 psi and high-heat conditions. A cooler with a ⅜-inch or -6 AN inlet and outlet is best suited for power steering applications. If it's a tube-style cooler, make sure the fittings are not soldered to the tube. The solder will melt and you will have a mess on your hands.

Size matters, too. A small 8x4x2-inch stacked plate or 6-inch round-tube cooler will be more than adequate for most

A common mistake in building custom power-steering hoses is using standard steel-braided rubber hose and aluminum fittings on the high-pressure side of the system. Pressures there can reach 1,350 lbs. This hose is only good for a fraction of that pressure.

Top racecars run Setrab coolers. If they can endure competition racing conditions, they can work well on a Restomod. Setrab offers stacked-plate coolers like this one in different sizes. The close-up on the right shows the cooling fins. (Photos courtesy Setrab)

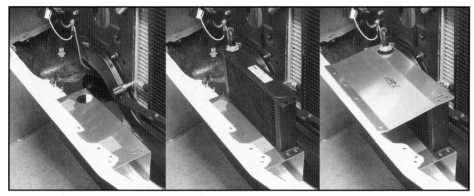

These sequence photos show a fairly simple bracket bent up to mount the Setrab cooler to the front of a Chevy Camaro. This cooler could be used for power steering, engine oil, and transmission fluid. For some reason, most people typically mount coolers to the radiator, where it can put undue stress on the radiator core. This cooler is mounted between top and bottom brackets made out of aluminum. I used light-tack masking tape to protect the paint surfaces and hold the brackets in place during installation and fabrication.

Here is the same Setrab cooler viewed from the front of the car. It gets more than enough air flowing through it. This idea can be applied to any car. Shelby Cobras have been taking advantage of this for decades. The aluminum brackets were hard-anodized for protection against the elements since this is a street-driven car.

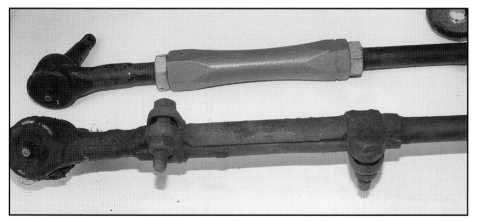

This tie-rod adjuster is offered by Detroit Speed & Engineering. It's made of 4140 1-inch hex stock, and it is much stronger than the stock unit. The hex allows for easy adjustment over stock adjustment sleeves. The stock sleeve adjusters are flexible sheetmetal. When they flex or bend, your suspension geometry and alignment changes. Why spend good money on aligning your car and not fully utilize the settings?

Restomods, even on a road course. Anything larger, and the cooling efficiency of the system will be hampered. Some production cars and trucks have been equipped with little in-line coolers. Installing one of these little coolers can reduce the fluid temperature by 30 degrees. The cooler fluid temperature will increase the life of the fluid, the pump, and steering assembly.

As with any cooler, if it's not placed where moving air can come into contact with the fins, it will be less effective. Place the cooler in a safe place where a rock off the tire or debris from an unplanned off-track excursion won't cause damage to any part of the system. The factory usually places its power-steering coolers on the frame rail in the engine compartment. Unlike with radiators, some moving air for the power steering cooler is better than none at all. Placing the cooler in front of the radiator where cool air is flowing is not always convenient.

Tie-Rod Adjustment Sleeves

Tie-rod adjustment sleeves are a weak link, but they are often overlooked as an upgrade. The stock adjusters are just sheetmetal formed into tubes. They flex under hard driving conditions, which causes variances in suspension geometry. The stock adjusters can also bend, causing the front suspension to be out of alignment. The stock adjustment clamps also make aligning a tough job at the track.

A couple of aftermarket companies offer beefy tie-rod adjusters. They're stronger than stock sleeves because they completely wrap around the tie rods and have full thread engagement. Their strength maintains more accurate alignment and suspension geometry under hard driving conditions. Hard driving conditions don't just happen on the track. The street is full of potholes, train tracks, and debris that can knock the suspension out of alignment. All performance-driven cars should upgrade to these adjusters. Adjusting the aftermarket sleeves is much easier for last-minute track adjustments and alignments at your local shop, because the adjustment sleeves and nuts can be turned with common wrenches.

REAR SUSPENSION

As with the front suspension, the rear suspension is very important when you're building a performance Restomod. These cars are supposed to be driven, and driven hard. This chapter will go over different factory and custom rear suspension systems for your Restomods. It will also explain how to get the best all-around performance out of your rear suspension

There are two typical types of rear axles: live axle and independent rear suspension (IRS). The live axle consists of a rigid housing that contains the axle shafts and differential, with wheels mounted solidly on both ends—this is the rear end that most of us are used to seeing under cars. Any travel or motion from the left tire directly affects the right tire, since they are both attached to the axle. A live axle is attached to the car's frame using links, bars, or leaf springs. There are many different link configurations. When it comes to locating the live axle, the concept is basic. The axle needs to have limited fore and aft movement. It also needs to have limited travel from side to side. All this is needed, while still allowing the axle to move up and down. From those basic principals, live-axle rear suspension gets complex.

Pinion Angle

The pinion angle is simply the angle between the rear end's pinion shaft and a true horizontal line. The transmission angle is the angle between the transmission's tail shaft and a true horizontal line. Together, these angles form the dri-

Here are two types of angle gauges. The analog gauge on the left can be purchased from most hardware stores. The digital SmartTool is more expensive. Both show that the rack is very close to zero degrees, which means the suspension is loaded correctly.

veline's phase angle. Pinion angles can make the difference between a smooth ride, or a noisy and shaking ride down the freeway. Correct pinion angles are also very important to the life of your U-joints. Over time, the angles can change and become incorrect due to loose factory tolerances, body and frame alignment, and changes in spring rates due to wear. You should check and correct pinion angles any time you change the ride height or modify the rear suspension. Even changing leaf springs can change the pinion angle.

Hot rod shops and seasoned backyard mechanics commonly overlook pinion angles. When I was doing research on this subject, I found out why it seems like there is very little information about it, and the little bit of information available seems to be con-

tradictory. After a lot of research, I decided to enlist the help of Kyle Tucker (an ex-GM suspension engineer).

It turns out that pinion angles are not a Jedi secret, though they differ for each application. Family trucks, production sports cars, and Restomods are not built for the same type of driving. I am going to cover pinion angle settings for Restomods built for street and road course racing, since the book isn't strictly covering drag racing, Baja racing, swamp buggy racing, or grandma cars.

Maybe you're building a full-tilt tube chassis to slide under a Fairlane shell. The best chassis designers determine the ride height first by positioning the rear axle, the correct size of tires, and the wheels under the body. Once they do that, they set the transmission height and angle, and then build the rest of the car

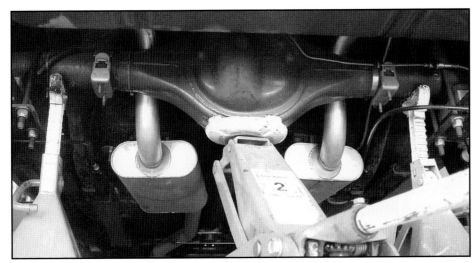

This is another way to lift the car up for measuring the pinion angle. Make sure to do this on a flat, safe surface. Place jack stands safely under the rear axle to compress the suspension as if the car were on the ground.

around that. If your car is finished or you are in the middle of a build-up, don't worry. These angles can be adjusted later, but it would be better if the car were designed around the correct angles to begin with.

Checking Pinion Angle

Checking pinion angle correctly is important. Start by getting an angle gauge. A few types are available. The most common is an analog magnetic-base protractor gauge (pictured in photos checking angles). These are available for about the cost of a meal at your local restaurant. Other types, such as digital angle gauges, are far more expensive. They basically do the same job, but they're much more precise.

Next, find a place to check your angles. Using a four-post rack or a pit is the most accurate way. The car should be on a level surface and at ride height. To get the ride height correct, you should fill the fuel tank. Fuel can add a lot of weight and change the ride height of the car. If the car is not level on the rack and resting on all four tires, your readings will not be accurate.

If you don't have access to a four-post rack or pit, you can use jack stands and/or ramps to simulate the fully loaded ride height. Do this on a hard, flat surface and make sure the car is level. You should place jack stands safely under the rear axle tubes. Do not use a floor-jack to support the front of the car. This is very unsafe. The front of the car needs to be lifted exactly as much as the rear of the car. If you are using jack stands under the front of the car, placement is very important. If you place the stands under the frame in front of the centerline of the spindle, you will be placing moren of the vehicle's weight on the rear suspension. If you place the jack stands under the frame behind the spindle centerline, you will be moving some of the load off the rear suspension. This factor will cause incorrect measurements.

The most precise way to set your car up for measuring pinion angle, without a four-post rack, is to use two sturdy car ramps and two sturdy jack stands. Start by driving the front of the car up on the ramps. Safely place jack stands under the left and right rear axle housing tubes. At this point, the front and rear of the car have to be raised evenly. If the ramps raise the front tires up 9.75 inches off the ground, the rear jack stands should support the rear axle so the rear tires are 9.75 inches off the ground. This will ensure you have lifted the front and the back of the car evenly for accurately measuring pinion angles. Don't forget: safety comes first.

The angle on the transmission is typically measured off the back of the transmission on the driveshaft yoke's seal surface. It can also be measured off the engine block, since the oil pan's gasket sealing surface is parallel to the crankshaft (just take into account that there is a 90-degree angle difference from the transmission angle). The pinion angle on the rear end is taken from the face of the pinion yoke. Finding the flat surface on the transmission and the pinion yoke is easy, but there may not be space to place your gauge. If you have a metal straight edge, you can rest it against the flat surface and attach your magnetic gauge to the straight edge.

For a car that is set up for handling around corners, the optimum pinion

The transmission angle can be measured off the yoke or off the tail-shaft seal. Here, a straight bar was pressed up against the seal with the magnetic-base angle gauge attached to read the transmission tail-shaft angle.

This picture shows phasing angles that should be used for most leaf-spring Restomods. Notice the pinion and transmission angles are both down.

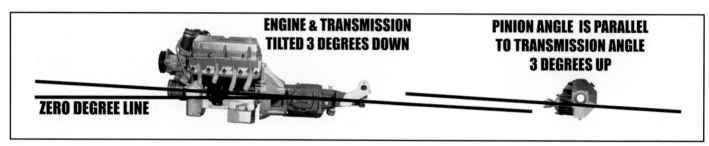

This picture shows how phasing angles are set up on most production passenger cars. Notice the differential pinion angle is as many degrees up as the transmission angle is down. The angles are parallel. Without load on the suspension, the angles total 6 degrees. These angles should add up to a maximum of 7 degrees.

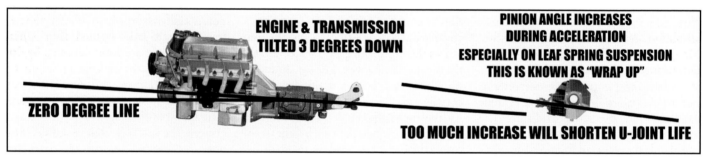

This picture illustrates the problems with running parallel phasing angles. The differential is shown with a torsional load from acceleration. The pinion tries to push upward, causing the springs to wrap up. At this point, the maximum tolerable angle of 7 degrees has been exceeded. This is bad for U-joints.

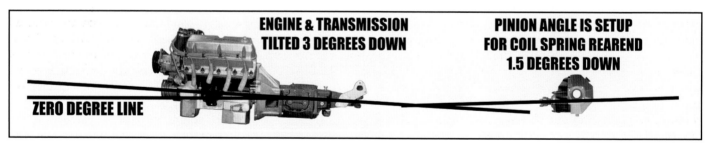

In this picture, you can see the pinion angle is set fewer degrees down than the leaf-spring set-up. This is how short-track coil-spring suspensions should be set up. Unlike leaf-spring suspensions, the trailing arms used in a coil-spring suspension typically minimize upward movement of the pinion.

angle is different than if you were setting your car up for serious drag racing. Incorrect pinion angles can cause chassis vibration and premature U-joint wear and failure. Without the correct angles, the needle bearings in the U-joint caps do not rotate (as shown in the U-joint section). Those needle bearings need to rotate in order for the U-joint to operate reliably and smoothly.

Optimum Pinion Angle

Now that you know how to measure pinion angle, it's time to find the optimum pinion angle. There are many different schools of thought in this area of suspension tuning. I am going to go over pinion and transmission angles. Both angles are equally important when it comes to optimum suspension tuning. When referring to both angles combined and their relation to each other, they are referred to as phasing angles.

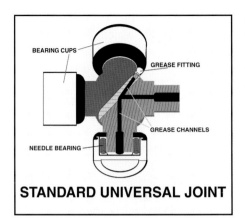

STANDARD UNIVERSAL JOINT

This is the standard U-joint. It is strong enough for everyday driving. If you are going to apply excessive torque and/or sticky tires, stepping up to an off-road-style U-joint is a good idea.

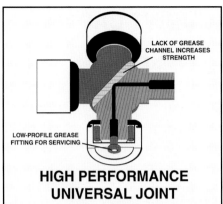

HIGH PERFORMANCE UNIVERSAL JOINT

This is an off-road U-joint. It has a grease canal and is made of stronger material than a standard U-joint. Off-road U-joints are a good compromise between standard and racing U-joints because they're stronger than standard units, but still serviceable.

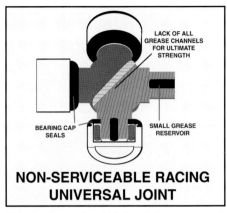

NON-SERVICEABLE RACING UNIVERSAL JOINT

This is the racing U-joint. It has no provisions for servicing. It does not have grease canals, which increase its strength. The only lubrication comes from small grease reservoirs in the end of the U-joint legs.

Pinion angle depends on your application. Production passenger cars and basic street cars operate fine with parallel pinion and transmission shaft angles. Many shops still use this old-school design for building cars, and it's fine for street use. However, if you are going to build a car that will be pushed to its limits on a road course, then forget that school of thought. During acceleration, torque causes the pinion to tilt upward. If you set your pinion angle a few degrees upward, the pinion will want to travel even further upward during acceleration. This is explained in more detail in the leaf spring section. The most common transmission shaft angle is 2 to 3 degrees down. Leaf-spring suspensions allow the pinion angle to rotate upward when the springs wrap up under acceleration. Angling the pinion downward compensates for this upward travel. Serious short-course racecars run a pinion angle of as much as 4.5 degrees down. A downward pinion angle of 2.5 to 3 degrees is a good place to start for Restomod (high-performance street and road course) applications.

The combined pinion and transmission angle should not exceed more than 7 degrees. A combined pinion angle of 3 degrees and transmission angle at 2.5 degrees add up to 5.5 degrees, which does not exceed the maximum. If you run parallel phasing angles like some old-school street rodders have been using, you can easily run into problems. For example, think of the transmission angle set at 3 degrees down and the pinion angle set up 3 degrees to run parallel with the transmission. When the leaf spring wraps up, the pinion angle can rotate upward 2 or more degrees. If you add the transmission angle at 3 degrees to the pinion angle of 3 degrees, it would add up to 6 degrees combined. During wrap-up, the 6 degrees can become 8 or more degrees, which exceeds the maximum allowable range totaling 7 degrees. This will dramatically shorten the life of your U-joints.

Restomods equipped with coil-spring rear suspensions can run with less downward pinion angle. The trailing arms on a coil-spring suspension typically limit the amount of pinion lift (where the front of the differential tilts upward), so pinion angle can be set at 1.5 degrees down.

Pinion Angle Adjustment For Leaf-Spring Suspensions

On leaf-spring suspensions, there are a couple of ways to adjust the pinion angle. The more common way is to install shim-style wedges, which are available in different degrees from several manufacturers. The other method is to install a pair of adjustable leaf-spring pads. These are great for project cars that will not be sitting at fully loaded ride height for quite some time. They can be installed early in the process of a project, then adjusted and welded later when you're close to finishing the car. They're a nice alternative to welding a stationary spring perch to the differential housing early on in a project, and having to use shims to adjust the pinion angle later.

There is an alternative to welding the adjustable perch, too. Once they're installed and the pinion angle is adjusted, carefully drill a hole through each perch and axle tube. Then thread the hole in the axle tube to accept a bolt. Disassemble the rear end to clean all metal debris from inside the axle housing, and then reassemble the rear end. This is not the easy or preferred method, but it is an alternative for people without welders.

Pinion Angle Adjustment For Coil-Spring Suspensions

Adjusting pinion angle on coil-spring suspension systems is completely different than on leaf-spring suspensions. There are three ways to adjust coil-spring suspension pinion angle. The third is the easiest and most common.

1. Cut the spring perches off the rear differential housing and weld them back on at a different angle.

2. Modify the length of the stock trailing arms.

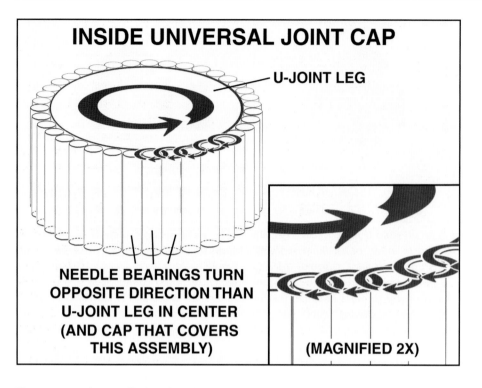

INSIDE UNIVERSAL JOINT CAP

U-JOINT LEG

NEEDLE BEARINGS TURN OPPOSITE DIRECTION THAN U-JOINT LEG IN CENTER (AND CAP THAT COVERS THIS ASSEMBLY)

(MAGNIFIED 2X)

You can see the needle bearings in the cap. When the joint turns, the needle bearings spin, keeping the U-joint from causing vibrations in the drivetrain and causing a shortened life.

A 2-degree wedge has been placed between the spring perch and the leaf spring. Shims typically come in 2- and 4-degree increments.

3. Purchase fully adjustable aftermarket control or trailing arms. These are readily available and are the most convenient way to get full adjustability from your coil spring rear suspension at any ride height.

Many different aftermarket companies offer adjustable upper control arms. These are easy to install, stronger than stock arms, and give you adjustability. More information on these arms is given later in this chapter.

Universal Joints

There are three types of universal joints available:

Standard-Duty U-Joint – This U-joint is great for everyday driving. It's completely serviceable, with a zerk fitting located on the body between two of the legs. However, the hole for the zerk fitting can be a weak area when a lot of torque is applied.

Off-Road U-Joint – This U-joint is for off-road/road-race applications. It's completely serviceable, but the zerk fitting is located at the tip of one of the U-joint caps. The body is much stronger since the fitting hole is not located near the center. This U-joint is also made of a stronger steel than the standard-duty U-joint.

Race-Only U-Joint – This U-joint is for racing uses only. It isn't serviceable and has no zerk fittings. The only way to service this U-joint is to completely remove it, lube it by hand, and then reinstall it. It's stronger because the U-joint body is solid steel, with no internal passages for grease.

Driveshaft angles of the driveshaft are very important to the life of the U-joint. Inside of the U-joint caps are needle bearings, which have to rotate inside of the cap when the U-joint is spinning. The needle bearings will not spin if the U-joint is installed incorrectly or the driveshaft angles are incorrect. If the needle bearings do not spin, they wear out. This will eventually cause strange drivetrain vibrations that are hard to pinpoint.

You can usually tell if your U-joints are worn excessively if you hear a clunking noise from the drivetrain when shifting from reverse to a drive gear. A worn U-joint can cause excessive vibrations in the drivetrain. The most sure-fire way to check the U-joints for wear is to safely put your car up on jack stands or a hoist. With the engine turned off, but in gear, physically attempt to rotate the driveshaft clockwise and counterclockwise. If you can feel play or see the pinion or transmission yoke not move in conjunction with the driveshaft, it's probably time to replace the U-joints. There should not be any visible play between the U-joint and its end caps.

Leaf Springs

Sometimes people overlook leaf springs as an important part of a car's performance. Leaf springs are not only an easy way to locate the differential housing, but they can also mean the difference between a comfortable or a harsh, uncontrollable ride. They also set the ride height for your car. Leaf springs are a single unit, but should be thought of as two separate units that do distinct jobs. The front half of the leaf spring locates the rear-end housing in the chassis. The rear half of the leaf spring is responsible for the ride quality. The spring effectiveness is affected by bias. Front leaf-spring bias means the front half of the spring has higher strength and spring rate than the rear. A spring with too little front bias will tend to promote leaf spring wrap-up (explained later in this chapter) and possibly induce wheel-hop. More front bias will help cure those problems, yet less rear bias will help the ride of the car be softer. More rear bias will also help make the rear of the car more stable around corners and firm up the ride a little.

This has a late-model Thunderbird four-bar suspension with stock trailing arms. These are not adjustable in any way except to cut them to the length you desire, which is more hassle than it is worth.

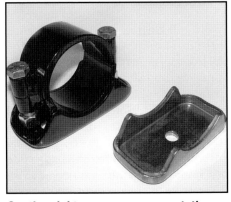

On the right, you can see a stationary spring perch. On the left, you see an adjustable perch. They are both offered by Detroit Speed & Engineering. There are many benefits to using adjustable spring perches.

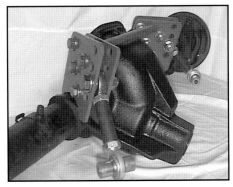

Pro Suspension Components offers this set-up that replaces the upper control arms on your 1979 to 2004 8.8-inch-equipped Fox-body. The system is called Pro-Link, and it allows easy pinion angle adjustment and change of instant center. (Photo courtesy Real Speed Parts)

having your own springs built is a company that has been in business of producing springs for manufacturers and some of the top custom car builders since 1937. Eaton Detroit Spring can build the perfect spring for your custom or stock application.

If you throw a set of 153-lb springs on your Mustang and install mismatched front and rear shocks and sway bars, you may get lucky and get a car that handles great. In most cases, mismatched components can leave much to be desired. This is a good reason to consult a knowledgeable suspension engineer or use a complete suspension package from a reputable company. At the very least, do some homework to increase your own knowledge before spending your hard-earned money on parts that might not work well together. Asking other enthusiasts what worked for them is a great way to get answers.

Wrap-Up

Leaf springs have a major enemy: wrap-up. Massive amounts of horsepower and torque under your hood will put a smile on your face. But if you can't get your power to the ground, it's less fun and sometimes it's downright frustrating.

When you hit the throttle, the torque of the engine is transferred to the rear end via the driveshaft. With the forces of the ring and pinion rotating against each other, the pinion is pushed upward. Since the rear end is mounted to the leaf springs, the springs try to change from their typical arc shape to the shape of an "S" as the rear-end housing rotates upward. This phenomenon is referred to as wrap-up. Wrap-up can be more or less extreme, depending on the leaf springs you have. With any hint of traction, the wrap-up can turn ugly and produce wheel-hop. The way to combat wrap-up is to install a set of leaf springs designed with more front bias.

Steel Multi-Leaves

Most Ford Motor Company vehicles are equipped with rear suspensions with steel multi-leaf springs. Not all aftermarket multi-leaves are created equal. I will point out the different fea-

Aftermarket companies offer many different spring configurations. Each company has a different idea about what design is best for each application. One company may believe that a 1971 Mustang would work better with a higher rate (stiffer) spring, which produces more oversteer. Another company may offer less front bias (less front spring strength), causing the leaves to wrap up

easier under hard acceleration. Some companies offer only leaf springs, while others offer leaf springs with rates that are balanced as a system with their other suspension components for a better overall package. Typical spring rates for leaf springs range from 85 to 250 lbs. The rates are determined by the vehicle's weight, model, year, and performance level. The best source for information on

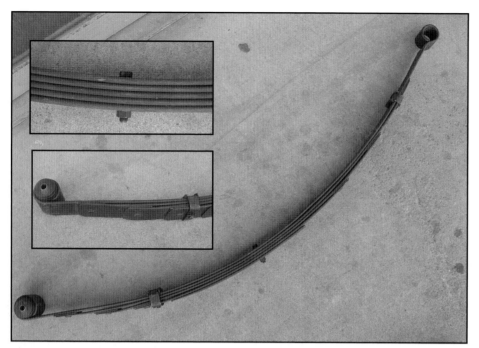

Here you can see the basic parts of a multi-leaf spring. A mono-leaf spring would only have one leaf. The center bolt holds the leafs together. The round portions at the ends of the spring are called spring eyes.

tures to help you decide what the best spring will be for your application.

Leaf Spring Rates

Spring rates are determined by placing the spring on a test table under a spring press. Mono-leaf springs are laid on the table with the arc facing down, opposite of the direction they're mounted on a car. If it takes 150 lbs of force to compress the spring 1 inch, it's a 150-lb spring. The higher the rate, the stiffer the spring. Mono-leaves are pretty basic in this aspect.

Multi-leafs are also rated on a test-table, but they have a progressive rate. The progressive rate comes from the secondary leafs that are stacked in succession with the main leaf. The extra leafs change the spring rate significantly. Before the main leaf can be compressed

1 inch, the secondary leafs begin to resist compression, and typically increase the amount of weight it takes to compress the spring.

Leaf Spring Features
Bias

Think of the leaf spring as a front section and a rear section that are separated at the axle-locating pin. A spring with more front bias will require more leverage to bow the front half of the leaf spring than the leverage required to bow the rear. The secondary leafs change the bias of the leaf spring as a complete package. A good spring for Restomod applications will have more front bias. This means that the secondary leafs are more prominent in the front half of the leaf spring unit. However, don't forget about the rear half of the leaf spring unit.

It's important too. Minimizing the number of leafs or their lengths in the rear half of the spring saves weight, but it can hamper your handling characteristics. Without the proper number of leafs in the rear half, the leaf spring may be too soft and better suited for drag racing.

Anti-Friction Pads

Multi-leaf springs are constructed of multiple steel leaves, and the friction between the leaves contributes to the spring's stiffness. To reduce the friction and noise, some manufacturers include anti-friction pads between the leaves to improve ride quality for street use. This is something to look for in a spring, since Restomods are meant to be driven as much as possible.

Lowered Springs

There are quite a few aftermarket companies producing lowered rear leaf springs. Lowering springs typically lowers the ride height of the car by changing the rate, arc, and overall length of the leaf spring. Some springs are available with the spring eye configured differently than the original spring. For instance, if the front spring eye is curled upward, the front spring eye can be built with the spring eye curled downward. This effectively lowers the car approximately 1.5 inches without using a lowering block. The benefits are not only the lower stance; you also get lower roll steer (steering changes induced by body roll), decreased torsional spring twist, decreased lateral movement, and a lower roll center (an imaginary line the body and frame pivot on during body roll). Beware: Installing lowered springs can change the pinion angle of your rear end. You might want to re-check your pinion angle after you lower your car to make sure everything lines up correctly.

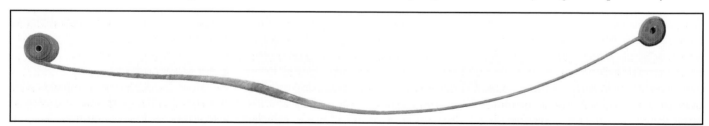

If you use sticky tires with a leaf-spring suspension, the leaf spring can be overpowered if the suspension is not set up correctly. The torque can turn the leaf spring into an "S" shape.

To eliminate bind and friction, pads are placed between leafs. Here you can see the anti-friction pad between the end of a secondary leaf and the main plate (primary leaf).

Leaf springs can be customized to lower or raise the ride height of your car. You may notice the leaf spring eye is reversed. See how the main leaf is on top and then curls down. This custom spring was made to lower the car.

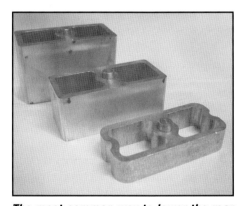

The most common way to lower the rear of a car with leaf-spring rear suspension is to install lowering blocks. Here you see the different sizes of lowering blocks. BellTech offers lowering-block kits, which include longer U-bolts, nuts, and blocks.

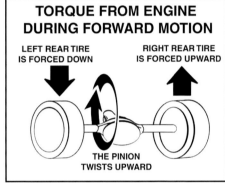

TORQUE FROM ENGINE DURING FORWARD MOTION

LEFT REAR TIRE IS FORCED DOWN

RIGHT REAR TIRE IS FORCED UPWARD

THE PINION TWISTS UPWARD

When the housing is separated from the leaf spring with more than a 2-inch block, the housing gets too much leverage. With power applied to the drivetrain, the rear-end housing can wrap-up the leaf springs into an "S," which can lead to wheel hop.

This Global West solid bushing does not bind in radial motion. The center and sides are not attached. The center is allowed to turn while the sides are bound. These bushings are equipped with grease fittings (not shown) so they can be serviced.

Lowering Blocks

The most common way to lower the rear of a leaf spring car is to install lowering blocks – basically a spacer that goes between the spring and the rear-end housing. Most Ford leaf spring cars have the rear-end housing located on top of the leaf springs. This makes lowering a car with blocks very easy. Trucks typically have the rear-end housing located under the leaf spring. Some early Ford cars are also designed this way. In this case, you can move the housing and relocate the rear axle mount pads to locate it on top of the leaf spring. After you do this, you can use the lowering block to further lower your vehicle.

Running more than a 2-inch block moves the axle housing too far from the leaf spring. This gives the axle housing more leverage when torque is applied, and will promote leaf spring wrap-up and wheel hop. If you have to run more than a 2-inch block, you should check into getting some lowered leaf springs.

Leaf-Spring Bushings

Leaf-spring bushings come in three types: rubber, urethane, and solid. Your choice of leaf-spring bushings should depend on what kind of driving you plan on doing. One builder may prefer using rubber in the front spring eye and urethane in the rear spring eye to keep road shock to a minimum. Since the front eye of the leaf spring takes most of the road shock, using rubber there makes sense. The urethane bushing in the rear eye minimizes lateral (side to side) leaf-spring movement. On the other hand, another builder may prefer to use solid Delrin and aluminum leaf-spring bushings front and rear for better handling performance, at the expense of ride quality.

Rubber

Rubber leaf-spring bushings are great for stock grocery getters. They minimize the transfer of road feel to the chassis because they absorb the shock from uneven road surfaces. On the other hand, rubber bushings allow the rear suspension to travel in ways you may not want it to, which can make the car unpredictable in high-performance driving.

Urethane

The next step up in performance is to replace the rubber spring-eye bushings with urethane bushings. Urethane bushings don't distort like rubber bushings, so they keep the springs in proper position. They help reduce body roll and torsional movement of the leaf spring. Urethane leaf-spring bushings should be installed with the manufacturer's suggested lubricant. Under harsh conditions, they

This is a parallel four-link rear suspension set up for cornering purposes. A panhard bar in front of the rear-end housing keeps it from moving from side to side. (Photo courtesy John Parsons)

These are leaf-spring bushings. They come in different forms: rubber, urethane, and solid. Each has different characteristics, so do your research and choose the best option for your car and the type of driving you're doing.

Three-link rear suspension systems have two lower links connected to the housing (like a four-link), but the upper links are replaced with a single link on the top of the differential housing. This set-up is not a typical three-link, because it has a decoupled torque arm just below the third link. This set-up works well, but it is not the best for regular street driving.

should be serviced on a regular basis to reduce squeaks. Since urethane is denser than rubber, some people feel the ride becomes too harsh, especially when using them in the rear spring eye. Using a urethane bushing in the front and rear spring eyes increases the transfer of road shock to the car. When pulling in and out of driveways at an angle, you will get some binding in the front spring eye. This binding can periodically cause noises under the rear seat. It sounds like someone dropped a water balloon on a car from a second story window (not that I would know). Even the twisting motion of the leaf springs under hard braking can produce this sound. Most of the road shock and binding come from the front

spring eye, which is why some people stick with a rubber bushing up front.

Solid

If you don't care about an extremely comfortable ride, you can completely do away with flexible bushings and install solid bushings made of aluminum and Delrin. Unlike urethane and rubber bushings, solid bushings have a solid center and separate solid sides. This allows the center to turn in a radial motion without binding on the sides. Solid bushings resist chassis roll, promote more predictable handling, and they do not bind. It is frustrating to drive a car on a road course and have it turn into a corner differently, even

though you entered it exactly as you had every other time. Solid bushings are a great fit for Restomods built for frequent outings at the road course. However, solid bushings create a harsh ride because they do not absorb as much energy from uneven road surfaces.

Coil Springs

In the U.S., Ford Motor Company has not used parallel leaf springs in any car line since 1980, but they are still used in trucks. The following is a list of a few of the cars equipped with coil spring rear suspensions: 1979 to present Mustangs; 1965 to 1978 LTDs and Galaxies; 1972 to 1979 Torinos and Rancheros; 1967 to 1988 Thunderbirds; 1965 to 1978 Marquis and Monterey; 1979 to 1986 Capris; 1974 to 1988 Cougars; 1972 to 1976 Montegos; 1978 to 1983 Zephyrs; 1968 to 1979 Lincolns; and more models and years. Typical Ford coil systems have two coils and four locating arms. The coil springs simply locate between two spring pockets. The length of the springs, the control arm articulation, and the weight of the vehicle all work to keep the springs in place.

Aftermarket coil springs are available from many different manufacturers. They come in stock and lowered heights. Different spring rates are also available. As with leaf springs, coil springs with higher rates are stiffer than lower rate springs and the rate is measured the same way.

As with leaf spring manufacturers, each coil maker has its own ideas about which rate will work best with your car. Some manufacturers design their systems to produce more or less oversteer than the others. They can accomplish these differences by changing spring rates or sway bar diameters front and rear. A good aftermarket suspension manufacturer carrying full front and rear packages can offer technical advice to help you with your application.

Trailing Arms for Coil-Spring Rear Suspension

Coil-spring and coil-over rear suspensions locate the rear-end housing with links commonly known as trailing arms or control arms. Many aftermarket companies offer upper and lower control arms with different bushing ends for different types of driving. Not all control arms are created equal. Some are better for drag racing than they are for running on a road course. Some arms are great for both. Restomods are meant to be driven as much as possible and would benefit from getting power to the ground in a straight line and around a corner.

Most aftermarket trailing arms have urethane bushings in each end. Urethane bushings have "stiction" (or static friction) and will wear out over time (as will any moving part). When the bushing wears out it distorts and allows fore and aft movement of the arms, which will change suspension geometry. These are better than stock, but are not the only designs available.

The most effective control arms available have spherical bearings on one or both ends. The spherical bearings offer full range of motion without bind or the possibility of distortion. Some applications will not benefit from having these spherical bearings at both ends, but require a more lateral "fixed" position of one end of the trailing arm. In these cases, one end may require a solid bushing and a spherical bearing in the other end. Each application is different.

Some rear trailing arms are designed to keep the rear axle housing in a certain position for proper geometry and articulation with a certain degree of bind. In these cases, one end may require a solid bushing and a spherical bearing in the other end. The spherical bearings offer full range of motion without bind or the possibility of distortion. Some aftermarket suspension companies offer upper control arms with adjustable length. After installing these on your car, you can adjust them to get optimum pinion angle for U-joint life and improved suspension geometry. Except for racing applications, aftermarket companies only offer adjustable upper control arms for adjusting pinion angle. The lowers are typically non-adjustable and rigid, since they need to take the brunt of most of the road shock.

Instead of replacing the upper control arms on your Fox-body with the typical boxed or adjustable arms, a com-

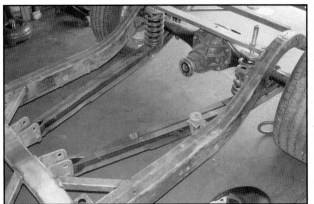

This is the Hot Rods to Hell Inc. Cassette Truck-Arm Suspension. It uses longer suspension arms like those used on Winston Cup series and other big-buck racing cars. This system has proven itself on the track, and now on the street. The set-up can be installed in leaf- and coil-spring-equipped Restomods.

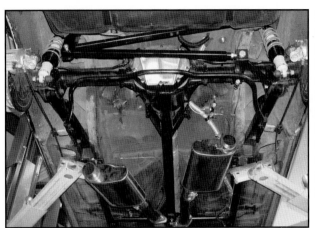

This Fox-body is equipped with a Griggs Racing rear suspension kit that replaces the upper links with a lower center-mounted torque arm that mounts to the differential and a special cross-member/subframe connector set-up. The lower links are replaced with a stronger set and an adjustable panhard-bar set-up has been installed.

Total Control Product's rear suspension system has a right and left lower link, a short lower torque arm, and a Watt's link mounted under differential housing. It also has lay-down coil-over shocks operated by rocker arms. The whole system bolts to a subframe, which bolts to four brackets that can easily be welded to the original frame.

pany named Real Speed Parts offers a product called Pro Link. Pro Link allows you to change the instant center by relocating the upper control arm points on the rear axle housing with a bolt-in bracket and link system that allows for multiple adjustments. It also allows for easy pinion-angle changes. This system has been proven to improve performance on road courses and drag strips. It has been tested to withstand up to 2,000-hp engines at the drag strip.

Real Speed Parts offers adjustable heavy-duty lower control arms to round out a completely adjustable Fox-body rear suspension.

Link/Bar Suspensions

The most common link system is the four-link. This is popular in drag racing, but unless it's modified slightly, it won't make for a very good candidate in a Restomod. Either the top or bottom

KEVIN MIKELONIS' 1972 GRAN TORINO

The '72 Gran Torino looks great, but it is very sedate compared to the $200K European cars that it races from coast to coast. Low-key is good, especially in the eyes of law enforcement agencies. (Photo courtesy Kevin Mikelonis)

If you are a true car enthusiast, you have heard of and/or seen classic movies such as *The Gumball Rally* and *Cannonball Run*. If you haven't, what are you waiting for? They aren't known for quality acting, but they are each classics because of the premise – a car race that starts at one side of the country and ends at the other. The kid in us knows it would be a total adrenaline rush to drive as fast as you can while breaking all traffic rules, not just a few minutes but for a few days. Kevin Mikelonis is a huge fan of the *Gumball* movies, so he jumped at the chance to race in a real-life rally. Yes, these rally races actually exist. T Gumball 3000 races are typically held in Europe, but they are periodically held in the United States. These modern-day versions of the *Gumball Rally* are mostly filled with $200K European cars.

As a die-hard fan of *The Gumball Rally*, Kevin wanted to enter his 1972 Ford Gran Torino. When he was accepted as a participant in the event, he started modifying his cherry, and basically stock, car into a rally-worthy contender. Since the car was going to need top-end power to compete with cars that not only have over a 200-mph top speed, but actually drive that fast during the event, Kevin needed to modify the original 351C 4V. These engines came from the factory with huge intake and exhaust ports. They were known for making top-end power on super speedways back in the early 1970s when rules forced Ford stock-car racing teams to stop running the Boss 429 engines. On public roads, this 351C was going to be following its roots with high-speed runs for long distances. An Edelbrock Performer intake and Holley 670 Street Avenger fed the big 4V heads. The heads were polished and stainless-steel valves were installed to help flow and durability. A custom-ground Ultradyne camshaft shoves a set of roller rockers. The short block was balanced and assembled with a forged crankshaft, heavy-duty rods, and Forged JE 9:1 pistons. Fuel ignition is handled by a full MSD ignition system. Frequent re-fueling stops are a great way to kill time between legs of the race, so Kevin installed a 22-gallon secondary fuel cell in the trunk. With a flick of the switch, the second tank would dump into the main tank. The increased capacity allows the car to be driven up to 540 miles at 100 mph between stops.

Kevin was going to need some serious speed, but he had to keep the RPMs down, so he installed a Transmission Specialties AOD. A 2,500 stall 10-inch lockup converter was chosen to optimize performance and drivability. The stock shifter was adapted to work with the AOD. To round out the overdrive, Kevin installed a 31-spline 3.50:1 gear set in the Ford 9-inch rear end. The next order of business was the suspension and braking. The suspension was firmed up with all-new polyurethane bushings. The factory four-link bars were boxed for strength. A set of 2.5-inch lowered 800-lb springs were used in the front and a set of 1.75–inch-drop 300-lb coils are assisted by an in-car controlled Air-Lift bag system (to help with the weight of extra fuel). A 1-1/8-inch front sway bar from a full-size sedan was installed, and the original 7/8-inch rear-bar was retained. KYB gas adjust shocks dampen each corner. A set of

Kevin built a custom console to match the footprint of the original one, but it's large enough to house the sound system, a laptop with GPS Co-Pilot software, a video screen for the front-and rear-facing cameras, and a fire extinguisher. (Photo Courtesy Kevin Mikelonis)

The heavy-breathing 351C 4V was built up with forged internals for strength, a well-designed cam, and reworked heads. An AOD transmission was chosen to lower the RPM at high speed so the car could get decent fuel mileage. (Photo Courtesy Kevin Mikelonis)

11-inch front brakes from a 429 equipped car were added, and the rear brakes were converted to 11-inch units as well. It hit the pavement on factory 15x8 Magnum wheels with a set of 255/60-15 and 275/50-15 BF Goodrich Radial TAs.

Kevin didn't want to change the interior too much, but knew he had to install some high-tech equipment to keep the team on the correct course and out of as much trouble as possible. The answer was to build a larger-than-stock custom console that could house the extra gear, but still be able to fit the footprint of the factory unit. On-board electronics include: Cobra 40 channel CB radio, Uniden 100 channel scanner, 7-inch LCD screen with front and rear mounted cameras, video recorder with in-car wireless microphone, and Bel-Tronics remote radar and laser detection system. The console also has room for the laptop computer that serves up direction via GPS Co-Pilot software. To help pass the time on the road, Kevin installed an I-Pod that drives JBL and Infinity components and speakers. With

the exception of all the high-tech gear, Grant steering wheel, and AutoMeter tachometer, vacuum, and trans temp gauges, the interior is all un-restored original and in excellent shape.

Kevin would like to thank his wife Joy for finding this car and standing by while he put senseless amounts of money and time into racing his car cross-country for no one's happiness but his own.

In 2002, the rally was run from New York to Los Angeles. In 2003, it was in the United States again, this time from San Francisco to Miami. Kevin was able to coerce Tommi Kukkonen to help with co-pilot duties for the 2002 and 2003 races. They have had a blast at these

events, which consist of approximately six days of driving to each destination city along the route and huge parties at each stop that rival the untouchable Hollywood parties you only hear about.

If you want to know more about Gumball 3000 rally events, go to www.gumball3000.com. If you would like to know more about the adventures of Kevin and Tommi, who make up Team Guts, go to their website at www.teamguts.com. If you ever see Kevin's Restomod with rally stickers plastered all over it, you can expect to see some expensive exotics close behind and putting some power down to catch up.

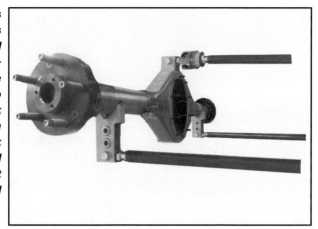

Three-link rear suspensions consist of two lower links and a third link centered above the differential housing. The system in this image shows a torque absorber to take out some of the shock caused by hard acceleration and deceleration. Three-link systems require a panhard rod or the equivalent (not shown) to keep the rear end centered in the chassis.

Martz Chassis has come out with a rear suspension kit for your early unibody Restomod. It features a non-parallel four-link, weld-in crossmembers, coil-over shocks, and a rear-mounted, stock-car-style sway bar. (Photo courtesy Martz Chassis, Inc.)

Bret Voelkel's '69 Mustang is shown tearing up the road course with its Air Ride Technologies AirBar four-link rear suspension and ShockWave front suspension kit. New technology has taken air-assisted suspension systems to the next level. (Photo courtesy Air Ride Technologies via Scott Killeen)

ment bolts, consider using airframe (also called AN bolts) bolts because they are very high-quality. The 3-link design, as well as the four-link, needs some type of side-to-side axle locating mechanism, such as a panhard bar or a Watt's link. The panhard bar attaches to the axle on one side and the frame rail on the other.

Martz Four-Bar

For your Restomod, you might decide you want to replace your rear leaf-spring suspension with a completely new custom four-bar rear suspension. Martz Chassis builds a complete rear suspension system to replace the traditional leaf-spring set-up. This system will allow you more adjustability over leaf spring rear suspension and can be finely tuned in the pursuit of better handling without the weight of leaf springs. This four-bar set-up has a weld-in support brace (with integral driveshaft safety loop) for the front of the links and a weld-in support brace for the integrated coil-overs; adjustable panhard bar; and optional sway bar. It includes all the proper brackets to attach the suspension parts to the rear axle housing. The kit options are solid rod ends or urethane bushing ends and a ⅞-inch stock-car style sway bar. This system has been tested at speeds over 150 mph on Martz's Mustang shop car. The kit allows you to keep your back seat, and it is perfect for cars with mini-tubs. Martz claims it can be completely installed in a weekend by a seasoned car guy with welding skills, so if you aren't up for some serious surgery, this might not be for you.

Air Ride Technologies AirBar

When you think of air ride suspension, you may think of boat-like cushy-handling characteristics. Bret Voelkel, the president of Air Ride Technologies, is changing those preconceived notions with new technology. Air Ride has been pumping new technology into its products for years. As of 2005, they are offering AirBar rear suspension systems for 1964-1/2 to 1970 Mustangs. It replaces the rear leaf springs with four-link rear suspension and the ShockWave 7000 units. A rigid cradle is bolted to the frame and underbody structure using

links need to be angled front to rear so that they converge as close as possible. This allows for more axle articulation than is possible with parallel links, which helps keep the tires planted in the turns. Angling two of the links approximately 20 to 30 degrees to the centerline of the car also eliminates the need for a panhard bar, which locates the axle side to side in the car.

Another common type of link system gaining popularity in the Restomod and Pro-Touring crowd is the 3-link. The 3-link uses two lower and one upper link to eliminate the inherent binding of the four-link design, and allows for complete axle articulation. Using only one upper link means that the link and its attaching mount must be extremely strong. Consider using at least 1½-inch diameter thick-wall tubing for this link, and no less than ¾-inch diameter bolts. For the lower links, use at least 1⅜-inch tube and ⅝-inch bolts. On the subject of attach-

existing factory bolt locations. AirBar lowers the car approximately 2 inches, with a deflated height typically 5 to 6 inches lower than stock. Bret installed the AirBar rear suspension with a ShockWave system in the front of his 1969 Mustang, which has proven itself street and road course worthy.

Independent Rear Suspension

If you want to switch to something completely different from the average Restomod's solid axle and leaf-spring suspension, an independent rear suspension (IRS) may be for you. With IRS, the left and right tires can move independently of the differential housing, which is solidly mounted to the frame. Two half-shafts (also known as drive axles) extend outward from the differential to rotate the hub assemblies and wheels. This design allows one tire to travel and move independently without affecting the other tire. A big benefit of the IRS is the possibility to have camber changes during suspension travel to increase the contact patch of the tire to the pavement when driving hard around corners.

Factory IRS

The most popular IRS for street rods is the early Jaguar rear end. The Jaguar IRS lacks forward trailing arms and upper locating links. It allows torque steer when high horsepower is supplied to sticky tires. Toe and camber problems are also common. For these reasons, consider one of the following set-ups instead.

Cobra and Thunderbird IRS

Your Restomod can be converted from the factory live-axle rear suspension to an IRS system for 1989 through 1997 Thunderbirds and Cougars or 1999 through 2004 Mustang Cobras. The Thunderbird and Cougar IRS subframes are not the same as the Cobra units. The Cobra IRS subframes and parts are stronger and have been found to adapt to older cars easier. The Thunderbird and Cougar have a wheel bolt pattern of 5 on 4.25 inches and the Cobra bolt pattern is 5 on 4.5 inches, which is more

The Cobra IRS is mounted to a bolt-in subframe. This set-up is waiting for engineers to fit it to the FR100 project. FR100 is a '53 Ford pickup, built by McLaren Technologies for Ford Racing Technology group. (Photo courtesy Ford Racing Performance Parts)

This is the same McLaren-built '53 Ford. Most of the original parts of the Cobra IRS have been replaced with fabricated parts. The strength of an IRS unit depends on the specific year, and some are stronger than others. This truck really gets flogged, and the IRS has worked exceptionally well on the road course and drag strip. (Photo courtesy Ford Racing Performance Parts)

common with muscle car-era Restomods. The T-bird and Cougar IRS hubs can be upgraded with Cobra hubs to convert the bolt pattern, but you will still have other inferior parts. The Cobra IRS units are the systems of choice.

These IRS systems are attached to a subframe unit. The coil springs and shocks do not attach to the subframe, so you need to fabricate mounts in the receiving chassis. An easy way to eliminate the need to make coil spring mounts is to convert the IRS to coil-over mounts. If you are going to mount the coil-over in the stock shock absorber position, be careful. The lower shock mount on the IRS control arm was originally designed to take the road shock. It was never intended to bear the load and weight of the vehicle, so the lower shock mount should be beefed up a bit.

DVS Restorations

The following information about the differences between Cobra IRS systems is

from David Stribling of DVS Restorations. The 1999 Cobra unit has 28-spline axles, a 3.27:1 gear ratio, Traction-Loc, and soft rubber frame mounts. The 2000 Cobra "R" unit (considered to be the best of the best) has larger 31-spline axles, 3.55:1 gear ratio, Gerodisc hydro-mechanical limited-slip unit (stronger and designed to handle the more powerful Cobra R DOHC 5.4-liter engine), improved CV Joints, improved upper camber slot location, and harder-durometer rubber frame mounts. Cobra units for 2001 had slightly improved axles (31 on the insides and 28-spline on the outsides), a 3.27:1 gear ratio, and Traction-Loc. Similar to the 2000 Cobra R, the 2003-2004 Cobra unit has 31-spline axles (redesigned again), 3.55:1 gears, Traction-Loc, redesigned camber, and redesigned tie-rod location for improved bumpsteer.

DVS Restorations has done all the homework on adapting Cobra IRS units into 1965 through 1970 Mustangs, including all the custom brackets and

It may raise your eyebrows a little, but the C4 Chevy Corvette IRS is lightweight, a completely self-contained unit, and has proven its great potential for street and track use. For various reasons, an IRS unit from one specific year may be more desirable than another from a different year.

Duane Carling at CTM Engineering did a ton of unbelievable research to put together the original IRS kit designed for the 1964-1/2 Mustang. If you want IRS for your Restomod Mustang or Falcon and don't want to do any welding or cutting, this may be the kit for you. (Photo Courtesy CTM Engineering)

flared quarter panels. The 1967 and newer Mustangs are wide enough to accept the IRS without flaring the quarter panels. The standard Cobra IRS subframe is a good fit with the DVS kit, but it leaves the car sitting a little too high for some builders, so DVS offers a modified IRS subframe for the builders who want their Restomod a little closer to the ground.

The Original T-5 IRS (for early Mustangs)

If you're looking for IRS for your early Mustang, Falcon, Comet, Cyclone, or Torino, and you want something rare without making any frame modifications, there is an independent rear suspension system is for you. A gentleman named Duane Carling from CTM Engineering has an incredible story about the IRS built for the Mustang back in 1964. The following information gives a little bit of the whole story. For more, get a hold of CTM Engineering. The company information is listed in the Source Guide in the back of this book.

Not a lot of people are aware of this IRS, but Ford had a team of designers building an independent rear suspension for the original Ford Mustang. In fact, the IRS made it onto a few test Falcons back in 1964 because the Mustang wasn't even available yet. Duane was looking at some pictures while doing research and found a picture of a 1964 Falcon with IRS that had been taken back in 1964. Soon Duane was on a quest to attain more information on this rare suspension system. One dead end led to another, until he eventually found the man who was the head of the IRS project. From there, the story goes beyond your wildest dreams. After many years, Duane found actual prints, original one-off parts, and other info that led him to piece together the original IRS built for Ford and tested by Shelby. The rumor is that it made an improvement in the handling of the Mustang, but the improvement didn't outweigh the cost of building it.

CTM Engineering now builds these systems just like they were back then. It uses custom parts, original parts from other cars, and a few Jaguar parts. The system bolts into the original factory locations on the 1964 and newer leaf-spring equipped chassis.

modifications necessary for each Mustang year. The 1965 and 1966 Mustangs are narrower than the 1967 and later cars. This proved to be a problem for the Cobra IRS, since the width of a 2000 Cobra R IRS is approximately 65 inches from hub to hub. The 1965 and 66 Mus-tangs' inner quarter panel lip to inner lip is approximately 66.25 inches. That only leaves 1.25 inches, or room to play with wheel backspace/offset and tire sizes—and that's not much! DVS offers a kit to bolt the IRS into the rear of the 1964-1/2, 1965, and 1966, but it works best with

FRAMES

Frame Types

Ford has used quite a few different frame designs over the years. Two basic frame construction types are full-frame and unit-body (or unibody).

Full-Frame

The oldest frame design is full-frame. Typically, the frame rails are constructed of .120-inch-wall stamped steel that runs the length of the vehicle. At present, Ford still uses full-frame construction in its full-size cars and trucks.

Ladder

The ladder frame is the oldest full-frame design. It typically consists of two long frame rails that run parallel for the length of the vehicle. The frame rails are separated by lateral supports. This design lacked strength in the early years. In 1932, Ford started adding diagonal cross-bracing (basically a big X-shaped frame structure) between the frame rails for strength. With the body bolted to the chassis, it became more rigid. From there, the ladder frame evolved until it was completely redesigned in 1965. Ford trucks continue to use the ladder frame today.

Perimeter

In 1965, Ford's ladder frame was redesigned and given a new name—the perimeter frame. The front and rear frame portions were approximately 12 inches inward of the external body panels. The frames are referred to as portions, not sections. This is a full frame,

A full-frame chassis has frame rails that run from one end of the car to the other. This '68 Galaxie has what is called a perimeter frame design, hence the frame rails running along the rocker panels (where the legs of the hoist are positioned).

made as one unit. The front and rear portions were not much different from the front and rear portions of the older ladder frame. The center portion of the frame was the difference in design. The center portion of the frame ran around the outside of the passenger compartment, usually only 1 to 2 inches inward from the external body panels. This design is much stronger in a side impact than the earlier ladder frames. This frame is also known as the "torque box frame"

because it uses structural supports called torque boxes that kick the frame rails outward to the edge of the rocker panels.

Unibody

Unitized body and frame construction is best described as body construction that incorporates body structure and chassis floorpan as a single structure. This single body and frame unit is made up of many different stamped sheetmetal pieces welded together. This makes the car lighter, keeps

A closer look shows the torque boxes that attach the outside frame rails in the center of the car, to the narrower front portion of the frame. These frames are heavy but strong, and they can be gusseted for extra strength

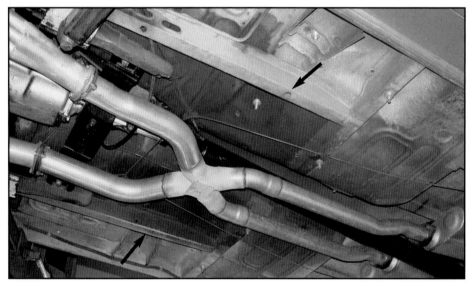

The unibody is the most common car frame on the planet. This '71 Torino is a good example. It has stamped sheetmetal frame rails (arrows) that run from the left of the photo to just past the X-pipe. The rear rails are surrounding the mufflers on the right of the photo.

it rigid, and keeps cost down at the assembly plant. Ford has been labeled by some as the pioneer of unitized frame construction in the United States. The 1935 Lincoln Zephyr was Ford's first try at the new frame design. By the 1960s, Ford and other American auto manufacturers were incorporating the unibody in full swing.

Subframe

A subframe is the lower section of the unibody that is formed into a frame rail. Suspension components and engines usually bolt to the subframe, due to its increased strength compared to the sheetmetal floorpan. A subframe can also be a bolt-in section of a frame that has suspension locating points.

Body Bushings

Stock Rubber

Full-frame constructed cars typically have bushings between the frame and the floorpan that they attach to. The factory bushings are usually made of rubber. These bushings help isolate the road noise and road feel to the chassis. For instance, when your tires hit the little reflectors that separate lanes on a highway, or they hit uneven pavement, the rubber factory bushings keep the jolt from being transferred to the body structure. That same design allows the frame to flex and twist under hard cornering.

Poly Compounds & Solid

As of writing this book, aftermarket companies are not offering body bushings for full-frame Fords made of poly compounds (commonly known as urethane, polyurethane, and Polygraphite). They also don't offer solid body bushings made of aluminum. These body bushings would be the same shape as the factory rubber bushings, and they would be installed the same way too. They add serious rigidity to the frame and body by tying them together as one unit, and not flexing or distorting like rubber bushings. They also add more road noise and allow more road feel as vibrations transfer from the frame to the body. Almost all applications would be best suited with polyurethane body bushings rather than solid ones.

Subframe Connectors

When building a car with a high-powered engine and a lot of torque, keep in mind that unibody cars tend to twist and flex. Forces from engine torque and flex from severe driving can cause fatigue in the body and frame structure, which makes the car more unpredictable on a road course or the street. To strengthen the structure of your unibody, you can install sub-frame connectors. Subframe connectors attach the front subframe to the rear frame. This reduces the torsional flex that the sheetmetal of the body structure usually absorbs and makes the car more predictable on a road course and the street.

Before installing subframe connectors in your car, be sure to inspect your frame and all of its components. If you install subframe connectors on a cracked frame, you will not be able to fully utilize the connectors. Repair any frame

In 1967, Ford added torque boxes to the Mustang driver's side footwell, tying the frame rail to the rocker panel. This sheet of metal added strength to the unitized frame on the driver's side to help with side impacts. Adding one on the passenger side would add rigidity to the unibody.

Here is a good view of a front sheetmetal frame rail. The rail is simply a folded-up piece of metal that's tack welded to the sheetmetal floorboard. It's strong enough for regular driving, but it could use some strengthening for the type of driving Restomods sometimes see.

damage from rust, stress, or an accident before installing subframe connectors.

Subframe connectors come in many shapes, sizes, and designs.

Non-Integral, Bolt-in Subframe Connectors

Bolt-in subframe connectors are the easiest to install, but they're also the least effective. These connectors are only as strong as the bolts that connect them to the chassis. If you want to keep the option of returning your Restomod to stock one day, bolt-in connectors may be your best option.

Bolt-in connectors could be welded in, but they're not intended for that pur-

pose. If you're going to weld them in, you may as well step up to stronger connectors that are meant to be welded. In most cases, bolt-in connectors greatly reduce the ground clearance, which can be a problem if your Restomod has a lowered suspension.

Non-Integral Weld-in Subframe Connectors

Non-integral weld-in subframe connectors need to be welded in place, but they don't require serious modification to the floorpan, if any at all. They perform better than the bolt-in type, but depending on the car, they can reduce ground clearance. If your Restomod is

like most, it's lower than stock height and can use all the ground clearance it can get.

A few companies offer non-integral subframe connectors, including Total Control Products, Global West, Maximum Motorsports, and more. Depending on the application, these types of connectors are still less effective than the integral type. For instance, a non-integral weld-in connector that hangs down under an early Mustang ties the front and rear frame together. However, the frame can still twist, unless you weld a gusset somewhere in the center of the connector to the frame. To get a mental picture of this, which do you think is going to resist twisting (not bending): a straight bar or a U-shaped piece of round tubing? Obviously, the straight piece is stronger, unless you add a gusset or two near the center of the bend.

Keep in mind, the only complaint ever heard about subframe connectors is about reduced ground clearance. I've never heard anyone complain about a chassis being too stiff. Weld-in connectors are typically noticeable the first time you pull your car into (or out of) an inclined driveway, at an angle. Chassis flex should be reduced.

Integral Weld-in Subframe Connectors

Integral weld-in subframe connectors are the mother of all connectors. They require the most work to install, including cutting the floorpan and welding, but they're also the most rigid. For all practical purposes, the strength you add with this type of connector is just short of installing a full frame in your vehicle. Integral weld-in connectors are typically stronger than the actual frames they connect. If done correctly, these connectors will not reduce your ground clearance either. Integral weld-in connectors protrude into the driver's compartment, but with a little creative insulation movement, they can be hardly noticeable.

Currently, there aren't any companies offering pre-built integral subframe connectors, but keep your eyes and ears open. If you want to build your own, you'll need hand tools, a welder, and preferably an air compressor and die

The Mustang was designed to be lightweight. The unibody front structure is not very strong without fenders attached. Don't forget to install all the fender-mounting bolts because the fenders tie the sheetmetal together as a unit.

Subframe connectors, like these from Global West, are used to tie the front and rear unitized frames (subframes) together. These are non-integral connectors, as they aren't installed through the floorpan between the front and rear subframes.

These connectors built and installed by Campbell Auto Restorations are considered integral subframe connectors because they are welded through the floorpan. These are built out of 2x3-inch rectangular tubing and extra gusset plates. Also notice that they don't hang down under the car, so they don't reduce ground clearance.

With a closer look, you can see how Campbell Auto Restorations tied the back of the connector to the rear frame with gussets and plates. Also notice the plate welded to the side of the actual frame rail to help tie everything to the bolt that holds the leaf spring. The front frame was boxed with steel plates as well.

Here's the rust-preventative POR Patch seam sealer and POR-15 paint. POR-15 Inc. offers a full line of rust preventative paint, primers, cleaners, sealers, and fillers. The products are so good that world-famous amusement parks use them.

Ford did a good job designing the front and rear '71 Torino subframes close together. Even though it's designed well, the Torino is a heavy car and could use the extra strength for hard driving around the racetrack.

grinder. You can purchase the metal tubing down at your local metal scrap yard. Most homemade connectors are made from 2x2-inch square or 2x3-inch rectangle tubing with .120-inch wall thickness. Using any smaller tubing or thinner wall thickness will minimize the effectiveness of all your hard work.

Before you get started, remove the seats, carpet, insulation, and any parts you want to save from welding slag and hot ground metal flack. If you are welding near any windows, cover them. You would be really surprised at the damage welding slag will leave behind. Take all safety precautions. Safely elevate your

car on level ground with car ramps or heavy-duty jack stands. Keep a fire extinguisher handy.

The most important part of a subframe connector is tying the front and rear subframes together, so locate them first. You'll need to plot out the most direct route between the two subframes. Some front and rear subframes will line straight up, but some chassis have a front subframe that is narrower than the rear (or vice versa). When you plot out the subframe connector location on a chassis where the subframes line up, the connectors will run parallel to the rocker panel. Running connectors straight from the

front to rear subframes will be the strongest. Make sure you connect the front and rear sections. If you fall an inch or two short of the actual subframe, the strength of the connector will fall short too. Figure out how you want the finished job to look. If you want the connector to be flush with the underside of the floorpan for ultimate clearance, then make your measurements to reflect your decision. If you don't mind it sitting a little lower than the floorpan, for instance ½-inch, then figure that measurement into your lines.

Plot out the sections of the floorpan you will need to remove. Make sure to make the lines ⅛-inch narrower than the width of your tubing. Measure two or three times –cut once! Figure the cutting wheel or blade will also remove metal, so take that into consideration. Make sure the lines are straight. There are a lot of contours on the floorpan, so plotting out straight lines is easier said than done. You can use a straight edge to assist, or if you're feeling punchy, get a laser level from your favorite hardware store and use the straight laser beam to plot out your lines. Make sure the laser is positioned straight over the floorpan for the most accurate results. If the floorpan curves upward more than the height of the tubing, leave the high areas when you cut the floorpan. Don't remove more metal than necessary. This is a tedious process, but well worth the effort. Before cutting anything, make sure you don't cut through a fuel line, a brake line, an emergency brake cable, or anything else important.

There are a few different ways to cut the floorpan. If you are tool-challenged and don't have an air compressor, you can use a hacksaw. Use the type with a small handle and a blade sticking out of it. I'm not proud of it, but I've used this method and it's not fun! Save yourself a bunch of grief and borrow an air compressor, a high-speed die grinder, and a cut-off wheel. In some cases, you can get away with a heavy-duty reciprocating saw. Almost anything is better than one of those little hacksaws.

Now cut the sections of metal from the floorpan. Trim the length of your tubing (subframe connector material). If you need to cut the connectors a little short (due to a strange angle), you can use 3/16-inch plate to make gussets to attach the connector to the subframe. Trial-fit the connectors to make sure they will fit before welding them in. Remove the connectors. For the ultimate strength of your work, you will need to weld every edge where the connector meets the floorpan and frame. For a clean weld, you will need to grind the paint off every edge of the sheetmetal with a grinding wheel. Clean the sheetmetal edges and the connector (bulk steel usually has oil on it from the manufacturing process and it will cause problems when welding). After welding in the connectors, use seam sealer to seal the elements out of the car. POR-15 products makes a seam sealer that inhibits rust called POR Patch; then use POR-15 to cover your work and keep it in good shape.

Front Support Systems

All manufacturers design braces into cars for increasing strength and keeping the car safe, without hampering the speed of the assembly line. Some of these braces are integrated into the chassis, and are welded to the car early in the process. The torque-box on the 1967 Mustang located under the left front foot well is a good example of a brace welded to the car for increased chassis strength. Bolted and welded braces are not extremely strong like separate pieces, but they are important to the strength of the chassis. If you're used to driving your car with them, you'd probably notice if they were gone. So, if your car is extremely rusty and the torque box is non-existent, replace it.

Export Braces

The factory added braces to shocktower-equipped cars such as the Mustang and Falcon. Non-Shelby Mustangs sold in the US were equipped with a pair of small braces that tie the shock towers to the firewall. The one-piece heavyduty brace that replaced them was called the Export brace. It was produced to add extra support to the shock towers on cars exported out of the United States. Shelby American installed this upgraded brace on its cars to add rigidity. Reproduction Export braces are available through many reproduction parts suppliers. If you are installing an intake system on your engine that does not leave you space to use the Export brace, then you should modify the brace or customize it to fit your application. The Export brace is just one part of the complete front structure of any of the early shock-tower-equipped cars. The front frame rails, fenderwells, and fenders are all constructed of thin sheetmetal. They are strengthened by the stronger, thicker metal of the shock towers. The factory Export brace is important because it helps keep the upper shock towers apart. I've heard of old, beat-up Mustangs that have seriously fatigued and cracked fenderwell structures because they were driven without their Export braces. The shock towers can get weak enough that when the car is let down off of a jack, the fenders and fenderwells move inward as much as a ½-inch. That might not seem like much, but any movement that can be measured by your eyes is too much. If your shock towers can flex and compress under hard cornering, it can cause changes in suspension geometry and unpredictable handling. The movement also weakens the entire structure, causing permanent damage, such as bent or cracked frame rails.

Monte Carlo Bars and Shock Tower Braces

There are many Restomod candidates that would benefit from horizontal bracing in the engine compartment. Shock tower and strut tower cars will benefit the most from a Monte Carlo bar since the weight of the vehicle rests on the tower structures. Tying the two towers together increases rigidity and reduces fatigue.

Not to be confused with the V-shaped Export brace described above, shock tower braces and Monte Carlo bars are the braces that cross in front of the air cleaner assembly. The Monte Carlo bar mounts between the two front fenderwells, just forward of the shock towers. The Monte Carlo bar comes in many shapes and sizes. They differ for model year and option packages. Sometimes they are a straight bar, and sometimes they are curved in the middle to allow for some special-option carburetion. Monte Carlo bars are usually used in addition to the Export Brace to promote structural integrity through triangulation.

You can replace the Export brace and Monte Carlo bar with tubular steel bars, or just plain add one if you don't have the any bracing to begin with. A

The Export brace ties the shock towers to an integral section of the firewall. This Mustang has a factory Export brace. The bar that runs in front of the engine between the shock towers is called a Monte Carlo bar. This bar is not a factory piece.

Total Control Products offers this fully adjustable shock-tower brace that takes place of the export brace and Monte Carlo bar. It's a nice piece that looks as good as it works. It can be installed with the factory upper shock mounts.

The TCP brace kit requires a few holes be drilled in the firewall and inner fenderwells to add strength with brackets by sandwiching the factory sheetmetal. This shows the bracket for the bar in front of the shock tower during installation. This kit could be installed in an afternoon.

Under the hood hinge on this Mustang, you can see a tube protruding through the firewall. It's welded to the roll cage inside the car and under the dashboard as well as to the back side of the shock tower in the engine compartment. This design adds rigidity to the whole chassis.

When removing the inner fenderwells, the front frame (factory or not) needs a pair of structure braces to add rigidity. Without the tubing that runs from a rigid point on the firewall or through the firewall attached to a roll cage, the frame will flex until it fractures or bends. (Photo Courtesy Greg Carter)

few companies offer these in different forms. Two common manufacturers are Total Control Products and MPG Head Service. Both of these companies offer different levels for its kits. A lower level kit simply replaces the export brace with an adjustable tubular unit. The higher-level kits offer the additional front tubular braces for improved strength and rigidity. The higher-level kits offer additional tubular braces for improved strength, rigidity, and full adjustability.

Strut Tower Braces

Late-model Fords have strut front suspensions, and they can be stiffened up with strut tower braces that are similar to the earlier models' shock tower braces. Quite a few companies offer these braces. On the late-model cars, engine compartments are smaller and crammed full of accessories, so the braces are specific to year and model. For example, a 2003 Mustang brace may not fit a 2003 Mustang Cobra due to supercharger clearance. Some late-model Mustangs also came with bars that resemble a combination of the Export brace and the Monte Carlo bar.

What if you have a '78 Ford Fairmont and you plan to turn it into a Restomod? There is a good chance aftermarket companies are not making strut tower braces for your car. Don't let that stop you. You could design and fabricate your own by cutting some 3/16-inch-thick steel plate to fit on the top of both strut towers and then mount it to a strong point on the firewall. Tie all three plates together with some round, steel tubing. For design ideas, take a look at some Mustang strut tower braces before you start.

Full-Frame Modifications

Some full-frame Restomod candidates came with C-section frames, also known as open-channel frames. These types of frames can be strengthened by a method called boxing. The object is to plate the open section of frame to box it. One trick is to use cardboard as a template for the boxing plates and then transfer the template onto the steel sheet. It's best to use material of the same thickness as the frame. Then just cut out the plates and deburr them after you have welded them in. This process significantly increases strength, and it has been used by hot rodders for decades.

If your frame is already capped from the factory, you can add strength to it by welding up the seams. Factory-welded seams are not always the best quality. This should only be done with the frame out of the car. Before you pull the body off the car, measure the frame for straightness. Then measure it again with the body off. Welding the seams is an easy way to warp the frame if you don't know what you are doing, so it's a good idea to weld the seams with the chassis on a frame rack. You should only weld a few inches at a time to prevent putting too much heat into the frame. The heat causes the frame to expand, which causes

Rear fenderwells are not always large enough to fit the rear tires you plan to install on your car. Replacing the inner and outer section of the fenderwell is referred to as tubbing a car. Widening only the inboard section of the inner fenderwell is known as mini-tubbing. (Photo courtesy Detroit Speed & Engineering)

Racing-style tubs can be used instead of stamped factory style replacements. The little wheel well inside this tub is about the same size as the earliest Falcon's, which can only comfortably fit 235-size tires in the stock rear wheel wells. (Photo courtesy John Parsons)

twisting and flexing. If your frame twists and you keep welding, the frame will be twisted for eternity. This error can cause all kinds of suspension alignment problems, not to mention the inability to mount the body back on the chassis without serious emotional anguish. If you are not an experienced welder, pay someone else to do the job right.

Front Braces

Unfortunately, front wheelwells don't always offer the clearance needed for tires of larger sizes. This is especially true when the ride height is reduced. Luckily, some full-frame Restomod cars have removable inner fenderwells. However, the structural integrity of the front sheetmetal and frame is reduced when the inner fenderwells are removed, and there may be more flex than desired. The inner fenderwells also protect the paint, engine, etc., from rocks that fly off of the tires. For these reasons, it's usually a good idea to either modify them or make some new ones that will fit.

Whether or not you decide to keep your fenderwells, it's a good idea to use some type of bracing to reduce flex. For instance, if you are going to remove the front inner fenderwells on your '72 Gran Torino, you should add front braces to put some strength back in the front body structure. Front braces are also known as forward struts or hoop bars. These are more commonly found

on extreme Restomods and drag cars. They can attach to a strong anchoring point on the firewall and run down to the frame structure next to the radiator. For the most rigidity, these bars can go right through the firewall and mount to a roll cage in the passenger compartment. This triangulates the front frame rails, which is especially important on extreme Restomods that are lacking the front inner fenderwells and shock towers. When you remove metal from the front structure, you will need to add bracing to put the strength back in.

If you decide to attach your front braces to the firewall, you should install some anchor plates to help distribute the load between the tubing and sheetmetal. The anchor plates should have the same wall thickness as the tubing used for the braces. A good rule of thumb is to make the anchor plate surface area about 2½ times the size of the tubing diameter you are welding it to. For instance, if the round front-brace tubing is 1 inch in diameter, the plate should be at least 2½x2½ inches square. It's not always possible to use such a big plate in tight spaces, but it's a good rule to keep in mind. It's best to weld continuously around the perimeter of these plates and plug-weld the plates to the host sheetmetal in a few places to further increase their resistance to fatigue.

Picking a strong anchor point is critical for strength and safety, so try to

attach the bars near bends or corners in the attachment area because these areas are inherently stronger. As with any design, the structure is only as strong as its weakest link. If you anchor the braces to a weak area of the firewall, the brace will eventually break the sheetmetal. Also be aware that during a frontal collision, a poorly placed brace could easily come into contact with the driver, injuring or killing him. To avoid that hazard, anchor the brace to the frame in more than one location to make the strongest and safest design. If you are planning on running with any racing associations, you may want to check their rulebooks before going through the process of any serious fabrication.

The majority of Ford Restomod candidates are unibody cars and they do not have removable inner fenderwells. The metal is needed to keep the structure strong. Keep in mind that the front frame rails on a unibody car are nothing more than stamped sheetmetal.

Rear Frame Rail Tricks

If you have to notch the frame to get clearance, it's a good idea to reinforce the area that gets cut out with sheet steel that is the same thickness as the original metal. It's also a good idea to use cold-rolled steel rather than hot-rolled, due to the increased strength of cold-rolled steel. When working with frames or suspension systems, excellent welding and fabrication skills are required to do this work safely. If you aren't 100 percent confident in your welding or fabrication skills, it's best to have this work done by a professional welder/fabricator.

In order to narrow the frame rails on a full-frame car, the rails are cut off about 18 inches forward of the rear axle centerline and moved inboard. When figuring out how far to move the rails inboard, make sure you end up with enough clearance on both sides of the tire. Try for at least 1 inch of clearance on each side of the tire, or more if possible. If you are going to reuse the original rails, the end of the forward rails need to be capped with a plate that covers the entire open end and continues inboard the distance you want to move the rail.

RICK CARLILE'S 1965 CYCLONE

Rick Carlile's 1965 Mercury Cyclone Restomod commands respect when the 525-hp small-block pushes the car to 150+ mph during track events. The car is seen here navigating turn 2 at Infineon Raceway. (Photo courtesy Bob Solorio)

This may sound like a familiar story. A friend talked Rick Carlile into taking his car out to the track. The day was going to be an exercise in adrenalin-pumping fun. Just one track-day was all it took – Rick was hooked! Knowing track excursions are not easy on cars, Rick started looking for a car he could build for strictly track use. He wanted something out of the ordinary, so a track Mustang was out of the question. Rick got the opportunity to pick up a 1965 Comet Caliente for $500. The rest is history.

While Rick's Comet Caliente isn't a streetable Restomod, it definitely deserves some attention. Rick thought the word Cyclone would command more attention than Caliente, so he re-badged the car. Other changes to the exterior are the additions of Crites Restoration Products fiberglass front and rear bumpers and a Crites fiberglass Ram Air hood. The quality hood comes with built-in ducting to make the Ram Air ducts functional. Rick engineered a custom air-

The sparse interior is all business. The driver is strapped to a Kirkey road-race aluminum seat and protected by a Safecraft fire system and 10-point roll cage. The Longacre Hot Lap timer on the dash keeps tabs of the on-track performance. (Photo Courtesy Rick Carlile)

The Crites Restoration fiberglass ram-air hood is functional. Rick custom built the air cleaner to adapt the hood to the Jet Performance-prepped 750-cfm Holley. Rick uses a stock-style Export brace and a non-adjustable shock tower brace to keep the front sheetmetal in check. (Photo courtesy Rick Carlile)

cleaner system from an air-cleaner base, and a custom plate that mounts the filter in the hood ducting.

The 1965 is equipped with all the right mechanical elements to keep it going during open-track events. For power, Rick had the 525-hp 347 prepared by Gerolamy. It's got a Ford Motorsports R302 block stuffed with Venolia pistons, Cunningham rods, a Moldex forged crank, Comp Cams flat-tappet cam, and Crane roller rockers. Bolted to the mill are World Products large Dart iron heads (turning the 347 into a 12.3-to--1 compression monster), dressed with Ferrara stainless valves and titanium retainers. A Jet Performance race-prepped 750-cfm 4150 Holley carburetor sits atop an Extrude Hone match-ported Cobra dual-plane intake. Lubrication is handled by a Fram HP-6 filter and mount, Canton 8-quart road-race pan, and blueprinted Melling high-volume oil pump. A Setrab 25-row stacked cooler handles oil cooling. The

David Klee race-prepped Ford Toploader 4-speed is engaged with a McLeod clutch, pressure plate, and aluminum fly-wheel. The transmission is solidly mounted with a McLeod scattershield, and it spins the 3-inch diameter aluminum driveshaft. The Ford 9-inch rear is stuffed with 3.70:1 gears mounted to a Detroit Locker, which turns the Summers Brothers 28-spline racing axles.

The interior follows the same racing plan, which only contains the essentials. You will find a Kirkey aluminum road race seat, Simpson 5-point harness, 13-inch Grant steering wheel, the essential AutoMeter gauges (clocked so the needles all point in the same direction during normal racing conditions), Safecraft fire system, video camera mount (for critiquing after the race), Longacre Hot Lap timer, and Wink mirror. Surrounding the interior is a 10-point roll cage, which protects the driver and ties the custom subframe connectors and entire chassis together for the ultimate in rigidity.

Handling the front suspension are TCP control arms, strut rods, and coil-over kit (using double adjustable Aldan Eagle shocks). Front braking is accomplished by a Baer 13-inch track system using Hawk Blue pads and cooled by a 3-inch Cobra Automotive front brake duct kit. The rear suspension has 4-leaf rear springs with bronze race bushings, which are dampened by Spax rear shocks. The rear braking is accomplished by 11-inch x 2.5-inch rear drum brakes wearing Porterfield R-4 compound shoes. The body sway is controlled by a 1¼-inch front bar and a ⅞-inch Addco rear bar.

Over a decade later, Rick is still hooked on open-track racing events. His Cyclone seems to be continuously evolving and picking up speed, just like any true-blooded Restomod. A street version of this car would stick out in a sea of Mustangs and be well received by other enthusiasts, but not by the competition.

If you are one of those guys who want the ultimate in strength for racing and street driving, you can build your own chassis like Preston Peterson did. There's more information about this frame's '67 Mustang within this book. The frame is shown before the top half was constructed. (Photo courtesy Preston Peterson)

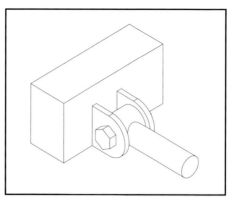

This illustration shows the proper way to mount a suspension or load-bearing link. The suspension link is located by two mounting tabs. This mounting method is referred to as double shear. A single mounting tab would be insufficient and unsafe. (Illustration courtesy Vince Asaro)

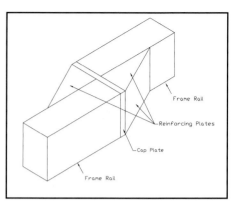

This illustration shows the method for narrowing rear frame rails. The frame is cut, a cap plate is welded into place, the frame is welded the desired distance inward, and then reinforcing plates are added for strength. (Illustration courtesy Vince Asaro)

You can purchase mandrel bent frame rails and build a new frame for your entire car. This in-progress shot shows custom exhaust routing through the frame and the integral driveshaft loop. (Photo Courtesy John Parsons)

Use 3/8-inch or thicker steel for these plates. Next, reattach the rear rails to the plated end of the forward rail, and then box in the areas ahead of and behind the plates with sheet steel that is the same thickness as the rails.

As you move the frame rails inboard, they are more likely to twist under suspension loads. You will need to add a fairly large X-member above the axle housing to prevent twisting. Use 2x3-inch box tube or something equivalent. The configuration should consist of a piece of tubing that attaches to the left side of the rear frame, a couple inches in front of the axle housing, and spans across to the right side of the frame behind the rear axle. Install a piece of tubing on the right side of the frame, in front of the axle housing, that spans across to the left side of the rear frame behind the rear-axle housing. Notching or cutting one of those tubes and joining it to the other tube will create a strong X-brace to strengthen your rear frame. When installing this X-member, make sure the axle won't hit it at full bump. You may end up moving the X-member to just above and behind the axle for clearance.

There are several companies that make universal rails out of 2x3-inch box tubing. Chris Alston's Chassis Works and Art Morrison Engineering are some of the best, but there are others. Similar construction techniques to narrow stock frame rails are used to install aftermarket frame rails. The majority of the time, when narrowing rear frame rails on leaf-spring rear suspensions, they are converted to coil-over suspension systems. If you use narrowed rear-frame rails, a narrower fuel tank or fuel cell will most likely be required.

Roll Bars and Roll Cages

Production bodies and frames were not originally designed to withstand the rigors Restomod guys put them through. Along with increased safety, the strength of the body and frame are increased with the addition of a roll bar or roll cage.

The following is an explanation of the terms used when dealing with roll bars and cages. Windshield posts are referred to as the A-pillars, and in succession, the next body posts toward the rear of the car are known as the B-pillars, then C-pillars, etc. Roll bars can be identified by the number of points that attach to the chassis or floorpan. A four-

This wagon seems to be a good car to explain pillar designations. The first pillar at the windshield is the A-pillar. The next one behind the front door is the B-pillar. The next pillar is the C-pillar, and so on.

The main hoop in this car is tied to the upper door bars with a smaller diameter tube. This distributes load better than any small gusset. The bars are closely contoured to the roof too.

Pinch weld guard comes in different colors, sizes, and types. The two on the left have metal inside them to help create a positive grip. The other type is just rubber, which can be seen between the radiator and core support. It helps cover sharp edges in interiors and engine compartments.

A roll cage can be tied to the shell of the car for added strength. You can use small tabs or larger, sheetmetal pieces. These panels have countersunk holes cut by a special punch and flare tool available from Mittler Brothers Machine and other fabrication tool shops. It adds a professional look to the job.

bars running through the firewall to the front frame horns, or shock towers on a unibody car. These two bars typically attach to the bars of the six-point where it passes the dashboard. Cages that are ten-point or more are basically eight-point cages with extra bracing for strength and safety.

When planning a roll bar or cage, it's a good idea to keep in mind that if you eventually want to race your car, your car will most likely have to pass a safety inspection and will need to be designed according to a rulebook. When building a Restomod, you'll most likely need to abide by rules established by the SCCA and/or NHRA. Each has its own requirements as far as tubing material, diameter, thickness, placement, etc., so if you plan on racing in more than one venue, it's a good idea to be sure you're legal for all the rules that apply. If your design doesn't follow exactly what is described in the rulebook, don't hesitate to call the technical inspector and ask questions before beginning work.

Roll Cage Safety

Roll bars and cages are there for your safety as well as the safety of those around you. Once again, if you're not extremely confident in your welding or fabrication skills, have this part done by an expert. An incorrectly designed or installed roll bar or cage could seriously injure you. If a bar breaks off in an accident, it could impale you. Make sure any companies or shops that you deal with have a good reputation and employ highly skilled workers. Again, if you have the slightest doubt about your design or welding abilities, have a professional fabricator do the job. Roll bar padding is another safety issue. An unpadded bar within arms-length or close to your head could cause a broken bone or worse. Also know that in an accident, seat belts can stretch as far as 12 inches.

If you are going to have a back seat for passengers, keep the passengers in mind when installing a roll bar or roll cage. On the street, passengers could easily come into contact with the bars too. If it's possible that they could be in danger, don't take the risk. Give them a ride some other day.

point cage consists of the main hoop and two rear braces that run from the top of the main hoop to the rear-frame rails, or anchor plates that reinforce the floorpan above the frame rails. A six-point cage adds another set of bars from a point between your shoulder and elbow on the main hoop to a reinforced area on the floor near your feet. Another version of the six-point uses bars that run forward from the top of the main hoop, follow the A-pillars down past the dash, and finally terminate at reinforcing plates on the floor near your feet. It's also common to combine the two versions of the six-point in one cage for more strength. An eight-point cage adds

There is a drawback to installing a roll cage with large obtrusive door bars for a street car. Even with the doors open, you are going to look like one of the Duke boys every time you get in and out of your car.

Vince Asaro put a lot of thought into installing these door bars. They match his seat angles and the downward bend is backed up with another bar for triangulation.

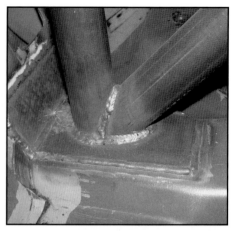

Attaching a roll bar or a cage requires a good foundation. Welding a bar straight to the sheetmetal is worthless. You must have an anchor plate to build strength. As with a building, starting with a good foundation is important.

Roll cages and roll bars benefit from the addition of gussets. The gussets add strength by triangulating the mounting point and distributing the loads over a larger surface area of the tubing. Be careful of any sharp edges on gussets or any other object within reach of your limbs or head. Sharp, exposed edges are extremely unsafe and have no place anywhere in your car, especially in the passenger compartment. Take a little extra time and smooth any exposed edges or burrs.

Exposed sharp edges that can't be reached with a file, sandpaper, etc., should be covered with some type of edge trim. Edge trim is available in a variety of different colors. Make your car as safe as possible. If your car gets damaged beyond repair in an accident, you can always build another one as long as you are still alive.

Weld-In Roll Bars/Cages

As with bolt-in roll bars and roll cages, make sure that you check the correct racing association rulebook that corresponds with your racing plans. It seems every sanctioning body has a slightly different idea of what design and tubing size is required to keep you safe. Some sanctioning bodies also requires the cage to be tied to the body for added strength.

Roll cages have been around for a long time, and there are some issues that keep surfacing. Two of the most common issues are headroom and door bars. Whether you plan to drive your car on the street on a regular basis or not, take entering and exiting the car into consideration. Some people choose cage integrity over ease of access. There should be a happy medium. On the one hand, you want the cage to be strong to absorb a hard impact; on the other hand, you need to be able to get out fast in case of a fire. An expertly designed and installed cage is not intrusive into the passenger compartment. The roll bar or cage should also be as close to the inside of the body as possible.

Buildings and roll cages have a few things in common, but the most important feature they share is the foundation. If the foundation isn't strong, the integrity of the roll cage will only be good for visual effect—and as a weapon. The floorpan and the frame must be in good shape. A rusted floorpan is not a good place to anchor the cage. Fabricators prefer to anchor a cage to frame structures rather than sheetmetal, but this isn't always possible. In the case of a unibody where the cage must attach to a sheetmetal structure, use large-load spreading anchor plates between the tubing and body metal. Again, use a rulebook as a guide to accepted practices. The rocker panels are typically made up of multiple sheets of formed steelsheet that are welded to create a strong structure. The steelsheet is also a good attaching point for the cage.

Roll bars and roll cage main hoops need to be anchored to the floor behind the front seats. In unibody cars, the rocker panels are the only place to anchor the main hoop. Most fabricators use 0.090- to .125-inch thick mild steel for fabricating anchor plates. The anchor plate is typically formed to take the shape of the floor area where it will be welded. Anchor plates need to be welded around the entire perimeter for maximum strength.

The main ingredient of a roll cage is the main hoop. The main hoop is the bar located just behind the front seats. All driver protection bars attach to the main hoop. Some racing rulebooks require the main hoop to be made out of tubing that is larger in diameter than the rest of the cage. In some rulebooks, the diameter of the main hoop tubing is determined by the weight of the car. Using larger diameter tubing, such as 2-inch, can cause headaches when attempting to bend it because most fabrication shops don't have the proper dies. If the fabrication shop you have in mind doesn't have the size of dies needed to bend your tubing, ask if they are willing to purchase them in order to do the job. A nearby shop may also be commissioned to bend the tubing. Either way, there are only two

The main hoop comes from the floor behind the passenger seat, goes up and over to the driver's side, and then flows down to the floor behind the driver's seat. Some racing classes require the main hoop to be larger than the rest of the cage, so check any rules if you plan to race.

Within this main hoop is a diagonal bar that ties the passenger side lower section to a point just over the driver's head. This bar is very important for strength if you plan on road-course racing. A horizontal bar without a diagonal bar does not limit torsional stress as well as a single diagonal bar does. The bar matters much less for drag racing.

ways to do things: the right way, or over and over again. Build the cage strong and safe from the start because it might save your life someday.

All roll cages are not created equal. Cages designed for drag racing are generally not as torsionally rigid as road race cages. In road racing, it's important that the chassis/cage be as rigid as possible so that the suspension can work under the extreme loads of braking and turning. Most road-racing roll bars and cages have a diagonal bar from the bottom of the right side of the main hoop, and running up to a point near the top of the main hoop on the left side. Adding this bar to the main hoop helps reduce twisting forces in the chassis, but more importantly, it helps keep the main hoop from trying to collapse downward in a rollover.

Bolt-In Roll Bars/Cages

Bolt-in roll bars and cages are for people who have commitment issues. Some people want to use their car for dual purposes. The car can be driven daily without the roll bar or cage, and it can later be installed on race days. Some people have plans to get their car back to "stock" condition someday. Yeah, right. Whatever your reason is, it's your car and bolt-in roll bars and cages are perfectly fine when they are welded and installed correctly.

If you ever plan to race, make sure to check the rules to find out if they accept bolt-in roll bars and cages. Some bolt-in cages are not legal at drag strips. Some racing associations accept bolt-in roll bars and cages only for specific classes. Other sanctioning bodies require the use of large, hardened washers or metal plates that sandwich the floorpan sheetmetal. The hardware helps ensure the bar or cage is anchored securely to the floorpan and will be harder to pull through the sheetmetal. Some associations also require the use of fine-threaded grade-8 bolts with two nuts locked together. The doubled nuts ensure the first nut won't come loose, causing the roll bar or cage to fail in an accident.

Quick Cage Tip

In the process of designing your bar/cage, keep in mind that the joints need to be welded all the way around. It isn't easy to do this with the cage tucked up against the sides of the body and headliner. First, you should form and install all of your floor-reinforcing plates. Lightly tack these in to keep them in position, but they will have to come out for the next step, so keep the tack welds small. The trick is to mock the cage together with light tack welds first, and then mark the floor around where each bar will attach with a Sharpie marker. Next, remove the cage pieces and floor plates. Now use a hole saw about 1/8-inch larger than the bar tubing and drill holes where you marked the floor. Deburr your holes and re-tack your floor plates in (they are coming out again shortly). Next, reinstall your cage bars and tack the cage together lightly. With the cage all tacked in, go around all the bars and put four or five tacks on each bar. Now remove the floor plates and let the cage slide through the holes in the floor a few inches. Voila! Now you can weld all the way around the tubes without having the sides of the body or headliner get in your way. When fitted tight to the inside of the body, a roll bar or cage will add considerable strength to your car and give it that wicked race-car look, while taking away as little interior space as possible.

Tubbing

For years, enthusiasts have resorted to tubbing to fit larger tires inside their fenderwells. To start off, there are two types of tubbing: tubbing and mini-tubbing. Both entail a ton of labor. Tubbing is what you generally see Pro-Street builders do. They remove the inner and outer fenderwells and replace them, along with making serious modifications to the frame rails. Mini-tubbing is the more recent style of getting more rubber under the rear of a car. You generally only remove part of the inner fenderwell to add a section for depth. With mini-tubbing, the frame may need a little surgery, but nothing major. The finished mini-tub typically looks like it came that way from the factory, instead of looking like a drag racer installed aluminum panels in his backyard. Now that you have

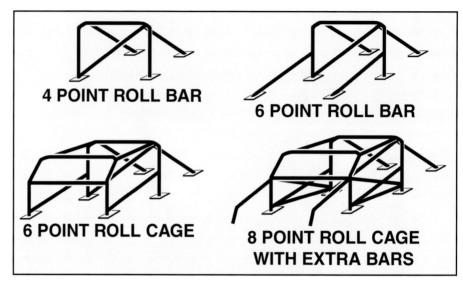

A roll cage is built off of the main hoop of a four-point roll bar. Roll cages come in many shapes and sizes. They are referred to as 6-point cages, 8-point cages, etc. Basically, the "point" designation comes from the number of points where the cage intersects the chassis.

an idea about the differences, we can read more about the processes of both types of tubbing.

Getting the widest tire possible under the rear fenderwell has been a goal since hot rodders figured out that wider is better for traction. It's not easy getting 13-inch-wide tires under the stock quarter panels of an early Mustang, or any other car for that matter. Tubbing involves removing the fenderwells and the floor from behind the front seat to the taillight panel. After all the original sheetmetal has been removed, the frame rails are cut off about 18 inches forward of the rear axle centerline and moved inboard enough to get the necessary clearance for the new tires. New wheelwells can be purchased from any number of companies, or they can be fabricated out of either sheet aluminum or steel. Steel tubs are stronger, more durable, and generally provide for a quieter interior. This is why the majority of Restomod cars are built with steel instead of aluminum tubs.

Mini-Tubbing

Mini-tubbing is the process of cutting the wheelwell front to back at the largest diameter, and widening the well by adding in a strip of sheetmetal between the inner and outer halves of the well. Sometimes it's also necessary to

When building your roll cage, take safety and function into consideration. David McMillan's '69 Mustang roll cage has a cross-bar positioned far enough forward to clear his noggin, but far enough back so he could use his sun visors.

notch the frame rail slightly to clear the tire. This process is less time-consuming and less expensive than a full tub job. This is the process used when the wheelwell can be enlarged enough to clear the desired tire without having to move the frame rails, but some frame notching is usually necessary. When properly installed by an experienced builder or a professional fabrication shop, mini-tubs look like factory sheetmetal fenderwells.

ENGINES

There are a few drivetrain parts that should receive extra attention when you're building a Restomod. Some of parts don't get much attention on street rods and Pro-Street cars. Most of those cars don't see the hard driving a Restomod car will see. When you push your car to the limit and beyond, weaknesses in your engine, cooling and oiling systems, transmission, and clutch will become more evident. This chapter is dedicated to these areas and more.

Engine Swaps

To start off, this section has information some purists will deem ludicrous and downright horrible. With that said, read on.

Swapping in a non-original engine is done for many reasons. Here are a few of them: gain more power, increase the "oooh" factor, save money, or just use what you have lying around. The most common engine swap in the early Mustang world is to swap from a stock 6-cylinder to a small-block V-8. I've included information on common and not-so-common engine swaps. I've also included some other things to keep in mind when you're thinking of swapping in a different engine. If you are reading this book, there is a good chance you are interested in building a car that will handle well. For instance, if you have a 300-pound 4-cylinder in your 1974 Pinto or 1976 Mustang II, dropping in a 720-pound 460 will probably not help your handling. A car like that makes a great drag racer, and that's about it. A few oth-

Just because a car didn't come from the factory with a certain engine as an option doesn't mean you can't make the swap. Probably the most labor-intensive engine swap is putting a 4.6- or 5.4-liter Modular engine into a shock-tower-equipped Restomod, because the shock towers have to be modified. (Photo courtesy The Mustang Shop)

er aspects to consider include the availability of engine mounts, headers, transmission, crossmembers, engine compartment size versus engine size, hood clearance, oil pan clearance, etc. I've gathered just a few possible Ford engine swaps, and some are only covered briefly. With all the engines Ford produced, someone could write a complete book on all the possible Ford engine swaps.

2.0 and 2.3-Liter 4-Cylinder Engine

If you've been around since the early 1970s, you may remember Ford's 2.3-liter coming with as little as 83 hp and 120 ft-lbs of torque. The factory stepped

it up with the 1984-1986 SVO Mustang, pumping the 2.3-liter up with as much 205 hp and 248 ft-lbs of torque using fuel injection and a turbocharger. The turbocharged 2.3-liter also appeared in the 1987 and 1988 Thunderbird Turbo Coupe with a whopping 190 hp (on the 5-speed model) and 240 ft-lbs of torque.

If you decide you want to keep your carbureted 4-cylinder, you might want to contact Esslinger Engineering in Southern California. Esslinger produces some serious parts for the 2.0 and 2.3-liter 4-cylinder engines. As noted earlier, the 1974 Pinto 2.3-liter pounded out an anemic 83 hp and 120 ft-lbs of torque.

This Mustang is being prepped for a Modular engine installation. Instead of removing the shock towers and installing a Mustang II suspension, The Mustang Shop has installed a late 1990s front suspension and strut towers for better handling. (Photo courtesy The Mustang Shop)

When installing different engines in your Restomod, getting the engine mounted at the correct angle and location can be tricky. Some applications require you to fabricate your own mounts. TCP makes mounts for small- and big-blocks. (Photo courtesy Total Control Products)

Restomods don't have to be V-8 powered. This little 2300 4-cylinder in a Pinto would put out some 12-second quarter-mile times (without a turbo). Esslinger Racing can assemble a 400-hp engine with a cast-iron block, as well as heads and valvetrain. (Photo courtesy Esslinger Racing)

Esslinger has been able to pump out 109 hp using a stock block, stock intake, and a carburetor, which is pretty impressive. With an upgrade to Esslinger's aluminum D-port head, you can see a whopping 40 to 50 hp over stock while still being able to keep your stock intake and exhaust manifolds. Plus, the aluminum head saves you 40 lbs over the stock cast-iron unit. Upgrading to Esslinger's SVO head and the matching custom intake manifold will net you an additional 20-hp gain. Esslinger also offers a complete aluminum block and

ARCA (Automobile Racing Club of America) aluminum head that will juice up your carbureted combination with another 20 hp (up to 170), and save you a combined 100 lbs over the stock cast-iron parts.

Now those numbers are only for naturally aspirated engines. With the right parts, Esslinger Engineering has been able to pump 400 hp out of the cast-iron 2.3-liter block. With Esslinger's aluminum block and all the right parts set up for drag racing, you can make up to 1,000 hp! Of course, that's with a tur-

bocharger running insane amounts of boost. Esslinger also sells fully assembled crate engines that have been fully dyno-tested. Or how about a stroker kit to turn the 2.3 into a 2.5-, 2.6-, or 2.85-liter? With a rare tall-deck engine block, you can even stroke it up to 3 liters of brutal mass.

If you'd rather go with a swap, the fuel-injected, turbocharged 2.3-liter is a direct bolt-in for the 1974 through 1980 Pintos, as well as many other 2.3-powered Fords. Of course, saying "bolt-in" means that the engine will bolt into the engine compartment with unmodified stock engine mounts. Putting the turbo 2.3-liter into a 1971 through 1973 Pinto can be done; you'll just have to cut off the 2.0-liter lower engine/frame mounts and weld in 2.3-liter lower mounts. A V-8 swap may be tempting, but you can buy a Thunderbird Turbo Coupe for very little money; take the engine, transmission, and computer out of it; and sell what's left to recoup most of your money or more.

If you're still wondering why I'm talking so much about 4-cylinder engines and Pintos, listen to this: The 1971 Pinto Sedan tips the scales at 1,949 lbs. By 1980, the 4-cylinder Pinto Sedan had slowly gained weight to an all-time high of 2,385 lbs, which is still really light. So, if you had a 2,000-lb Pinto, and put in a stock 190-hp 2.3-liter from an '88 Turbo Coupe, the power-to-weight ratio would be approximately 10.5 pounds per horsepower. For comparison, let's look at a 3,300-lb '68 Mustang with a stock 230-hp, 302-ci engine. That works out to a much weaker power-to-weight ratio (PTWR) of approximately 14.5 lbs per horsepower. Pump the 2.3-liter Pinto up to 400 hp, and the PTWR changes to 5 lbs per horsepower—the Mustang would need 660 hp to match that.

If I have not persuaded you to keep the front of your Pinto light, there are a few companies offering headers and engine mounts for V-8 swaps. Contact info for these companies can be found in the Source Guide in the back of this book. Total Performance has engine mounts, oil pans, and headers. Hedman Hedders and Hooker Headers sell engine swap headers.

Of course not everyone can afford a Cosworth-built 358-ci NASCAR engine, but it sure would be nice to pop the hood on your Falcon or Maverick and see this thing staring back at you. With a Restomod, any extra horsepower is appreciated.

Supercharged V-6 engines can be found in 1989-1995 Thunderbird Super Coupes. These engines can be adapted and modified to power some of the smaller Fords. These engines are lighter than V-8s, which can help you build a balanced, great-handling Restomod.

Ford V-8 Swaps

You have many engines to pick from when building your Restomod. Each engine has benefits and drawbacks. Picking the right V-8 for your application is not easy. It's kind of like walking into a donut shop and seeing all those little round treats staring back at you through the glass case. Sure, you have your favorites, but your mind wanders. So, which one's the right one? The small-block comes in many different flavors, as do the FE and 385-series big-blocks. Add to that the tasty new overhead-cam 4.6- and 5.4-liter Modular engines, and it's easy to get overwhelmed. It goes without saying that each of these engines

can be stroked and over-bored for even more cubic inches.

I'd like to send a special thanks out to Marlin Davis of *Car Craft* magazine, and Jim Smart of *Mustang & Fords* magazine, for their help on some of this hard-to-find engine information.

Small-Blocks

Collectors have picked up a decent portion of the factory-equipped V-8 cars on the road and started restoring them, especially the well-optioned V-8 models. This leaves mostly 6-cylinder-equipped cars for the serious Restomodders. According to Jim Smart of Mustang & Fords magazine, the most common engine swaps in the early Mustangs and other shock-tower-equipped cars are from the old inline 6-cylinder to the small-block Ford engine. The second most common swap is from the 289 or 302 to the 351W. Swapping the 289 or 302 for the fuel-injected 5.0-liter (late model 302 ci) is the next most popular after that. Jim also notes that the popularity of the 5.0 swap is beginning to overtake the 351W swap with Restomodders.

Small-block Fords come in three different flavors. The first is the 90-degree Windsor V-8 family, the 221, 225, 260, 289, 302, Boss 302, and 351W (ranging in weight from 460 to 525 pounds). The second is the 335 Series, or Cleveland engines including the 351C and the Boss 351, each weighing 550 lbs. Last are the Modifieds, the 351M and 400M, weighing 575 lbs.

When you're swapping in any of these small-block Fords, you need to know the overall dimensions. These differences can cause installation clearance issues. Small-block Fords range from 24 to 26 inches wide.

The 1962 through 1965 small-block Fords have a five-bolt bellhousing. After that, all small-block Fords, except for the Modifieds, switched to a 6-bolt bellhousing. All small-block Fords, again except for the Modifieds, share the same engine mount configuration on the sides of the engine.

The Modified engines are beasts unlike any other. They're similar to Cleveland, but with taller deck surfaces. The "M" shares the transmission bellhousing surface with 385 Series 429 and 460 big-blocks, but its engine mounts are not shared by any other Ford engine.

For more general info on small-block Ford engines, check out any one of the small-block Ford titles from CarTech Books.

FE Big-Blocks

The FE family consists of the 332, 352, 360, 361, 390, 406, 410, 427, and 428-ci engines, each weighing 625 lbs. The rarest FE is the 427 SOHC, which tips the scales at 680 lbs. FE engines produced before 1965 had one type of 2-bolt engine mount on the sides of the block. The 1965 and later FEs had the same early production 2-bolt mount provisions and an additional set of later 2-bolt mounts.

With the exception of the 410 and 428, the FEs are internally balanced, so make sure you have the correct weight of flywheel and harmonic balancer to fit your application. The FEs (with the exception of the 427 SOHC) are approximately 27 inches wide. If you are or were privileged enough to own a rare 427 SOHC engine, you will have a hard time fitting this 32-inch-wide monster in the engine compartment of early shock-tower-equipped cars.

385 Series Big-blocks

The redesigned 429 and 460 big-blocks are known as the 385 Series engines. They tip the scales at 720 lbs. Then there is the Boss 429, which only weighed 635 lbs. It was a heavy hitter in NASCAR with its big top-end torque numbers. Only a few '69 and '70 Mustangs were produced with the Boss 429 wedged between factory-modified shock towers. You can wedge a 429 (non-BOSS) and a 460 between the shock-towers of 1967 through 1973 Mustangs and Cougars, as well as a few other models, with parts from Crites Restoration. Heavy modifications would be necessary to fit these engines in Mustangs and Cougars built before 1967. If you ever found a Boss 429 block, you could identify it by the screw-in freeze plugs and four-bolt mains. The 429/460 blocks can't be identified as two- or four-bolt mains without pulling the pan, but the

Not only is it unusual to see a '53 Ford truck built as a Restomod, it's also unusual to see one powered by a 4.6-liter Modular engine and a 6-speed transmission. Keep your options open if you want a Restomod that will stand out in a crowd.

four-bolt main blocks are more desirable. The 429 and 460 share the same block, and the displacement depended on the crankshaft. All the factory 429 and 460 engines were filled with cast-iron crankshafts. The 1979 and newer 460s were externally balanced.

Modular Engines

Ford's latest V-8s are the 4.6- and 5.4-liter Modular engines. There is a 16-valve, single overhead-cam (SOHC) and 32-valve, dual-overhead cam (DOHC) version of each displacement. These engines differ from year to year and are available with either aluminum or cast-iron blocks.

Modular Ford engines hit the streets in 1991 in the Lincoln Town Car. These early 4.6-liter blocks had a different bolt-pattern from later Modular engines because they were bolted to an automatic overdrive transmission that had been used with the older 5.0-liter engine. Some 4.6-liter blocks are made to bolt up to front-wheel-drive (FWD) transaxles and will not bolt to any RWD transmissions, rendering them useless for Restomods. With those exceptions, all other 4.6-liter, 5.4-liter, and 6.8-liter (V-10) Modular engines share the same transmission bellhousing bolt pattern, which is different from all other Ford engines. The front timing cover changed from model to model and year to year. They can have different, bolt-boss configurations and bolt sizes, so builders suggest keeping your parts together when building Modular engines. The

One definite complaint about the earlier shock-tower-equipped cars is the narrow space between the shock towers. This '66 Mustang has a 351W wedged in place. The stock exhaust manifolds barely fit. JBA headers and a few other companies make tight fitting headers for this application.

main caps are different too. The Windsor (Canada) engine plant builds with main dowel pins and cross-bolts; the Romeo (Michigan) plant builds its mains with jack-screw cross-bolts. Windsor engines use floating wrist pins, and Romeo engines use press-fit pins. The pistons are different dish sizes, too. Windsor iron blocks have a "W" cast in the valley area and in the front of the block. Make sure you know which one you have before you start ordering parts.

The 4.6-liter and 5.4-liter engines share the same engine mounts. The 4.6- and 5.4-liter DOHC and SOHC blocks are different, but can be made to accept either DOHC or SOHC heads with some simple modifications. That way, you can build a screaming 5.4-liter engine with DOHC heads. The Lincoln Navigator came with this combination, putting out 300 hp and 360 ft-lbs of torque, but the supercharged 5.4-liter lightning belted out 380 hp and 450 ft-lbs of torque with SOHC heads. Those are just factory power numbers; imagine what can be done with camshaft swaps, head work, intake manifold swaps, superchargers, turbochargers, and more. Sean Hyland Motorsports has been able to create some amazing power, and it offers Modular performance parts and completely modified crate motors. For more info, check out his book *How to Build Max Performance 4.6-Liter Ford Engines*, available from CarTech Books.

Ford Racing Performance Parts offers complete DOHC Modular crate

How about building a mid-engined Restomod with a 2005 Ford GT 5.4L supercharged modular engine? It pumps out 500 hp and 500 ft-lbs of torque. Imagine this beast sitting behind the seats of a '66 Mustang mounted in a custom chassis. The options are endless.

Mark Deshetler was building this '66 Mustang and had a chance to get a well-built engine for a great price. However, the engine was a small-block Chevy. He adapted the chassis and made it work. It's been open road racing at speeds around 180 mph. Though it's sacrilegious to some, to others it's a great use of available parts.

the supercharger, intercooler, and forged crankshaft, weighing in at 543 lbs. Another great option is the 5.0-liter DOHC "Cammer" crate engine, which is rated at approximately 500 hp (with free-flowing exhaust) and a broad torque curve with a peak of 365 ft-lbs. It is equipped with an aluminum block, high-flow DOHC heads, performance rods, 11.0:1 compression ratio, fuel injection, and all accessories. These crate engines are a really great option if you're looking for something to swap into your Restomod, and Ford is supposed to be coming out with a stand-alone wiring harness to make things even easier.

Superior Custom Classics offers stand-alone wiring harnesses for just about any engine combination you can imagine or build. Street & Performance also offers wire harnesses for installing a 4.6-liter Modular engine in your Restomod. Of course, you can always get a wiring harness and all the accessories you'll need out of a donor car.

DVS Restorations makes engine mounts for bolting Modular engines into 1964 through 1970 Mustangs and 1967 through 1970 Cougars using their original suspension. However, no matter which Modular you choose to swap, if you have shock towers, you will need to modify or remove the shock towers to make room. There are two companies offering shock tower modification kits. Revelation Racing Supplies sells kits to convert the front suspension to smaller-diameter coil-overs, which gives you room to modify the shock towers. DVS Restorations also offers shock-tower modification at its facility. The DVS shock tower modification kit requires lowering the upper control-arm attachment points. The other option for installing Modular engines into shock-tower cars is to completely remove the shock towers and weld in a whole new front suspension, which does not require any suspension member located above the upper control arm. If you are installing a Modular engine in a full-frame car, such as a Galaxie or Gran Torino, currently there aren't any companies offering engine mounts. With some fabricating knowledge and tools, you could design some of your own.

motors in 4.6-, 5.0-, and 5.4-liter sizes. One of the 4.6-liter options includes a complete 1999 Cobra engine with exhaust and a T-56 six-speed transmission bolted together as one complete unit that, when complete, weighs 1,010 lbs. Another option is a complete (with supercharger) 390-hp 2003 Cobra Supercharged 4.6-liter crate engine with cast-iron block, forged crankshaft, Manley SVT I-beam rods, and all accessories, which weighs 762 lbs. Ford Racing also offers the 2003 5.4-liter supercharged Lightning crate engine that comes with

The engine block is a P-Ayr composite replica block. It weighs about 15 lbs, has all the factory bolt-bosses, and works great for building a custom chassis, running a turbocharger, or doing any kind of serious modification. This one is waiting for custom engine-mount fabrication. (Photo courtesy Greg Carter)

Engine Swapping Parts

When it comes to engine swaps, the most common engine swap is ditching a 6-cylinder in an early Mustang to move up to a small-block 302 or 351W. Take into account that when you upgrade from a smaller engine to a larger one in any car, you will need to upgrade suspension (springs, braces, and steering) components to support the extra weight. You should also upgrade the braking system, the fuel system, and the cooling system.

Some cars had different steering components for 6- and 8-cylinder models, so you'll need to make sure your parts are up to the task of working with the extra power. Using stock 6-cylinder brakes on your Restomod after installing a 400-hp 347 is also a bad idea. Not only have you added weight to the nose of your car, but you have increased the power output to make it even faster. Different engine sizes and performance also need differently sized fuel lines. Don't expect your new V-8 to reach its potential using the original fuel line from your 6-cylinder equipped Mustang. The same is true for the cooling system – a radiator designed to cool a 6-cylinder is not going to keep your V-8 cool on a hot day.

If you are going to install a fuel-injected 5.0L engine in your older Restomod, you should perform the items previously listed along with a fuel-injection fuel pump and filter, a 130-amp alternator, and some specialty brackets and adapters from Windsor-Fox Performance Engineering. Of course, you will need the complete 5.0L- engine from a donor vehicle with the fuel injection, ignition, engine control module (ECM), and wiring harness.

There are many companies offering parts to make life easier when bolting an engine into your Restomod. For instance, you may want to bolt a big-block 460 in your 1968 Ford Fairlane, or a 351 Cleveland in your 1965 Mustang. Either way, you'll need at least one of the following custom engine swap parts: engine mounts, headers, oil pan and pickup, accessory brackets, radiator, and transmission adapter.

I've put together a pretty good (but by no means comprehensive) list of swap parts manufacturers. Some of the companies manufacture the products they offer, and a few of them offer products for other manufacturers. Not all manufacturers sell parts directly to the public, so purchasing parts from a distributor like Mustangs Plus or Dark Horse Performance is much faster and easier. Some of them offer swap parts I don't have room to list, so search around these companies and you may find the parts you need.

Hedman Hedders and Hooker Headers sell engine swap headers and brackets for a lot of different applications. Trans-Dapt Performance sells engine mounts, transmission adapters, and transmission mounts. Ford Powertrain Applications (FPA) offers custom tri-Y, shorty, and long-tube headers for many common and uncommon applications from 1955 through 1993 and for stock and aftermarket heads. FPA even has headers for applications using Total Control Products rack-and-pinion steering. They are very high-quality and tuck up tight to the floorpan, which is a great feature for the lowered stance of the Restomod crowd.

D&D Automotive Specialties offers swap kits and components for early Fords, but its largest offering of parts are for Fox-bodies (Mustangs, Fairmonts, Zephyrs, Cougars, Capris, and T-Birds). Kaufmann Products sells custom engine mounts and headers for early Mustangs, most Fox-body applications (using stock and aftermarket heads), Rangers, and Broncos. Coast High Performance offers Pro Mustang Performance headers for engine swaps. Mustangs Plus and Year One both sell some engine swap parts. Total Performance manufactures engine swap headers for many of the 1960 through 1978 shock-tower-equipped Fords. Tubular Automotive sells the hard-to-find tight-fitting headers for early shock-tower cars, which allow you to install a 351C in 1964-1/2 to 1966 Mustangs without modifying the shock towers. If you have an old or newer Restomod and you want to swap in a big-block, you should try Crites Restoration Products. Crites offers headers, swap kits, and all the necessary parts to swap engines into full-frame and unibody Fords and Mercurys from 1957 through 1988. Crites also has the knowledge of its kits to let you know what other parts you will need during your swap.

Total Control Products produces heavy-duty interlocking engine mounts made for installing the FE (except the 427 SOHC) and small-blocks in the 1964-1/2 through 1970 Mustangs and Cougars. The mounts are bushed with polyurethane inserts and will not separate, even if the urethane were to somehow deteriorate.

These Jomar stud girdles are worth their weight in gold. They reduce rocker-arm stud flex, which helps keep the valves in adjustment and reduces stud failure.

When swapping newer engines into older Restomods with original Z-bar style clutch linkage, you will find out there is no provision on the side of the late-model 5.0 block to bolt the ball stud. Without that ball stud, you can't use the original linkage. For some reason, you have to be "in the know" to find an adapter bracket to mount the pivot ball to the newer blocks. Well, I'll let you in on the secret. Kaufmann Products and Total Performance are at least two companies producing such a bracket.

In some cases, you may need to relocate your oil filter from the stock location due to engine swap headers or engine mounts. It's actually a good idea to convert to a larger racing oil filter for higher oil pressure and better lubrication. Check the oiling system section later in this chapter for more details.

The large water pump inlet is on different sides of the crankshaft for different engines. If you put a 351W in a 1965 Mustang, you'll need to change the radiator. The original 289 water pump inlet is on the right side of the crankshaft, and so is the lower radiator outlet. The 351W water pump inlet is on the left side of the crankshaft. In this case, you would need to install a new radiator with the outlet on the left side. Aftermarket radiator companies like Griffin Radiators make custom radiators that are direct bolt-ins.

Accessory mounting is also important when swapping engines. In most cases, you can use the accessories and brackets designed for the new engine.

For instance, if you are swapping from a 351C to a big-block 460 in your 1972 Gran Torino, you can go to a wrecking yard and pull a 460 out of a truck, rebuild it, and then swap it in. You have a few options of what accessories and brackets to use. You can either use the brackets that came with the 460, or scour the wrecking yards for brackets that will put things in their stock locations, or you can find an aftermarket accessory bracket company that offers something in the positions you need.

Accessory brackets are available from many aftermarket companies. The following is a list of companies and the applications they support. March Performance, Zoops, and Street & Performance offer aluminum bracket and pulley systems for the following accessories: belt tensioner/idler, power steering, alternator, water pump, and A/C. FPA offers high and low-mount alternator brackets for big-block FEs. Jones Racing Products (JRP) offers small-block accessory brackets and pulleys. The JRP high-mount alternator bracket can be used with the mechanical water pump and pulley removed from the front of the engine (for use with some electric pump applications). Powermaster Motorsports is mainly known for manufacturing performance alternators and starters, but they also offer accessory brackets for Ford engines.

Engine Parts

Restomod engines are usually loaded with performance parts. I could write a separate book on engine upgrades, but there are plenty of other S-A Design CarTech books covering the subject. I will keep this section fairly short, and try to include parts that sometimes increase the durability of your engine, especially if you plan on driving it hard on the street and at the track. Some of these parts also give the engine back its horsepower. For instance, a cooling fan bolted to the front of the water pump robs power from the engine. The inertia of its rotating mass and wind drag reduces your engine's overall output. When you remove the manual fan and install an electric fan,

A rev-kit for your roller cam is another "must-have" part. These help keep tension on the lifters when you are revving up your engine, and they reduce valve float at high RPM. Getting a kit that fits your lifters can be tricky, but it's well worth the money.

you give the power back to the engine. Of course, the fans would draw more electrical current from the alternator, so it has to work a little harder, but the power difference between manual and electric fans is substantial.

Bolts

Some people find it hard to justify spending money on engine bolts, since they don't increase your power. However, they are very important in certain applications. Going to your local hardware store to purchase bolts to use for bolting on your timing cover is okay, but buying hardware-store bolts for your heads and main caps is a really bad idea. Even if you bought some grade-8 bolts from the hardware store, they aren't designed to work inside an engine, so you'd just be asking for trouble. I've been around cars long enough to see people build engines with grade-5 bolts as head and main bolts. Even if you're on a budget, any good engine builder will tell you to spend the extra money to buy good, quality fasteners. The professionals I asked said they would use a minimum of quality rod bolts, main bolts or main studs, and head bolts when building an engine. They all recommended using Automotive Racing Products (ARP) fasteners.

If you have the extra money, you should consider replacing all your engine fasteners with high-quality nuts and bolts. Some of you may be thinking

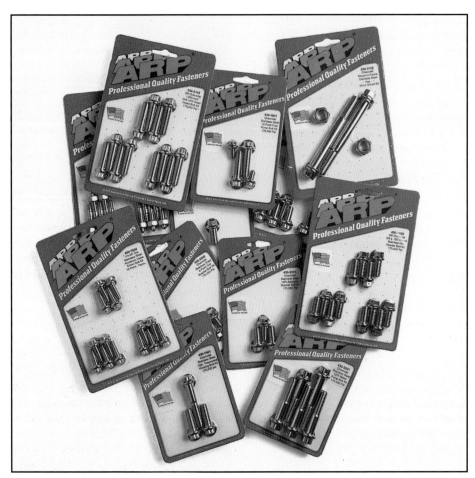

The most popular bolt company in the aftermarket industry is ARP. ARP offers bolt kits for just about every engine component, including all the accessories on the outside such as water pumps, starters, etc. ARP also offers bolts in bulk if you're interested in getting the best quality bolts for your body or suspension components. Don't be fooled by other bolts that are advertised as aircraft quality. ARP has higher standards than aircraft applications require. (Photo Courtesy ARP)

that using ARP fasteners in areas like the oil pan and the intake manifold is overkill. Figure that most small engine bolts are commonly over-torqued. Now think of the hassle involved with removing the remains of a broken intake manifold bolt that ended up breaking the third time you reinstalled it. Maybe you think you'll never remove your intake manifold or timing cover after you install them the first time, but that probably won't be the case. Quality fasteners will save you the threads in your block, untimely hassles, and money in the long run.

Bolts are different from studs. A stud only has to be installed once. For instance, a main bolt must be removed every time you remove a main cap. If you remove a main cap attached with main studs, you only have to remove the

nut. This saves the threads in the block. When installing studs in the mains or any other blind location (a hole that does not have an opening at the bottom), it's best to bottom-tap the hole. This means that the threads need to extend to the bottom of the hole so the bottom face of the stud will have positive contact with the block. This gives the studs more integrity. Since you're using studs because you want more strength, you should do the job completely.

Using head studs can save the threads in the deck of your block, since you can leave them screwed into the block during head service. Imagine how much deterioration the cooling system can cause to the head-bolt threads in the block. Removing the bolts time and again can eventually pull the threads out

of the block, necessitating a Heli-Coil. The only drawback to running head studs is lack of serviceability when the engine is in the car. The head must have room to slide perpendicular to the block's deck (head mounting surface) for the length of the studs. This is especially troublesome on shock-tower-equipped cars. Stepping up to quality head bolts instead of head studs will not help you save the threads in the block, but they do make it easier to work on the heads while the engine is in the car. Usually, serious racers with head studs don't have any obstruction for head removal, or they have spare engines to swap for faster repair.

Before assembling the important engine parts, you should clean the threads in the engine block so you get a good torque reading. Some people use a bolt tap to clean the threads. This is a bad idea. Every time you run a tap through the threads in the block, it takes away thread material. If you do it enough times on a new block, or just one time on an old block with 30-year-old threads, you could take away enough material for the threads to pull out when you try to torque things down. The best way to clean the threads is with a heavy-duty rifle brush, or a set of Thread Cleaning Chasers from ARP. Thread Cleaning Chasers are undersized taps that safely clean out the gunk, but leave the threads. They are a good investment.

Breslin Performance Products also offers high-quality bolts with a feature that no other bolts have – Split-Lock technology. There is a set pin in the center of the bolt that spreads the special split-threaded end of the bolt to lock it into place. Vibration, heat, and torque dependence will not effect the bolt's locking ability. Once the bolt is torqued, the set pin is tightened, and the bolt is locked in place. Breslin currently offers header and header-flange bolt kits, but more applications are on the way.

Cooling System

Internal combustion engines create enough heat to destroy themselves if they are not equipped with a good cooling system. The cooling system also circulates hot water to warm the engine in colder climates. In simple terms, the cooling system consists of a few basic components: a radiator, a pump, water, and a fan. The stock cooling system is great for a stock engine in a moderate climate, but stock systems from the 1960s, 1970s, and 1980s are inadequate in extremely hot environments. With the addition of computer-controlled engine management systems, cooling systems have become more efficient.

The block and reciprocating assemblies operate efficiently and wear less when the temperature is in the range of 190 to 210 degrees Fahrenheit. The wear on the cylinder walls decreases dramatically when the cooling system operating temperature is 180 degrees Fahrenheit or hotter. If your cooling system is running too cool, you can damage the engine. Keep that in mind when messing around with the cooling system components.

Ford, Lincoln, and Mercury engines all have similar cooling systems. The coolant is drawn out of the lower portion of the radiator and forced into the front of the block. The water flows around the cylinder walls, up into the heads through holes in the head gaskets, and up even further to the crossover under the thermostat, where it is restricted until it gets hot enough to open the thermostat. After the water flows through the open thermostat, it travels through a hose into the top of the radiator. Once the water enters the radiator, it transfers heat to the cooling fins and starts the whole process all over again.

Ford first introduced the 221-ci V-8 in 1962. Due to its crankshaft and accessory pulley configuration, its water pump rotated clockwise (looking at the front of the engine). This has been labeled standard rotation. In 1986, Ford introduced the serpentine belt accessory system. Because of the way the serpentine belt ran through the pulleys and accessories, it turned the water pump in the opposite direction. Everyone calls this reverse rotation. The impeller in the pump had to be redesigned to efficiently pump water through the engine cooling system. Standard-rotation pumps will not work on reverse-rotation accessory-

This WP362 electric water pump offered by Meziere mounts to a plate that is welded to the Saldana radiator, instead of to the front of the engine block. These water pumps are rated at 2,400 hours of operation before servicing. That adds up to a lot of hours. After you drove your car for 2 hours every single day for three years, then you would need to start thinking about servicing the electric motor.

drive systems, and vice-versa. They might fit, but the blades on the impeller are designed to turn in only one direction. If you have some serious cooling problems with your car, and you have checked every part of the system and still can't figure it out, check to see if your car has the correct water pump. This problem has baffled many seasoned mechanics.

While not necessarily a Restomod part, I'm including these heater-hose fittings because of the high quality Restomods should reach. Corrosion of original heater hoses and bypass hose fittings are common problems with older cooling systems. Old fittings not only look bad on the engine, but they become difficult to remove from intake manifolds and water pumps without damaging the threads. Replace your corroded, ugly heater and bypass hose fittings with new, high-quality stainless steel fittings from Performance Stainless Steel. They will always look good and will not damage the threads in your water pump, block, or intake manifold if you need to remove them.

Water Pumps

Every cooling system needs a pump to circulate fluid, which helps to minimize hot spots; automotive cooling systems are no exception. If your pump fails to circulate water through the engine, the water surrounding the cylinder walls would boil. That boiling would allow air pockets, or hot spots, to form around the cylinder walls. Air doesn't cool as efficiently as water, so these hot spots would allow the cylinders to over-

The original timing cover on this engine was modified to accept fittings so that coolant lines could be run to the Meziere electric water pump. Meziere also makes remote water pumps that mount anywhere, just in case you don't have room at the bottom of the radiator for the WP362.

Not all water fittings are created equal. If you want a better-looking fitting that won't rust and corrode, you should check out the full line of Performance Stainless Steel fittings. These fittings will look good forever.

heat and cause severe block expansion. These extreme conditions could cause the block to crack and other engine parts to seize or fail. A functioning pump moves water around inside the engine and through the radiator, where cooler water resides. The cooler water helps to equalize the system temperature.

As mentioned above, the impeller inside the water-pump case circulates the water. The impeller has small blades that cup the water and force it through the engine.

Stock Water Pumps

Most stock water pumps have a stamped-steel impeller. They work great on low-horsepower daily drivers. The impeller fins are designed to move coolant into the engine block at normal driving RPM, but it loses efficiency because of the straight-blade design and loose tolerances between the case and the blades. Ford did not design the stock cooling system with high RPM and excessive heat-producing horsepower in mind. At high RPM, the pump cavitates because the impeller turns too fast. When the pump cavitates, it fails to pump cool water into the hot engine. Without cool water cycling into the engine, the water gets even hotter. This is not efficient and can cause damage, or at least headaches, if the system goes through this cycle too often within a short period of time.

Belt-Driven Aftermarket Water Pumps

It's a good idea to upgrade to an aftermarket water pump if you boost your horsepower, take your car to the track, or just want to improve the efficiency of your cooling system. Aftermarket pumps are available in cast iron and aluminum. Meziere, Milodon, Stewart Components, Edelbrock, and FlowKooler are just a few companies offering these pumps. Some pumps are designed to flow better at lower RPM for streetability, and some are designed to operate at high RPM for full-race applications. Make sure to contact the manufacturer for guidance on its products before making a purchase.

Some companies offer OEM-style housings with upgraded impellers. Others offer their own housings and impellers. Most aftermarket pumps are equipped with low-drag bearings to reduce the horsepower needed to drive the unit. If you are worried about weight, aluminum housings are lighter than cast-iron units, and can shave approximately 10 lbs off the nose of your engine. Although 10 lbs does not seem like a lot, it can add up when coupled with other weight-saving parts. The aluminum also dissipates heat better than cast iron.

The higher-performance water pumps have larger bearings and pump shafts for strength in higher-performance applications. The larger shaft will require a pulley with a larger shaft hole, or you can modify your current pulley. Ford small- and big-block water pumps are available with standard and reverse rotation, so be sure to get the right pump for your application.

Electric Water Pumps

In the past, electric units were made for drag racing only. A drag-racing cooling system has minimal requirements: the pump doesn't need to produce much pressure and the engine is producing extreme heat for 12 seconds or less.

Car owners tried the original belt-driven electric and stand-alone electric water pumps on their street cars with very little success. These bad experiences gave electric water pumps a bad name, but there have been some superior advances in electric water pumps in the last 10 years. Not only have the designs changed for the better, but they have also become more reliable.

A few aftermarket companies offer reliable, high-quality electric water pumps, including Meziere Enterprises Inc. Meziere offers electric units for the Ford small-blocks, Clevelands, Modifieds, 385-series big-blocks, FE big-blocks, and Modulars. The 5.0-liter and Modular 4.6-liter electric pumps work an idler pulley so you can use the stock accessory belt configuration, or you can run without the pulley. In some applications, these pumps can free up as much as 15 hp. Depending on the application, these pumps flow from 35 to 55 gallons per minute (gpm). These aluminum-bodied pumps are available polished or in red, blue, purple, and black.

When you're running an electric water pump, it should always be running when the engine is on. At any time the pump is not running, the engine could be building up air pockets around the cylinder walls, insulating them from water. This can happen before the water-temp gauge will even register. The beauty of the electric pump is the ability to run the pump even after you shut off the engine.

Electric water pumps also operate at the same RPM, no matter how fast the engine is running. If you have a 35-gpm water pump, it will be pumping at the same rate at 1,000 or 6,000 rpm. This helps keep the engine cool at an idle, as well as high RPM. If you get stuck in traffic, which can spell trouble for high-horsepower engines, the system will be flowing better than a belt-driven system.

New remote water pumps are also becoming available. They can help you free up some space on the front of your engine. This can be useful in custom applications where space between the radiator and a conventional water pump is cramped. Whether you've swapped in a physically larger engine or you're running turbos or a blower, a remote pump can get some extra space. If you simply want to clean up the front of the engine for an ultra-clean look, a remote pump might be the ticket.

Meziere also offers remote-mounted water pumps. One version mounts directly to the radiator with a special bracket that can be tig-welded to most aluminum radiators. When you completely remove the water pump off the

Mr. Gasket offers the Robertshaw thermostat, which is the highest flowing performance thermostat on the market. If you're not running a bypass in your cooling system, air bubbles can get trapped under the thermostat. The air won't open a thermostat until it's too late. The way to get the air to bleed past the thermostat is to drill two ⅛-inch holes in the thermostat. The holes allow air to travel through the thermostat, so the water will be able to activate it.

front of your engine, you need special port adapters to run hoses directly from the pump to the front of the block.

Thermostats

The engine's operating temperature is regulated by the thermostat. Every thermostat has a temperature rating, which is where it is supposed to open. The ratings typically range from 160 to 190 degrees. For instance, a 160-degree thermostat will stay closed until the coolant behind it reaches 160 degrees. When the thermostat opens, hot coolant flows through it. Once the coolant flowing through it drops below 160 degrees, the thermostat closes so the coolant can reach 160 degrees again.

Drag-racing applications can benefit from replacing the thermostat with a restrictor plate, since the cooling system only needs to operate for short bursts of time. Restomods should be running a thermostat. With the exception of extreme Restomods, our cars will probably be driven on the street on a regular basis. On the street, the thermostat is necessary for bringing the car up to operating temperature. Most people think a cool running engine makes more power, since the colder the air-fuel mixture is, the better it burns. This is correct

for the intake system, but the block and reciprocating assembly operate better and wear less when the engine is in the range of 190 to 210 degrees Fahrenheit.

Cooling system experts choose Robertshaw thermostats and Stant Superstats. The Robertshaw is available from many manufacturers, including Mr. Gasket and FlowKooler. It's the most desirable thermostat since it's the least restrictive when fully open.

Cooling experts suggest drilling two small holes in the outer ring of the thermostat if your cooling system does not have a bypass. Without a bypass system, air pockets can form under the thermostat. The hot air doesn't heat the thermostat to its opening temperature, so it stays closed. If this happens, your system will fail and your engine will overheat in a hurry. The two small holes allow the hot air to get through the thermostat, so your cooling system will operate correctly.

Radiator

The cooling system is made up of many important components; the radiator is the key to dissipating heat. The radiator is made of tanks, tubes, and fins. Hot coolant flows into one of the radiator tanks. The coolant is pushed through tubes on its way to the tank on the opposite side. During this movement, the heat transfers to the tubes and into the cooling fins. The fins are cooled by the air flowing around them (through the radiator), which allows more heat to be transferred from the tubes.

Until the mid-1980s, most production radiators were constructed of copper and brass. When manufacturers started trying to make their systems more efficient, the copper/brass tube thickness was causing radiators to weigh too much. They had to find alternative material to make radiators lighter, without losing strength. Instead of running four half-inch-diameter copper brass tubes with .015-inch wall thickness, radiators could be constructed of two one-inch aluminum tubes with .016-inch walls, with half the weight and better cooling capacity. If you're just trying to lighten up your front end, you may want to take into consideration that an

aluminum radiator may weigh less, but the bigger tubes hold more coolant. In Restomod applications, cooling properties should be a higher goal than saving a few pounds, so don't skimp out on a radiator that's too small.

Griffin Radiator, BeCool, C&R Racing Inc, and Saldana Racing Products are just a few companies offering aftermarket aluminum radiators. Each company has a different construction process, and some may not offer direct bolt-in units for your application. Griffin Radiators welds its tubes to the headers (where the tubes meet the side tanks) like the other companies, but unlike other manufacturers, Griffin also adds epoxy where the tubes meet the headers. The epoxy adds extra strength to the tube-to-header joints, and adds an extra level of leak protection.. If you want a direct bolt-in radiator for your '66 Mustang with a 351W, you may be limited to one or two radiator companies. Radiators made specifically for 351W swaps use original mounting brackets and have the correct inlet and outlet sizes and locations. If you're building a custom cooling system and don't require a bolt-in radiator, universal radiators are available from most companies. The universal radiators are usually cheaper, but since they don't have any mounting provisions, some custom mounting and fabrication skill is required. Universals are sold by overall width and height, and they are not always offered with different sizes of inlets and outlets.

Custom radiators are available in single- and dual-pass versions. A single-pass radiator is most common. The hot coolant is forced into the left tank, at the upper left corner of the radiator, where it works its way to the tank on the right side of the radiator and flows back into the engine through the lower right corner. The dual-pass radiator is essentially two single-pass radiators stacked on top of each other. A typical dual-pass design will have the hot coolant enter the upper right corner of the upper right tank. The coolant is forced across the upper section of the radiator to the left tank, where it travels down the left side of the tank and into the lower half of the radi-

A fan shroud has an inlet and an outlet. The inlet is the area closest to the radiator. The outlet is the section closest to the engine. The inlet is most effective when it is close to the same size as the radiator core. This stock fan shroud seals to the radiator all the way around. This is a late-model truck fan bolted to a 351W in a '71 Torino.

ator. The coolant then has to pass from the left side to the lower right side of the tank, where it enters the engine.

Cooling Fans

The cooling system is put to the ultimate test—not only in road-course racing, but in traffic as well. The system builds heat in the engine as usual, but the heat is trapped under the hood, where it heat-soaks the engine compartment. The worst part of traffic is not getting flow through the radiator.

I was once told, "If your car overheats in traffic but runs cool at 60 miles per hour, your radiator is big enough, but you are not getting enough airflow through your radiator." You can dig a little deeper and say: The cooling fans may not flow enough cfm, or you may need a fan shroud to effectively direct air through the entire radiator.

Stock flex fans, like stock clutch fans, are great for moderate performance engines. There are a few aftermarket companies making high-performance flex fans. Aftermarket flex fans usually have less reciprocating weight than stock solid and flex fans, but not all flex fans are created equal. Flex fans are rated by their maximum RPM and by engine size, so make sure you get the right one for your application.

Flex fans get their names from their flexible, steel fan blades. At low RPM,

the blades keep their pre-formed curves, so they can pull as much air through the radiator as possible. This is great for when you are idling in traffic. At high RPM, the blades lose their curve and flatten out. The flat fan blade has less drag on the engine which, along with the blades' lighter weight, increases power output. This is great for racing. Since your car will be moving when your engine is at high RPM, your fan doesn't need to feed the radiator with air.

When using a stock or aftermarket flex fan, make sure you periodically check the fan blades for defects and cracks. Since the blades flex back and forth constantly, the metal can get fatigued and crack. Think of bending or twisting an aluminum can for a few minutes. It will eventually crack and break. I'm not saying flex fans break a lot, but if they do, they can be very dangerous. I had a stock flex fan break at about 4,000 rpm on one of my old cars. The fan blade went through the layers of metal in my hood. I never found the blade. Minutes before that, a friend was leaning over my engine, revving the engine after he tuned my carburetor. Be aware of the state of your car and its parts.

Electric Fans

Deciding which electric fan set-up to run can be overwhelming if you don't know what to look for. Besides looking for a fan that will fit in the space you have, the most important thing to look at is the amount of air a fan moves. For instance, a single 15-inch-diameter electric fan might move 2,800 cfm, while a 14.45-inch fan from another company might only move 1,350 cfm. That's a big difference. Another feature to look for is the amperage drawn by the fan. Of those two fans, the 15-inch model draws 13.9 amps, and the 14.45-inch model draws 10.5 amps. The higher the draw, the more power your alternator will need to generate.

Each company offers a variety of single- and dual-fan set-ups with different widths, heights, and depths, along with cfm and amperage ratings. In some instances, you may get stuck with a low-performance fan due to cramped space. If your car heats up driving around town but stays cool on the freeway, you

may need a fan that moves more cfm. If you have only 3 inches of clearance between your water pump pulley and the radiator, it may mean you're stuck with a fan set-up that moves half the cfm of a set-up that requires 4½ inches of clearance. It might cost you more money, but if clearance is your problem, you can switch to a remote-mounted electric water pump. Driving around with an inferior set-up that overheats under normal driving conditions can be unnerving and embarrassing.

You can mount electric fans directly to the radiator, to brackets, or to a fan shroud. Mounting fans to the radiator can be done by using plastic or metal rod kits that slide through the radiator cooling fins. The rod kits come with little locks to prevent them from coming loose and causing the fan assembly to fall into the engine. When you cut the excess rod off, leave about 3/8-inch of rod sticking out. The excess rod sticking out is a very dangerous cutting hazard, especially if it's metal. Go to your local hardware store and get some rubber screw caps or some small-engine vacuum caps to slip over the protruding rod tips. The first time you are working on your car and rub on one of those caps, you will be thankful you took a little time to do this right. Some fans or integrated fan and shroud systems can be mounted to metal or aluminum straps specifically for the job, or you can fabricate your own.

Fans come as pushers and pullers. A pusher fan will need to go in front of the radiator so it can push air in. A puller fan needs to be mounted in the rear of the radiator so it can pull air through. Most electric fans with integral fan shrouds are puller types, since if it was mounted in front of the radiator, the fan shroud would block the path of airflow. Pusher fans work well as a booster fan if you're running a mechanical fan and need some extra help cooling, or for custom applications without clearance between the radiator and engine.

High-output Restomods need an electric fan set-up that flows 2,800 cfm. This might require running dual fans. I've seen 550-hp small-blocks get by with a single 15-inch puller that moves

This electric fan will help cool, but the only section of the radiator getting cooled is the diameter of the fan itself. A fan with a shroud would help pull air through a larger section of the radiator. The area of the radiator not covered by the fan does not get any airflow while the car is sitting still.

Delta Current Control is designed to gradually turn the fan on, rather than giving it a big surge of power and shocking your electrical system. The controller also helps maintain a constant system temperature, rather than hot and cold coolant cycling that can hamper engine life and performance.

Electric fans can be triggered by a manual switch on your dashboard, or by a thermostatic switch. Fixed-range thermostatic switches screw into a water port on the engine or the radiator and have an operating range of 10 to 15 degrees. They can be purchased for the range that you determine is best for your application. Adjustable thermostatic switches have a probe that either screws into a water port in the cooling system, or they have a probe that pushes into the radiator fins near the inlet where the heated water enters. You can adjust them to turn the fans on at whatever temperature you choose. Either way, electric fans draw enough amperage that powering them without a relay can cause enough resistance in the wire to get it real hot. In some cases, the wire can get hot enough to drop the speed of your fans after 15 minutes of running time, or melt the insulation off the wire and cause serious problems. A relay mounted close to the fans will run the load-bearing hot wire a much shorter distance for a much safer connection. If you connect the fan relay with a constant hot, the fans will be able to run even after the key is turned off. They'll turn off after the engine temperature drops below the switch's operating temperature. Most companies will tell you not to wire it like this because there is a possibility the fans will stay on and drain your battery. With a "keyed" hotwire to the fan relay, the power is cut off when the ignition key is turned off.

2,800 cfm. I've also seen 480-hp big-block cars have lots of issues with dual 12-inch electric fans pulling 2,500 cfm. An engine that is out of tune can run hotter, and big-block engines historically run hotter than small-blocks. Cooling systems on moderate-to high-horsepower engines in hotter climates would be better with at least 3,600 cfm. Getting too much cfm is almost impossible, at least according to Tim "The Tool Man" Taylor.

Factory production cars are another good source for electric fan set-ups. For instance, 1993 to 1997 LT1 Camaros and Firebirds came equipped from the factory with dual 12-inch electric fans and a fan shroud. Due to overall size, this fan is good for full-size Restomods. It's approximately 28x18x5 inches, and supposedly moves 3,600 cfm. This set-up draws 10 to 15 amps while running, and has a 15-to 20-amp surge on start-up.

The most common factory fan set-up used for older cars is the 1997-1998 18-inch Lincoln Mark VIII fan with built-in shroud, part number F8LH-8C607-AA. Its overall dimensions (not including factory mounting tabs, which are typically removed for installation) are 22x18.5x6.25-inches deep at the cen-

ter of the electric motor. The set-up moves approximately 4,500 cfm. It draws 33 amps while running and 100 amps during the surge at start-up. When using this fan, it's imperative to swap out the alternator and run at least a 130-amp unit to make up for the current draw. For your exact electrical system amp draw, check the formula for picking the correct alternator.

The other imperative part of installing the Mark VIII fan, or any other fan that draws a lot of amperage, is getting the correct high amp relay, wire gauge size, and wiring configuration. Using the wrong parts will cause disastrous failure to your electrical system; this is not an area to cut corners in. Putting in a standard 30-amp relay to operate the fan's power circuit is a good way to smoke your wiring harness. There are two ways to get switched high-amp power to high-amp fans. The most common way is to use a Bosch 75-amp relay (part number 0-332-002-156) that is meant to be used for Mercedes diesel glow-plugs. The second, more elegant way of regulating high-amp power to an electric fan is to install a high-amp fan controller. One controller from

Fan Shrouds

A fan shroud is an important part of getting optimum performance out of your manual or electric cooling fan. The shroud helps channel the airflow through the radiator for optimum cooling. Without a shroud, even a fan will draw air through a limited section of the radiator, depending on the size of the fan. Obviously, if you don't have enough

DERRICK YEE'S 1973 MAVERICK

Derrick Yee is a big fan of the Ford Maverick. As you can see, his passion for them is shown by this great example of an unique Restomod. The lack of bumper guards and the prominent carbon fiber hood give this Maverick a powerful look. The Mav' has a great stance: Not too low, not too high. It has great ground clearance for added drivability, and looks right at home on this mountain road. The smoked taillight lenses and barely visible stainless exhaust tips work well together. (Photo s courtesy Phil Royle)

What is the first car that comes to mind when you read the word Restomod? If you're from the same country I'm from, you will probably have the same initial thought that I do – Mustang. That's understandable. We probably read the same magazines and books. What's the second car to come to mind? Maybe your next answer is a Cougar, Fairlane, or Falcon. Well, when will your response be the Maverick? What's wrong with the Maverick? It was built to replace the Falcon and compete with the import cars coming to the US in the early 1970s. Its platform is very similar to the Mustang, but it has more rounded and swoopier body lines.

Derrick Yee has held Mavericks high on his list of cool cars for many years. He's even a big enough fan of them to create his own website called Maverick-Man.com, where he is the Maverick Man. The Maverick in these pictures is just one in his collection of many. One is built with straight-line racing in mind, and the other is a straight-6 gem. This one is known as the Baby Blue Maverick. It is built for all-around performance driving, which makes it a Restomod. He wanted something different, something that

exuded performance, so he had some connections build a custom carbon-fiber cowl hood (which he sells as a product on his website). Just so the hood wasn't the only carbon-fiber part on the car, he put a set of APR carbon-fiber race mirrors with bases custom-made to fit the original mirror mounting holes. The two-tone roof helps balance the dark-colored hood. To lighten things up, the Mav has Hella H4 conversion headlights, Koito White Beam H4 bulbs, clear turn signals, and smoked Plexiglas taillight lenses. Other external touches include removal of the huge front and rear bumper guards, the addition of Boyd Coddington Dictator 17x7-inch and 18x8-inch wheels wearing 245/40-17 and 255/45-18 Bridgestone Potenza S-03 Pole Position rubber, and the menacing stance. The car has a completely different look than I've ever seen on a Maverick. To get the big tires to fit, Derrick used the combination of 4-inch backspacing on the wheels and rolled the front and rear inner fender lips.

If the looks alone aren't enough to get you to change your mind about Mavericks, maybe looking under its baby-blue skin will. The powerplant is a 302

The Boyd Coddington Dictator 17x7 and 18x8-inch wheels work well with the overall look of the car. They also display the Wilwood 4-piston Dynalite calipers and the drilled and slotted brakes through the polished spokes. (Photo courtesy Phil Royle)

stuffed with 8.5:1 forged JE slugs, compressing air up against 1966 52-cc heads with 1.94-inch intake, and 1.6-inch exhaust valves. The Lunati cam operates the Comp Cams 1.6:1 ratio roller-tipped rocker arms. The engine is force-fed through a Holley 750 double pumper by a Holley 174 Power Charger running 6 lbs of boost. Compressed air is ignited by Taylor wires, MSD BTM ignition box, Blaster 2 coil, and Mallory distributor. The boost wasn't enough for Derrick, so he threw a pair of Nitrous Express polished bottles in the trunk with an automatic bottle opener, which feeds the blower through a Nitrous Express Phase 3 Gemini Twin Plate. For accessories, the engine was dressed with K&N air and valve cover breathers, Ford Motorsports valve covers, and March pulleys and brackets. Cooling is handled by a GMB pump, Cool Flex hoses, and a Griffin aluminum radiator. The spent gasses flow through Hedman Hedders, 2.5-inch pipes to 2.5-inch Magnaflow Tru-X Pipe to 3-inch pipes, complimented by Magnaflow XL stainless mufflers to 3-inch mandrel bent tubing piped out the rear.

A C4 automatic transmission powers a Ford 9-inch rear end. Derrick knew a standard 9-inch wouldn't hold up, so he contacted Moser Engineering. Moser came up with a heavy-duty housing capped with a nodular case and a 1350 yoke. Inside is a 3.50:1 gear set on a Trac-Loc limited slip diff and a pair of 31-spline Moser custom alloy axles. The rear end is kept in place by stock leaves, but assisted by Cal Trac traction bars

and a 0.5-inch ADDCO sway bar. The front suspension consists of all polyurethane bushed parts, 1-inch TMC Mustang sway bar (not an exact fit, about a half-inch wider than the Maverick bar), TMC 600-lb springs, and other TMC hardware. All four corners are wearing KYB gas shocks. The best drivability modification Derrick made so far was the addition of Wilwood Dynalite Pro disc brakes on all four corners. He made slight modifications to fit a Mustang kit on the Maverick front spindles, and easily installed a 9-inch Ford rear kit. After driving with 4-wheel discs, he wants to upgrade all his Mavericks, even the 6-cylinder.

An often-overlooked part of a Restomod is the interior. Derrick didn't leave this stone unturned. He had the Cobra Daytona front buckets and rear seats covered by Katzkins with leather to match the color of the Auto Custom Carpet kit and original interior. Derrick positioned the AutoMeter gauges so they could be read clearly through the leather-wrapped Dino steering wheel. The centerpiece is a B&M Starshifter. When he gets tired of listening to the engine, he has a sound system consisting of all the right Panasonic pieces. To power the grid, he uses a chrome 100-amp alternator and Optima Red Top.

The 302 is force-fed 6 psi by a Holley 174 Power Charger. Derrick added two polished Nitrous Express bottles in the trunk so he can put the squeeze on unsuspecting competition. (Photo courtesy Phil Royle)

Derrick would like to thank his wife, mom, dad, God, Matt Held at Holley, Chris Coddington at Boyd Coddington Wheels, Allen Nicholas at Wilwood Brakes, Eric Knappenberger at McCullough PR, Todd Ryden at MSD, Carol Yohe at Edelbrock, Brian Havins at Nitrous Express, Jon Bennet and Bruce Wood at Moser Engineering, Chad Dimarco at Sube Sports, Lisa Cerda at Katzkins, Randy Killingbeck at March Perfromance, Ron Piasecki at Autometer, Tanya Axford at Magnaflow, John Hrinsin and Mike Golding at Mr. Gasket, Jay Hess and Kathy Flack at JE Pistons, KC Chow at APR Performance, Chris Chan at VIS Racing Sports, Crystal Nelson at Stir Marketing, Shane Reichart at K&N Filters, Carl at Viking Fabricators, Phil Royle, at Eurotuner, and Greg Yamamoto at Super Street.

If you think the car looks familiar, it's possible you've seen it on *Hot Rod TV*. It also showed up (with yellow paint) on the cover of the January 2000 issue of *Hot Rod* magazine. Maybe now that you've seen what can be done to a car with lower popularity numbers than the Mustang, you may want to add Maverick to your Restomod vocabulary.

The Cobra Daytona front and rear seats were covered in leather by Katzkins to match the original interior and Auto Custom Carpet. The addition of AutoMeter gauges, B&M shifter, and Dino wheel round out the interior. (Photo courtesy Phil Royle)

cool air flowing through the radiator, you might have overheating problems.

Running a manual fan without a shroud can produce similar cooling issues, especially since they aren't as close to the radiator as most electric units. The fan will just whip the air around in the engine compartment instead of pulling it through the radiator effectively. Without a shroud, the air that does get pulled through the radiator only comes through an area about the same diameter as the fan. Increasing the shroud inlet size increases the cooling area. The best design would have a shroud inlet that is the same size as the radiator core. The fan diameter should be about 1 inch less than the diameter of the shroud's outlet opening.

Along with helping airflow, the shroud also helps keep the engine compartment safer while the engine is running. The fan, whether it's electric or manual, can be dangerous when you are working on your engine. Electric fans wired to engage solely by a thermostatic temperature sensor can turn on at any time. Fingers or loose clothing pose a safety hazard if the fan kicks on when you least expect it. The same can be said for a manual fan while the engine is running, so don't lean over your engine while wearing a necktie. The fan shroud doesn't eliminate the danger, but it helps.

Oiling System

The stock engine oiling system consists of oil, oil pump, pump pickup, oil pan, oil filter, and the engine block's oil passages. There are two types of oil systems available for engines: wet-sump and dry-sump systems. Of the two systems, I will be covering wet-sump systems more than dry sumps, since the latter is very uncommon on street-driven cars.

A wet-sump system is the most common and holds the majority of its oil in the oil pan sump, hence the term "wet sump." Ford production cars, except for the 2005 Ford GT, run wet-sump systems. They are cheaper to build and maintain. Wet-sump systems are self-contained with an internal oil pump that is indirectly driven by the camshaft, and a pickup in the oil pan.

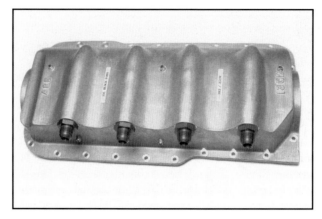

This cast-aluminum dry-sump oil pan is manufactured by Armstrong Race Engineering (ARE). ARE sells cast valve covers, oil pans, and dry-sump pump kits for multiple Ford engines. These pans are very beefy parts so they offer extra rigidity to the engine block. (Photo courtesy Armstrong Race Engineering)

The capacity of a wet-sump oil system is determined by how much oil the oil-pan sump will hold. Adding an external filter and/or cooler adds capacity to your oiling system, but that doesn't change the amount of oil in the oil pan. If you're worried about your oil pump running dry, some builders suggest putting oil restrictors in the block to allow less oil to get to the top end of the engine. This helps, but adding a higher-capacity oil pan will help even more. Some engine builders prefer to use high-pressure oil pumps in engines with stock-size pans. This increases oil pressure, but won't suck a stock pan dry like a high-volume oil pump will in the right conditions.

Dry-sump systems hold the majority of their oil in an external oil tank, not in the sump of the oil pan, hence the term "dry sump." Dry-sump systems require an external pump turned by the camshaft or a crank-driven belt. Any problem with the drive system or hose failure will cause serious engine failure. Dry-sump systems are more expensive than wet-sump systems due to the added components and plumbing, but they are the safest way to keep your engine pressurized with oil. In a dry-sump system, oil is continuously pumped by one chamber of the pump into the external oil tank. There is a constant supply of oil available in the external oil tank for another chamber of the pump to feed the engine. Depending upon the application, the available capacity of a dry-sump system ranges from 4 to 14 quarts. They allow for a very low-profile oil pan, which allows racers to set the engine closer to the ground for a lower center of gravity. Under harsh acceleration, brak-

ing, and cornering, the wet-sump pickups in the oil pan will be sucking air, which could cause damage to the engine. The dry-sump pump removes the oil from the pan to stop it from sloshing up during extreme conditions and hitting the crankshaft and rods, where it robs power from the engine. Moving up to 14 quarts of oil in a dry-sump tank, toward the center or the rear of the car, also helps transfer weight for a more balanced car.

Oil Filters

Not all oil filters are created equal. There are many different oil filters on the market, but only a few of them are suited for performance applications. If you're going to drive your car hard, you should get a performance filter. Performance filters have better filtering media and thicker cases, which increase the burst pressure to at least 500 psi and protect against rock and stone damage. Wix Racing filters are distinguished by the "R" after the part number. They're also individually wrapped to keep out contaminants. K&N Filters offers Performance Gold filters that have an additional 1-inch wrench nut on the end with a provision for safety wiring (specialty stainless steel wire used in racing and aircraft to keep bolts from vibrating loose). Fram also offers Racing series filters for performance applications.

Oil Filter Relocation

A common problem with Ford's stock oiling system is the restrictive oil filter and its mount. Upgrading to an aftermarket, remote oil filter helps combat oil pressure problems and helps

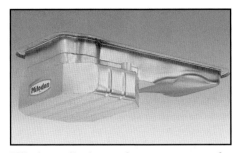

Milodon sells dry- and wet-sump pans for most Ford applications. This one is a low-profile road-race version. It doesn't hang down as far as the street/strip oil pans, so your ground clearance won't suffer. (Photo courtesy Milodon)

increase bearing life. These problems don't pop up on the street with mild engine combinations, but when you start pumping high horsepower at a high RPM, you should upgrade to a remote-mounted filter to protect your powerplant. When I mention remote oil filters, I don't mean those cheap remote kits that use the stock size filter. I'm talking about installing a remote oil filter adapter, like a Fram HPK600 or Moroso #23766 and a high-flowing, high-capacity Fram HP6 or WIX 51222R filter. This is a trick known to Ford road racers, and now the secret is out. Canton Racing Products and other manufacturers offer oil filter adapters that accept fittings large enough not to restrict the oil flow from the block to the remote filter, or the flow of oil back to the engine. Use at least -10 AN fittings and hoses to plumb the system to keep the oil flowing freely. Just swapping from a high-performance filter in the stock location to a system like the one mentioned here has been documented to increase oil pressure to 6 psi at idle. That might not seem like much, but imagine how happy your bearings will be at high RPM.

Windage Trays

During harsh driving conditions, oil sloshes around enough in the oil pan to come into contact with the crankshaft. This contact creates drag on the crank and robs power from the engine. A windage tray is basically a shield located between the crankshaft and the oil. It not only keeps the oil off the rotating assembly, but it also keeps it in the pan,

making it harder for the sump to suck air into the oil pump and the system.

Windage trays are connected to the oil pan, or bolted to crankshaft main studs and the oil-pump bolt or stud. If your frame and suspension limits your oil-pan clearance, you can use a stock or stock-shaped aftermarket oil pan. Some of these oil pans have windage trays welded inside, near the top of the sump. The bolt-in windage trays require a windage tray install kit, which includes main studs that feature extra threads on the ends for the tray's height adjustment. Milodon recommends adjusting the windage tray to no closer than .100 inch to the rotating assembly. These studs typically have 5/16 inch of extended thread length on the end of the main stud. The extra length should be left as long as possible (without interfering with the oil pan), just in case you eventually want to switch the style of tray or spend some more money on getting a stroker upgrade. Replacing the main studs on your second build-up because the studs were cut 1/2 inch too short is an unnecessary expense.

Many aftermarket manufacturers offer their own windage trays. Milodon offers louvered windage trays for most Fords. Their testing has shown real-world gains of up to 12- to 15-hp on 400-hp engines. The louvers allow the oil to fly off the crank and back into the pan, where the tray keeps it until it's sucked up by the sump.

Dry-Sump Oil Pans

Very few Restomods have dry-sump systems. Dry-sump pans are very low profile; they usually only have about 1 inch of clearance between the rotating assembly and the bottom of the oil pan. They either have pickup tubes that run the length of the pan with little inertia-baffles, or they have multiple pickups so the oil can be picked up during hard acceleration, braking, and cornering. Since the dry-sump system does not rely on the pan for its oil supply, a little air sucked up in the pan pickup won't kill the engine. As with most parts, dry-sump oil pans are designed differently for road racing, circle tracking, and drag racing. Make sure you buy the right pan for your application.

Wet-Sump Oil Pans

Since Restomods are meant to be driven fast around corners, a stock pan might not be adequate for your application. Stock pans don't hold much oil compared to aftermarket oil pans, and they are barely suited for mild performance engines and/or road-course driving. Aftermarket street/strip pans are designed to control the oil from front to rear, but the oil pickup can still get uncovered if you corner hard. Aftermarket wet-sump pans typically hold 2 to 2.5 quarts more oil than a stock pan. They also hang further down, which can limit your ground clearance.

A road-race wet-sump pan has trap doors to control the oil from moving in every direction. This keeps the oil pickup covered with oil, so the engine components will stay happy. Installing a street/strip pan is adequate for mild performance driving on a road course, but when you dial in your suspension, have extremely good brakes, and run sticky tires on a road course, you'll need an oil pan designed for road racing. Road-race pans have a wider sump than street/strip pans, so they can hold as much oil or more. They're also typically shallower than street/strip pans, so ground clearance can be even better, while still increasing the oil capacity.

The downside to road-race pans is that because they are bigger, it can be hard to find one that fits your application. They can interfere with headers, or

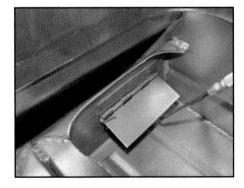

This is called a trap door. Behind this trap door is a hole in the baffle wall. Oil on the other side of this baffle can push through this door during a hard right-hand corner, so it can keep the oil-pump pickup covered. The wire on the hinge will only allow it to move up a limited amount.

at least get close enough to heat up your oil without a thermal barrier. The biggest hurdle to jump is possible interference with steering linkage. Consult the manufacturer's technical department about your engine size and chassis type for the correct road-race pan before laying down your money.

When upgrading to a new oil pan, you'll need to buy the proper oil pump pickup. A given pickup is designed for a specific pan, and probably a specific oil pump too. Oil pump companies don't have any kind of standard. So, it's a good idea to purchase your oil pump and oil-pump pickup from the same company you purchase your oil pan from. That way you know the pan, pump, and pickup will all fit when you go to bolt them up. It's pretty frustrating to buy a pan and pickup, hope to bolt it all on over a weekend, and then find out they don't fit. You may later find that your oil pump was made by a manufacturer that changed the pump design four times within a couple of years. A ⅜-inch change is huge when you are working with tight tolerances in the oil pan. The oil pump pickup is supposed to be ⅜ of an inch from the bottom of the oil pan. If it's too far from the bottom of the pan, it could starve under hard driving conditions. If the pickup is too close to the bottom of the pan, it will be too restrict-ed and not able to feed enough oil to the engine. If the engine does not get enough oil, it could cause enough suction to pull the pan in and out at different RPM and eventually cause the bottom of the pan to fail from fatigue.

All this information about oil pans, pumps, and pickups is not just a scare tactic – it's written from personal experience. These problems can happen to anyone. So, the moral to all this is: Don't mess around with your oil system. The oiling system is very fickle and it doesn't take much to cause expensive problems, let alone just a headache.

Oil Cooling

When driving your Restomod hard at a road course, your engine oil temperature will climb higher than you have ever imagined. On a road course, you keep the RPM up and the engine working harder than in any other type of driving you do. The water-cooling system is usually hotter, too. All the components under the hood are hot from trapped air under the hood. The temperature of your engine oil can climb to 260 degrees or more, but there are a few ways to cool it. You can run an external cooler in front of your radiator, a cooler built into the radiator, or a heat exchanger.

Aftermarket radiators are available for serious performance applications

Racers have found less restriction from the Fram HP6 and WIX 51222R filters. To mount these, you'll need a block adapter and a remote filter mount like this Fram unit. Moroso also makes a mount for these big filters. It's suggested to plumb these with -10AN hoses and fittings.

with oil coolers built directly into the radiator. This helps keep the oil cooler, but at the same time, it heats up your coolant. Think of your engine oil running about 265 degrees, and your engine coolant running about 215 degrees. The oil will be trying to dissipate heat to the coolant, and since the water is considerably cooler, it will cool the oil. This can be a happy relationship if your coolant system is extremely efficient. The oil cooler in the radiator can also work in the opposite way during normal day-to-day driving conditions. The engine could take forever to heat up to operating temperatures. The water could cool the oil too much to effectively protect your engine.

An external oil cooler in front of the radiator will transfer less heat to the cooling system directly, but since there will be hot air flowing through the oil cooler into the radiator, you'll get some extra heating in the coolant system. The best external coolers on the market are Setrab coolers. They are known worldwide and supply many manufacturers. They are a stacked-plate design and are durable in racing environments. There are a few companies offering copies of lesser quality, and there are a few companies re-labeling Setrab coolers as their own.

A heat exchanger also works as an oil cooler. Coolant runs through plumbing that runs through the oil system, which allows the heat from the oil to transfer to the cooling system and vice

Dry-sump oiling systems are typically only used on road-racing and open-track cars. These systems offer the ultimate in oil control. If your car can out-handle its oiling system and you see your pressure gauge drop during corners, it's time to upgrade.

Dyno-tuning is a good way to get the optimum power out of your Restomod. Dynos are very helpful in tuning fuel-injection set-ups as well as carburetors. This Dynapack chassis dyno is more accurate than roller dynos, since it can actually put a load on the chassis, unlike the freewheeling drum type. (Photo courtesy Mustang Corral)

versa. This system helps equalize the two temperatures for better performance and longevity. An aftermarket external heat exchanger is good enough for just about any horsepower level, depending on the system. Typically you will only find heat exchangers on high-dollar racecars. They use bypass systems that close off the oil going to the exchanger until oil-operating temperatures have been met. The bypass systems combat the problem of getting engine fluids up to proper operating temperature. The car will have faster warm-up times and better (less) engine wear.

Induction and Fuel Systems

The most important elements in making power are air and fuel. Getting the correct air/fuel ratio into and out of the combustion chamber is the key to making power. There are a few ways to get the mixture in. Natural aspiration through a carburetor is the traditional way to feed an engine, but fuel injection can be more efficient if it's tuned properly. To increase power, you can cram more air and fuel into the engine by bolting on a turbocharger or supercharger. Whatever you choose, remember that first you have to get the fuel to the carburetor or fuel-injection system.

There are entire books written on carburetors (even on specific carburetors), fuel-injection systems, and superchargers. For more specific info on any of these topics, check out the CarTech Books website at www.cartechbooks. com.

Carburetors

Carburetors are rated by how many cubic feet per minute (cfm) they flow. This rating is helpful in choosing a carburetor, depending on the number of cubic inches or potential horsepower output of your engine. It is possible to over-carb an engine. Bolting a big 750-cfm carb on a stock small-block 302 is overkill, and the engine will not operate at its optimum potential. If you bolt a little 600-cfm carb on a 460 built for high-RPM power, it will not run correctly. There are charts and information to help find the carb for your application, but it's best to consult an experienced professional. You can ask a technician from the carb company, or an experienced carburetor guy at a speed shop. If you get the wrong size of carb, your performance potential can be limited by over carbureting and running too rich, or by under carbureting and running too lean. In extreme cases, running excessively rich can cause fuel contamination in the oil, which thins the oil and

can lead to internal engine failure. Running too lean can cause overheating and possible piston failure. These conditions can even happen with a correct-sized carb that's just seriously out of tune, so if you don't know what you're doing, be sure to consult a professional who does.

Before choosing a carburetor size, choose your carburetor company. There are a few common brands on the market today, and each has its benefits. Some carburetors are better for trouble-free street driving, some are best for street/strip driving, and some are better for road-course racing. The well-known aftermarket carburetor companies include Holley, Barry Grant Demon Carbs, Carter, and Edelbrock. Factory remanufactured replacement carbs are also available from a few companies. There are even shops that rebuild and power-tune factory and aftermarket carburetors. The best way to tune a carburetor for optimum fuel efficiency and power is to take your car to a shop equipped with a dynamometer, where an air/fuel meter can be connected to the exhaust. With this equipment, the shop can fine-tune your car's fuel system while putting the entire mechanical drivetrain under load.

This MoTeC air/fuel ratio meter is used to help tune the carburetor or fuel injection. By installing an oxygen sensor in the exhaust system just after the header collector, you can correctly read the air/fuel mixture. The MoTeC meter shows the mixture ratio in an easy-to-read digital display that will read to two decimal points. It's an indispensable tool for fuel-injection tuning. By checking the readout, you can easily tell if you're getting lean or rich conditions anywhere in the entire RPM range.

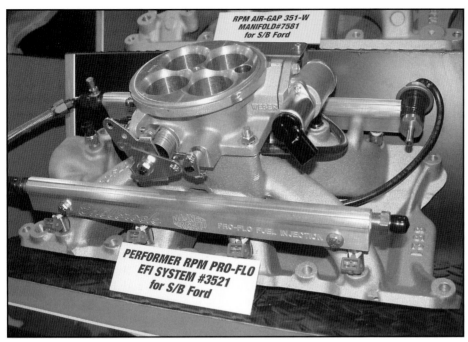

Aftermarket companies have stepped up to the plate and are offering fuel-injection systems for just about any application. This Edelbrock small-block Ford intake comes with small Weber injectors.

Fuel-Injection

If you're tired of tuning your carburetor, you can step up to a fuel-injection system. Compared to carburetors, fuel-injection systems are completely tunable, and the torque curve is usually more level and kicks in earlier in the RPM range. There are throttle-body injection (TBI) systems and direct-point fuel-injection (DPFI) systems. Throttle-body injection has a single point of injection (one area, on top of the intake manifold), where port injection has multiple ports, such as an injector for each cylinder. DPFI has many other commonly known names, such as direct-port fuel injection, direct fuel injection, multi-port fuel injection, port fuel injection, and more. These systems are available from factory donor vehicles and aftermarket companies.

Fuel-injection systems are built from two types of components: electronics and hardware. Electronic components include the computer, wire harness, and sensors. The hardware components are the manifold, throttle body, injectors, fuel rails, fuel pressure regulator, and fuel pump.

Fuel-injection systems come in many different configurations and manifold designs. Direct-port fuel-injection (DPFI) systems are superior to throttle-body injection (TBI) systems and are the only systems we will be considering for Restomod use. TBI systems were used early on in Ford's quest for fuel-injection performance. TBI systems are not generally thought of as much of a performance upgrade over a good carburetor set-up, so they are not common today.

Don't get the term "throttle body" confused with TBI injection. A throttle body of some kind is also used on all DPFI systems. The difference is that in a TBI system, the throttle body actually contains two fuel injectors. Since the air and fuel all flow into the manifold at a single point, a TBI system still utilizes the intake manifold to try and distribute the air-fuel mixture evenly to all the cylinders.

All manifolds and throttle bodies in DPFI systems deliver air only. In almost every configuration, fuel is injected at the base of the intake manifold almost directly into the cylinder head. Therefore, there must be an injector for every cylinder. There are two distinct styles of intake manifold designs: plenum-style manifolds and individual-runner manifolds. Plenum-style manifolds have central throttle body that feeds into a central common plenum. The plenum branches off into individual runners that flow to each intake port in the heads. Individual-runner manifolds do not share any common area, and they have individual throttle bodies and injectors for each runner.

Examples of plenum-style systems are 1986-1995 5.0-liter intake manifolds and converted single-plane or open-plenum carburetor manifolds. Examples

This Trick Flow intake manifold has eight runners fed by a single open chamber in the top section. This type of set-up can be referred to as a common-plenum system.

of individual-runner systems are converted stack or ram injector intakes like the ones available from Hilborn, or Weber-style manifolds with throttle body replacements made to replace the Weber carbs.

One of the fun things about fuel-injection conversions is the fact that almost any manifold and throttle body combo that will deliver air can be made to work as a fuel-injection intake. With some creative thinking, some builders have merged vintage intake styles with updated electronic fuel injection. An original intake manifold can be modified to accept fuel injectors, and even vintage-looking carburetors can be altered to serve as throttle bodies, making for a nice blend of performance and classic looks.

Aftermarket companies have been producing fuel-injection conversion kits since the mid-1990s. These early kits only replaced the 4-barrel carburetor with a throttle body injection unit. In the late 1990s, a few companies started offering DPFI kits for Chevy applications. If you wanted a DPFI for your Ford, you had to buy a DPFI system without the intake manifold and have the injector bungs welded to your aluminum intake manifold. In 2004, Edelbrock and ACCEL introduced standalone DPFI systems with pre-fabricated small-block Ford intake manifolds that you can tune with a laptop computer. These systems come with almost everything you need including a throttle body, fuel injectors, intake manifold, fuel rails, regulator, wiring harness, ECM, tuning software, and more. Some systems come more complete and support different horsepower levels than others. ACCEL, Edelbrock, and other manufacturers have seen the demand for DPFI systems for Fords increase, so development of more parts and Ford applications are on the way.

For more on custom and aftermarket fuel injection systems, check out the CarTech title *Building and Tuning High-Performance Electronic Fuel Injection* by Ben Strader.

Fuel Feed Systems

Before it ends up in the engine, the fuel has to get to the carburetor or fuel-injection system from the fuel tank. The fuel feed system consists of the fuel, tank, pickup, filter, pump, and line. If you don't upgrade your fuel-feed system when you upgrade your engine and its induction system, you won't be able to optimize the performance. In some cases, you can damage the engine by starving it and running lean.

Fuel Tanks

In the past, fuel tanks were not designed very well. Fuel tanks in cars built after the mid-1980s were designed with baffles around the fuel pump and pickup. Flaws in older designs first became evident to drag racers. During straight-line acceleration, the fuel would rush to the rear of the fuel tank, leaving the fuel pickup uncovered. Without fuel covering the pickup, the pump could not suck fuel from the tank. The fuel in the system would feed the carb until the line ran dry, which could happen in a matter of seconds. Once the car stumbled and slowed down from running out of fuel, the fuel would slosh toward the front of the tank, where the pickup could suck fuel again instead of fumes.

Restomods have the same problem, but not necessarily from straight-line acceleration. The pickup gets uncovered when you make hard lefts and rights. Drag racers found resolution by putting a sump in the rear of the tank, since that's where the fuel ends up during straight-line acceleration. Although this move isn't common for Restomod builders, they can gain some resolution by installing a sump in the rear, as long as it's baffled. A non-baffled lower sump doesn't keep the fuel from sloshing during cornering. A few companies offer fuel tanks for older cars with built-in baffles to keep the fuel trapped around the fuel-pump pickup. Aeromotive offers a tank with a baffled rear sump that is a direct replacement for many popular Fords. Rock Valley Antique Auto Parts offers stainless-steel replacement fuel tanks with internal baffling (without lower rear sump). They also have options for installing in-tank fuel-injection pumps, and offer tanks for selected Ford cars from 1928 to 1957.

If you're building a Restomod or racer and don't have the constraints of using a stock fuel tank, you can step up to a fuel cell. They come in different forms. Unlike stock fuel tanks, fuel cells can be purchased with internal baffling and foam to keep the fuel from sloshing around and uncovering the pickup. Racing fuel cells are safer than a standard metal fuel tank that came from the factory in your car because they are more pliable and resilient in a crash. The less-expensive fuel cells are typically a polyethylene outer shell with aviation

Each runner on this Roush-built engine's intake manifold operates individually. They don't share a plenum or any airflow.

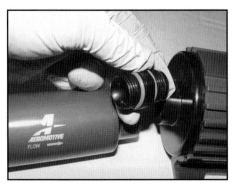

This Aeromotive 11101 fuel pump has a large aluminum body and a flat mounting flange. It requires O-ring-sealed -10AN fittings, not pipe-thread fittings. Do not use any type of sealant on the threads. To make things easy, an Aeromotive fuel filter can be threaded right into the fuel pump using the fitting shown.

Not all fittings are created equal. As you can see, the fitting on the left has a huge step on its inlet. The XRP fitting on the right is flowed much better and has a gradual inlet. With fuel- and oil-system plumbing, restrictions like the one on the left can add up fast and really hurt your flow.

Your Restomod can hold its fuel in a small, stock fuel tank, or for more mileage you can install a larger aftermarket fuel tank or fuel cell. Rock Valley makes stainless fuel tanks for Restomods. The fuel cell in this Year One-built Mustang is from Fuel Safe.

This Aeromotive fuel pressure regulator, part number 13204, is used with carbureted applications. This bypass-style regulator requires an -8AN return line, and is adjustable from 3 to 14 psi. It requires AN fittings with O-rings, not pipe-thread fittings. Don't use any thread sealer. Using 90-degree fittings to feed the carburetor can be a little restrictive, so 45-degree bends should be used for better flow.

foam inside to assist in baffling. The safer and more expensive fuel cells have a metal outer shell with an inner bladder filled with internal fuel strainers and foam baffles. The inner bladder is the wearing part. If you are purchasing a fuel cell for a long-term project car, make sure to check the company's fuel cell warranty. If the warranty is for 5 years or less, and your car isn't running for 2 years, you will be limiting the lifespan of the bladder. You may want to purchase your fuel cell toward the end of your project. Fuel Safe makes custom fuel cells and some specific bolt-in units for early Mustangs. The bolt-in Mustang cells come in 16- and 22-gallon versions.

Fuel Pumps

There are performance mechanical and electric fuel pumps available for all power ranges. Fuel pumps are rated in gallons per hour (gph) and how many psi they maintain. For a carbureted engine, you need a fuel pressure of 6.5 to 7.5 psi, depending on your horsepower level. Any more than that, and the fuel will push past the needle, seat in the carburetor, and cause a rich running condition or flooding, depending on the severity. If you install a pump that builds more psi, you'll need a fuel pressure reg-

ulator in between the fuel pump and carburetor. Mechanical fuel pumps are all pretty similar and basic, since they have a specific place they mount on the block. They're available up to 130 gph and 15 psi for high-revving engines.

Most builders prefer to have their higher-output engines fed by electric fuel pumps, which take away much less power from the engine than a mechanical pump, and also transfer less heat into the fuel. For standard applications, electric fuel pumps mount in two places: either in the fuel tank or outside it. In-tank pumps are mounted inside the fuel tank and are immersed in the fuel. Ninety-nine percent of externally mounted electric fuel pumps are "pushers," which means they push fuel better than they suck it from the tank. Pushers need to be mounted as close to the tank and its fuel pump pickup as possible; most manufacturers suggest mounting it within 12 inches from the tank. If you mount a pusher too far from the tank, it will not be able to supply the engine with enough fuel and your car will be plagued with driveability problems.

Regulators

Fuel pressure regulators do as their name suggests. Performance fuel pumps push more pressure than the carburetor or fuel injection can handle. This is necessary to keep fuel flowing to the engine under load when it demands more. Non-adjustable fuel-pressure regulators regulate the pressure to the predetermined amount, while you can adjust the pressure according to engine's demand with an adjustable regulator. Each regulator is designed for a specific job. High-performance regulators are designed to operate at full potential with a specific fuel pump, so if you are running an Aeromotive fuel pump, you should get the properly matched regulator. Some are also designed specifically for turbocharged and supercharged boost demands. These regulators use a vacuum boost port for increasing fuel pressure during boost conditions.

Follow the manufacturer's suggestions for mounting your fuel-pressure regulator. The regulator is typically mounted within 12 inches of the carbu-

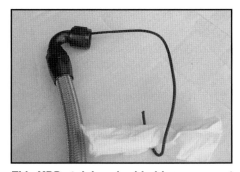

This XRP stainless braided hose was cut with a high-speed cut-off wheel. Unfortunately, these wheels create a lot of rubber and particle dust in the hose. It needs to be cleaned out before you install it on your car.

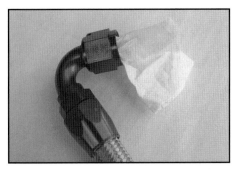

To clean the hose, I used a section of 18-gauge electrical wire and a piece of quality paper towel. With the wire still hooked to the small piece of paper towel, slowly pull the 18-gauge wire through the section of hose.

When the paper towel comes out, you may be surprised at how much debris is in the hose. Wipe the wire off, get another piece of towel, and repeat. Compressed air doesn't remove this junk. This debris would not be great in your bearings or carburetor, so take a little time to clean your hoses.

retor or fuel-injection system. Some racetracks won't let you race if your fuel pressure regulator is mounted on the firewall, since it would be in the path of the flywheel and clutch if either were to fail and scatter. It's also a good idea to mount the regulator in a place that is not too close to a heat source, unless it's shielded. On carbureted cars, you could mount it on the engine close to the carburetor. However, it will be close to a heat source, and if you need to work on the carb or adjust the valves it may get in the way. A less obstructive place to mount the regulator is on the inner fenderwell.

Some regulators work without a return line to the fuel tank, which is called a static or dead-head set-up. Dead-head systems require the fuel pump to cavitate, since the pump has to pressurize the feed line up to the regula-

tor. The feed line is kept at a higher pressure than what the regulator allows, so the pump cavitates. Some dead-head regulators make loud knocking noises, caused by the piston or ball cavitating while the pump keeps higher pressure against it. This cavitation can also cause the engine to run lean because the fuel is sitting in the line, rather than constantly flowing through it like it would on a system with a return line to the tank.

The other type of regulators operate in return-style systems. Regulators for carbureted systems with a fuel return line have one feed line plumbed from the fuel tank and a separate line that returns extra fuel to the tank, once a predetermined pressure has been reached. Since this system is able to return extra fuel to the tank, there's no need for the pump to cavitate. Fuel-pressure regulators on fuel-injection systems work the same way, returning

the excess fuel to the tank. The fuel return system allows the fuel pump to constantly flow at its full potential, while the regulator keeps only the necessary fuel where your engine needs it.

Fuel Line

High-performance engines demand more fuel. You can upgrade all the components of your fuel system, but you will be limiting the system's potential if you don't upgrade the fuel lines all the way from the engine to the tank. For instance, a '65 Mustang equipped with a 289 had a 5/16-inch fuel line that ran from the tank to the fuel pump. This fuel line will not support the volume of fuel a pumped-up 347 will require. A 3/8-inch fuel line running from front to rear is great for big- and small-blocks up to the 400-hp range, but not much more. Once you move into the 400+ horsepower area, you need to upgrade to a larger fuel line. Aeromotive suggests running a -10AN (5/8-inch) feed line and an -8-AN (1/2-inch) return line with a 500-hp engine built for street and road-course racing. A 5/8-inch fuel line might seem like a lot, but if you spend the money on the pump and regulator, you should listen to what the company suggests because it knows the products' capabilities. High-performance engines are demanding at high RPM, and the fuel line sizes need to be stepped up. It's very annoying to spin the motor up and have it cut out because the fuel pump just can't get the volume to the engine.

When bending aluminum tubing, it's more work to use a spring-type tubing bender, but they work great and they're not too expensive. The bender was fairly easy to slide over this 5/8-inch Moroso fuel line.

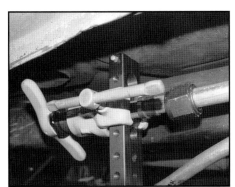

This Rigid flaring tool is used to put a 37-degree flare on the aluminum tubing. Make sure to slide the tube nut and sleeve over the tube before flaring. This tool put a perfect flare on the tubing every time.

It's a good idea to install a secondary fuel filter before the carburetor. The Mr. Gasket billet fuel filter with -10AN fittings is a perfect choice for the ⅝-inch fuel line. XRP tube nuts and sleeves are shown installed in the spliced area.

To cut down on heat getting to my fuel line, I covered it with Thermotec Thermo-Sleeve. Think carefully about your fuel system before starting. If it's the lowest point of the car, re-route it somewhere else and it will be protected from speed bumps. If it's near exhaust heat, protect it or re-route it.

The other fuel lines need to be upgraded, too. Sucking fuel out of the tank through a stock ⅜-inch fuel pump pickup will defeat the purpose of upgrading the size of the fuel feed line. Make sure your fuel hoses and fuel fittings aren't too restrictive. Running a ⅝-inch feed line into a -6-AN (⅜-inch) fuel filter creates a bottleneck and defeats the purpose of running a large feed line. Be careful when using fuel fittings. Bent fittings come in two different types. There is a forged style and a less restrictive tube style. Every 90-degree forged fitting decreases the flow. Some companies offer fittings that are "flowed" better than others for less restriction. A few restrictive fittings will hurt the engine's performance potential.

When running feed and return lines, I have found the Moroso aluminum fuel line is easiest to use. It can be easily bent by using a hand-operated spring-type tubing bender. Be aware that you can kink it if you bend it too far. Before installing the aluminum hard line, take a few things into consideration. Don't run fuel line (or any line that carries important or flammable liquid) in the transmission tunnel, because if you ever break a universal joint or a driveshaft, the flying parts can possibly damage the lines within reach. The lines should not be the lowest hanging part on the underside of your car, where they could be ripped or damaged if you were to drive off the road course or pull off the highway onto a soft or uneven shoulder. Every 90-degree bend is another restriction in the system. If a 90-degree bend is necessary, try to make it a sweeping bend rather than a tight bend. With the aluminum hard line, you can use tube nuts so that the fittings connect it to accessories. Otherwise, you'll need to run a short section of hose between the hard line and the accessory.

Fuel Filters

On carbureted systems, at least one filter should be mounted between the tank and the pump. Some pumps have such tight tolerance that a small piece of debris will cause the pump to jam. On fuel-injection systems, filtering is even more important. The injectors are much more susceptible to getting clogged than a fuel pump, because the injector clear-

ances are so precise. A clogged injector has the potential to burn a hole in your piston. That's why it is suggested to run a filter between the tank and the pump, and another between the pump and the fuel rails, just for an extra point of filtering protection.

Turbocharging

Turbocharged street cars have become more common in the last few years. With the introduction of computer-controlled fuel-injection systems and new turbo technology, some of the turbo woes of the past have diminished. One of the problems that still exists is that the boost can kick in suddenly and isn't necessarily proportional to RPM, which makes it harder to modulate on a road racing set-up.

Running an intercooler is beneficial on a system running above 6 to 7 lbs of boost. An intercooler will help keep your intake temperatures down, which can keep your engine from detonating. Intercoolers come in two types: air-to-air and air-to-liquid/water. If you have a way to feed a steady supply of cooled water to the intercooler, the air-to-liquid units are more efficient. They just require more plumbing and weigh more, due to the liquid and extra equipment necessary to cool it.

Supercharging

There are a few types of superchargers available. The two most common superchargers are the Roots type and the centrifugal. The most popular type in

All electric pump equipped fuel systems require a fuel filter installed before the pump. Fuel-injection systems should have an additional filter between the pump and the fuel injection. This Aeromotive fuel filter is 5 inches long and 2 inches in diameter, and it has a cleanable stainless-steel 100-micron filter media. O-ring style -10AN fittings are required to plumb it into the fuel system.

This is a Paxton centrifugal supercharger and intercooler kit for a 4.6-liter DOHC Cobra engine. As long as you're swapping in an engine like this, you might as well go for a blower too, right?

Superchargers have found their way under the hoods of a lot of cars. Smaller roots-type and centrifugal superchargers produce gobs of power without showing people and authorities what is nestled between the fenderwells. Vortech offers quiet centrifugal superchargers to keep the power up and the noise down.

the 1980s was the Roots-type supercharger. It was really cool to have a big 6-71 or 8-71 Roots blower sticking out of your hood with the carbs and air cleaner sitting as high as the roofline of your car. These big Roots blowers are not fuel-efficient. They also generate lots of heat, obstruct the driver's vision, and make a lot of noise. Every once in a while, auto manufacturers play around with blowers and offer them to the public on special-option vehicles. In 1989, Ford started introducing smaller Roots-type blowers on production vehicles like the Thunderbird Supercoupe, SVT Lightning, and SVT Cobra. These Roots-type blowers are starting to be more common on production cars and trucks, but they are smaller and quieter than the 6-71.

Hot rodders in the 1990s changed their building style to make it a little more subtle. They were building more hot rods with all the performance parts under uncut hoods. Car guys still want big power, but they don't want their source of power to be obvious to everyone, including local authorities. For this reason and others, people started moving to centrifugal superchargers.

Centrifugal superchargers had been around for at least 70 years in one form or another, but a drive design change in the early 1990s made them more bearable on the ears. By the late 1990s, centrifugal supercharger technology had vastly improved. The newer centrifugal units are built better. They are more suited for fuel-injection systems, available for more applications, and some even include a warranty.

The small-block Ford is one of the most popular centrifugal supercharger applications. The most popular centrifugal supercharger companies are Paxton, Vortech Engineering, Accessible Technologies Inc (ATI), and Paxton Automotive.

For more on supercharging, check out the CarTech title *Street Supercharging* by Pat Ganahl.

CHAPTER 6

DRIVETRAIN

For better fuel economy and all-around performance driving, most Restomod guys swap in late-model transmissions with extra gears or overdrives. This section will cover the most popular manual and automatic transmission swapping info, where to get the parts, and what is offered by each manufacturer. Selecting a transmission to run in your car is determined by a few factors, including but not limited to: your everyday driving style, frequency, and distance; the condition of your clutch knee; whether or not you want to cut a hole in your floorpan; whether you drag race, road race, or both; and the size of your wallet. If you decide on a stick shift, do you want the smoother shift of an internal-rail shifted Tremec TKO or T-56? Would you rather have more gear ratio selections like a Richmond 6-speed? If you pick an automatic overdrive, do you want it to be manually controlled like the Ford AOD, or do you want to fork out the extra dough for the computer controller so you can use a 4R70W transmission? New transmissions might come out that will work even better for you. Maybe Ford will come out with newer and stronger transmissions, like a 7-speed manual, or maybe a 6-speed automatic.

Manual Transmissions

This section is devoted to technical information about a couple of companies offering Tremec TKOs and T-56 variants, Richmond 6-speed transmissions,

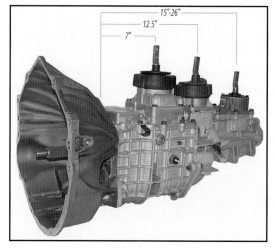

In 2004, Tremec came out with the TKO-500 and TKO-600 5-speeds to replace the earlier TKO models. The updated transmissions handle more horsepower and have more gear options. The image shows three shifter locations at 7, 12.5, and 15 to 26 inches from the mounting face of the transmission. These shifter locations are offered exclusively by Keisler Automotive Engineering. (Photo courtesy Keisler Automotive Engineering)

and conversion kits. There are a lot of companies offering conversion parts and some incomplete kits, so space limits the company coverage to a select few.

If you want to drop a bunch of extra money for transmissions that will hold the loads a standard production transmission won't, you can check offerings from G-Force Transmissions, Tex Racing, or Quaife. For instance, the standard production Borg Warner T-5 is rated to a capacity of 300 ft-lbs, while the reworked G-Force T-5 is rated at 500. Depending on the model of the production T-56, it can be rated as high as 550-ft-lbs, and the reworked G-Force T-56 handles around 800. Tex Racing Enterprises offers racing 4-speed transmissions with a Chevrolet mounting pattern (an adapter bellhousing is required) for Extreme Restomods built mostly for track racing. Quaife makes outrageous racing drivetrain parts for

racing cars, with prices to match the level of performance and quality. The old adage "You get what you pay for." applies to these companies. These transmissions may be a cut above an average Restomod unit, but if you're making that kind of power, you'll end up needing one sooner or later.

If you want 5 gears, don't have excessive amounts of power, and don't want to modify the transmission tunnel, get yourself a Borg Warner T-5. You should be aware that the production T-5s come in different flavors and ratings from 230 to 330 ft-lbs of torque. When swapping a T-5 into a small-block Ford Restomod, for best results, you should get a T-5 from a V-8-powered 1990 to 1993 Mustang.

For those of you putting a late-model 5.0-liter engine in an early car equipped with mechanical Z-bar clutch linkage, you will run into problems.

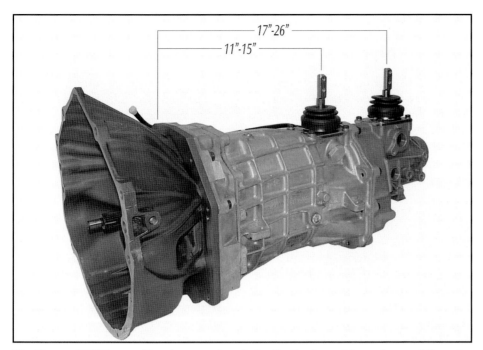

The Tremec T-56 6-speed has been a wise choice for Restomodders who want the extra overdrive gear on the freeway. The picture shows two shifter positions at 11 to 15 and 17 to 26 inches. These are exclusive to Keisler Automotive Engineering. (Photo courtesy Keisler Automotive Engineering)

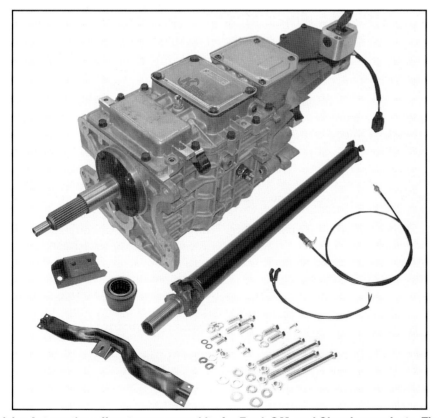

Keisler Automotive offers tranny-swap kits for Ford, GM, and Chrysler products. Their kits include all the necessary hardware, crossmember, driveshaft, transmission, and more. They have done all the research to make sure the angles are correct, and if transmission tunnel modifications are necessary, they also have computer-designed add-on sheetmetal covers. (Photo courtesy Keisler Automotive Engineering)

The later model blocks don't have the boss on the side of the block for the Z-bar linkage stud. You can make your own, or purchase an adapter bracket from Kaufmann Products and Total Performance.

Tremec TKO 5-speed

Swapping in any of the TKO 5-speeds into an early shock-tower car is tricky. There is a lot of different information available on what cars the TKO fits in, with and without modifying the transmission tunnel. The TKO has two large high-mounted inspection covers and the shifter. These covers are tall enough that they can hit the underside of the transmission tunnel when you install the transmission and engine with the correct pinion angle (as seen in the pinion-angle diagram in Chapter 3). For Falcons and 1964-1/2 to 1970 Mustangs, the transmission tunnel needs to be raised about 1 inch to clear the top of the TKO. There are companies selling transmission crossmembers that allow you to install the TKO in these early Mustangs without modifying the transmission tunnel. They say, "It only gives you an extra 3 degrees down on the transmission, but that's not a problem." There is a problem with this logic. The transmission is originally 3 degrees down, so when you add 3 more degrees, it adds up to a total of 6 degrees down. This angle can spell problems for your U-joints. Add a bunch of extra stress from increased horsepower and torque, and it will spell trouble. You may get lucky and never have a failure, but your chances are greatly increased. Shops that have a serious understanding of pinion and driveshaft angles would not cut corners. These shops would install the transmission at the correct angle and modify your transmission tunnel if necessary. If you want to purchase one of these "pinion-angle-challenged" crossmembers and install shims between the crossmember and trans mount to raise it to get the correct angle, you would at least save some time fabricating the entire unit. Then you just need to modify the trans tunnel since you raised the transmission to the proper height. For the various other Restomod candidates

Campbell Auto Restoration Services offers this cool converter box. The pulse signal from the transmission goes into the box, which converts the signal to an electrical motor that accepts and drives the standard GM mechanical speedo cable. It is fully programmable for different gear ratios and tire diameters.

out there, the best way to see what will fit is to start measuring.

Keisler Automotive Engineering

The people over at Keisler Automotive Engineering do all the homework for you. They offer kits for Ford Restomods, as well as Chevrolet and Mopar muscle cars. The TKO 500 and 600 offered by Keisler Automotive Engineering have a few different shifter locations (not including the different locations available straight from Tremec), so depending on your application, you may be able to use the stock shifter location and keep your factory console. Keisler takes pride in making its kits correct and complete. When I say "correct," I mean that the kits are designed to allow for the correct pinion angles. To achieve the correct angle, it may be necessary to modify the transmission tunnel. If it is, Keisler includes the templates for cutting and the necessary sheetmetal cover to finish the job like a professional. The bolt-in kit includes all the parts necessary to bolt everything in, including the driveshaft for your specific application, wiring, and the crossmember. Keisler is constantly adding new kits, so if you go to the website and don't see your application, make a call and check, just to be sure.

Tremec T-56

The most popular 6-speed manual transmission (production or aftermarket) from the late 1990s to present is the Tremec T-56 (formerly BorgWarner T-56). Tremec saw a market for offering T-56s for Fords and an aftermarket T-56 (Tremec part # 1386-000-012) to fit small-block Fords. The resulting transmissions have been a huge help for Restomodders looking for a sixth gear. The additional overdrive in the T-56 allows for better fuel economy and higher top speeds. Tremec's aftermarket T-56 fits the 1965 to 1993 289, 302 (and 5.0), and 351C/W with a 6-bolt transmission mounting face. The T-56 does not fit the Modified small-blocks or any of the big-blocks. If you want a T-56 to fit a Modular engine, that's easy, since Ford started offering it in the production 2003 and 2004 Cobra.

The Tremec T-56 is rated at 450 ft-lbs of torque. It requires a cable-operated clutch set-up and it is longer than any other manual transmission in overall length, so a shorter driveshaft will be needed. The transmission mount is also further back than any other Ford transmission mount, so you'll need to modify the crossmember or get a new one. It shares the 10-spline Ford-style input shaft with the T5. The output shaft is a 31-spline unit, so unless you are upgrading from a T5, you will need a new transmission yoke.

The following is a list of 4-speeds for comparison against the T-56:

1966 4-speed Ford Syncromesh Borg-Warner T-10
Gear Ratios: First 2.36:1, Second 1.62:1, Third 1.20:1, and Fourth 1.00:1

1964-1973 4-speed Ford Top Loader – close ratio
Gear Ratios: First 2.32:1, Second 1.69:1, Third 1.29:1, and Fourth 1.00:1

1964-1973 4-speed Ford Top Loader – wide ratio
Gear Ratios: First 2.78:1, Second 1.93:1, Third 1.36:1, and Fourth 1.00:1

Tremec Aftermarket T-56 for Fords
Gear Ratios: First 2.97:1, Second 2.07:1, Third 1.43:1, Fourth 1.00:1, Fifth 0.80:1, Sixth 0.62:1, Reverse 3.28:1
Design Torque Rating: 450 ft-lbs

Keisler Automotive Engineering

The T-56 offered by Keisler Automotive Engineering has a few different shifter locations, so depending on your application, you may be able to use the stock shifter location and your factory console. Keisler manufactures a unique shifter mounting location for the T-56, which allows it to be used with street rods, trucks, and cars with bench seats. This is a typical shortcoming of the T-56, but Keisler's custom T-56 eliminates this problem completely. Keisler offers bolt-in kits that include all the parts necessary to bolt everything in, including the driveshaft for your specific application, wiring, and the crossmember. Even if the guys at Keisler don't have a kit for your specific application, they may be able piece together a kit from the parts they already have in stock.

D&D Performance

The D&D Performance T-56 starts life as a Viper model transmission, rated at 550 ft-lbs of torque. To get that increased strength, the Viper T-56 has a larger input and output shaft than the Tremec aftermarket unit. While D&D has the transmission taken apart for blueprinting, it also gets upgraded shift forks and rings as well as some other modifications performed by D&D. D&D installs a custom mid-plate (front cover for end-loading), an output shaft modified to accept a mechanical gear-driven speedometer, and tailshaft housing modified to house the speedometer gear assembly. These upgraded units fit the same small-block applications as the Tremec aftermarket unit, and D&D offers them for bolting behind the Modular engines as well. The large 30-spline Viper output shaft requires a Viper driveshaft yoke.

D&D Viper conversion T-56
Gear Ratios: First 2.66:1, Second 1.78:1, Third 1.30:1, Fourth 1.00:1, Fifth 0.74:1, Sixth 0.50:1, Reverse 3.28:1
Design Torque Rating: 550 ft-lbs

T-56 Speedometer
You'll need a speedometer to know how fast you're going. There are two

The Richmond overdrive 6-speed transmission is available with plenty of different gear ratios to meet your needs. They used NASCAR-proven technology from their Super T-10 racing transmissions to aid in its initial design. This is a cutaway display model that shows the gears, syncros, and other internal parts. The shifter location and overall length are close to the dimensions of some early Muncie 4-speeds, but the transmission mount is 4 inches farther rearward than the mount on those same Muncies.

types of speedometers: electronic and mechanical. Some modified T-56s are offered with a mechanical speedometer. Most factory (GM and Viper) T-56 transmissions are equipped with an electronic speedometer that reads a signal from the reluctor ring on the output shaft in the tail-shaft housing. To pick up this signal, you have to get a factory vehicle speed sensor (VSS) that attaches to the transmission. There are aftermarket speedometers that read this signal and convert it to operate the indicator needle. If you want to keep the stock mechanical speedo or use an aftermarket mechanical unit, but don't have a mechanical speedo-cable receiver on the tail-shaft housing, you're in luck. There is a little black box on the market that converts the pulse signal to an electric drive motor that accepts the mechanical speedo cable. By moving some simple dip switches, you can program the output for different rear-end gear ratios and tire diameters.

If you'd rather have a mechanical speedo gear straight out of the transmission, you can pick up a modified tail-shaft housing from Jags That Run (JTR). They also offer services to put in a mechanical speedometer, relocate the VSS, and install a reluctor ring. Having both a mechanical speedometer and a VSS would be necessary if you have a mechanical speedometer and a computer-controlled fuel-injection system that requires a VSS signal to operate.

Richmond Performance Products

Richmond Performance Products offers ring-and-pinion gears and transmissions. The line includes 2-speeds, 4-speeds, 5-speeds (street and road-race versions), and 6-speeds. Since I can't remember the last time I saw someone swapping in a Richmond 5-speed, I'll focus on the 6-speed.

The Richmond 6-speed (aka ROD – Richmond OverDrive) is put together using NASCAR-proven technology. Its shifter has external arms and side levers. The transmission mount is located approximately 5 inches rearward of the standard top-loader 4-speed, so the cross-member will have to be modified. The centerline of the shifter location is closer to the position of 4-speed shifters than the Tremec aftermarket T-56. You'll also have to modify the transmission tunnel for the shifter location. The ROD overall length is within a 1/2-inch of the T-10 and top loader. It is not as large as the T-56 in overall case diameter, which makes it easier to swap without modifying the tunnel.

Richmond 6-speeds are available with two different drive ratios, along with multiple gear ratios.

1.682:1 Drive Ratio

First 4.41:1 thru 3.04:1, Second and Third 2.75:1 thru 1.57:1, Fourth 1.24:1 and 1.74, Fifth 1.00:1, Sixth .76:1 thru .91:1

1.148:1 Drive Ratio

First 3.01:1 thru 2.08:1, Second and Third 1.88:1 thru 1.07:1, Fourth .84:1 and 1.19:1, Fifth 1.00:1, Sixth .52:1 thru .62:1

Bellhousing Set-ups

When bolting on any stock or aftermarket bellhousing with a centering hole that locates the transmission front-bearing retainer, you need to check some critical measurements. If you just bolt one on your car and throw in a transmission, you run a high probability of destroying your pilot bearing, input shaft bearing, input shaft, and other internal parts. The symptoms can be extreme clutch chatter, engagement problems, and erratic clutch operation. Aftermarket companies typically have a maximum specified run-out of .010 inch. Check with the manufacturer of your bellhousing for exact measurements and instructions. There are two bellhousing alignments to check. First, check the run-out on the inside circumference of the pilot hole compared to concentricity of the crankshaft centerline. You do this by mounting a dial indicator on the end of a stand, with a magnetic base centered on the end of the crankshaft. Turn the crankshaft and check for a minimum of

PRESTON PETERSON'S 1967 MUSTANG

One look at Preston Peterson's 1967 Mustang, and you know this isn't your average Restomod. The prominent European-style flares help house the extra wide stance of the fabricated chassis and suspension. (Photo courtesy Preston Peterson)

The radiator and intercooler are mounted at an angle so air entering the grill will produce ultimate cooling. The hot air flowing through the radiator exits through the large vents in the custom hood. (Photo courtesy Preston Peterson)

When you look up the word "extreme" in the dictionary, you will find that it means (A) existing in a very high degree, (B) going to great or exaggerated lengths, or (C) exceeding the ordinary, usual, or expected. All three definitions fit when you try to describe Preston Peterson's 1967 Mustang. Usually you can put cars in the *extreme* Restomod or Pro-Touring category if a car is equipped with a fully fabricated tubular chassis. Preston has taken the term to an entirely new level.

From a distance, you see an extremely low Mustang with big flares attached to the fenders. These types of flares can be found on European racing cars, such as entries in the Deutsche Tourenwagen Meisterschaft or DTM racing series. The 1967 was wider than the previous 1966 body, but it wasn't wide enough for what Preston wanted to do with the car. He already had a full set of Shelby flares, but they were not extreme enough.

What you don't see from a distance is that under the flares and stock sheet metal is a full-tilt racecar. The body panels were cut off the original chassis. This car has been in more pieces than a 1/25-scale model car. The body sec-

tions were the roof, the quarter panels, the tail panel, doors, and the front sheet metal. The original unibody underbody was discarded. This was so he could start from scratch and fit the 18-inch CCW wheels. Yes, the car was built to fit the wheel package.

The frame design is mostly based on late-model Trans-Am series cars. The frame is underslung in the front and rear, and it doesn't kick up on either end for suspension. The rear axle has frame rails under and over the top. The design was analyzed with Grape, a Finite Element Analysis (FEA) shareware program he received from *RaceCar Engineering* magazine, using a torsional analysis spreadsheet. Preston picked tubing size, wall thickness, and design from his extensive chassis research of Trans-Am, NASCAR, drag race, and street-rod frame construction and SCCA rules. Once he finished construction of the frame, he started fitting body panels on the chassis so he could build the rest of the car to fit under the skin. Every part of the car was engineered to the gills. For example, the exhaust is routed up into the quarter panel where the Dynomax SuperTurbo mufflers are tucked away for

Even though the car has a full-tube chassis, Preston did a great job making the interior appear similar to a production car. The seats are Kirkey Road Race Deluxe items. The car has a stereo, as well as power locks and windows. (Photo courtesy Preston Peterson)

the ultimate ground clearance. Up front, he built a custom set of headers with 34-inch long 1.75-inch primaries and 3-inch collectors.

Preston wants to thank C&D Machine in Kirkland, California, for build-

From the rear, the vents for relieving air pressure under the hood are evident. The CCW 18x10.5 and 18x13-inch wheels are wrapped in Michelin Pilots and keep the Mustang going in the direction the steering wheel is pointing. (Photo courtesy Preston Peterson)

Without the Howe radiator in place, you get a good view of the 396-ci small-block. The Novi 2000 Race supercharger helped the engine produce 791 hp at 5,800 rpm with 13 psi of boost. (Photo courtesy Preston Peterson)

ing the 396-ci stroker using a Ford Motorsports A351 block that has been modified to hold four-bolt main caps and Scat 3.85-inch forged stroker crankshaft with Eagle H-beam rods spinning on Chevrolet rods journals. Slugs are forged Probe 0.040s with a 27-cc dish. The air-and-fuel mixture is pressurized to 13 psi by a Novi 2000 Race supercharger, and cooled by a ProCharger 3-core intercooler. The Carb Shop built the blow-through 750-cfm carburetor, which sits atop an Edelbrock Victor, Jr. and AFR 205 heads with a C&D Machine valve job. Preston installed a Probe stud girdle to keep the FlowTech Induction hydraulic roller 232/240-degree, 0.566/0.555-inch-lift camshaft

in check. Fuel is supplied by a Product Engineering Sportsman 310 pump and an Aeromotive bypass regulator. Fire is supplied by an MSD boost retard and Crane Hi-6 box. Other electric accessories include an FJO wideband oxygen sensor and MSD knock sensor. The pressurized package is kept cool by a Weiand water pump and a custom Howe Racing radiator with internal oil cooler, using a Lincoln Mark VIII fan to keep excessive amounts of air flowing. To keep the stroker fully lubricated while keeping the engine placed low in the chassis, he installed a Weaver dry-sump system with the tank in the trunk. Gears are selected by a Tremec 5-speed, while the McLeod 10.5-inch dual-disc Street Twin and 157-tooth aluminum flywheel keeps everything engaged and able to spin quickly. The complete package hammered the dyno with 791 hp at 5,800 rpm with 13 psi.

In extreme fashion, Preston made the upper and lower control arms from Coleman Racing stock car parts, which swing a custom set of Coleman spindles. Steering is accomplished by a KRC pump and a BRT rack and pinion. Combined with the 285/30-18 Michelin Pilots and CCW 18x10-inch wheels with 9 inches of backspacing, it only has a 0.5-inch scrub radius. A Speedway 1.25-inch 0.180 wall

tubular sway bar keeps sway under control. Neatly tucked in the rear of the chassis are a Coleman full-floater 9-inch rear end with 0.5-degree negative camber, 3.55:1 gears, Auburn limited-slip differential, and a differential cooler. The 3-link suspension is made from a Hoerr racing panhard bar and Coleman links. The front and rear corners are dampened by AFCO double adjustable coil-over shocks. Sticking to the ground in the rear is a pair of Michelin Pilot 335/30-18 tires coupled with CCW 18x13-inch wheels with 7 inches of backspace. Braking is handled by Sierra Grand National billet calipers and 13-inch Coleman rotors and hats in the front and PBR calipers on 13-inch rotors in the rear.

After building the entire chassis, Preston attached all the body panels to it. Then he built the flares from scratch and installed ducting around the radiator, positioned so air could flow through the radiator and exit through the top of the hood, instead of pressurizing the engine compartment. Once all the custom work was done, he had Jim Maesner cover the external surfaces with a medium blue. Then it was time for Preston to turn the interior of this racecar into something that looked and felt more like a street car, since he plans to put about 7,000 miles on the car annually. He installed Kirkey Road Race Deluxe seats, Simpson harnesses, a Grant steering wheel, and AutoMeter and VDO gauges. For creature comforts, he added a Kenwood stereo system and power locks/windows.

If it wasn't extreme enough, he has decided that he wants a twin turbo setup, upgraded to the latest Tremec TKO offering. He also wants to install a new gear set, make some more modifications to the front suspension, and install bigger brakes. If you were writing a car dictionary, you may find a picture of Preston's 1967 Mustang to help demonstrate what the word "extreme" means.

The transmission pilot hole must be within .010 inch of the concentricity of the crankshaft. You can measure the run-out with a dial indicator by turning the crankshaft. The dial indicator must be connected to an extended magnetic base centered on the end of the crankshaft. Without ensuring the correct run-out on the pilot hole and mounting face, you will severely shorten the life of your transmission.

The transmission mounting face is as important as the pilot-hole run-out. With an extension, place the dial indicator on the face with the magnetic base connected to the end of the crankshaft. Then check the side-to-side and top-to-bottom run-out. The dial indicator should spin around the outside of the pilot hole and not have more than .010 inch of run-out.

.010 inch. The second measurement to check is the mounting surface of the bellhousing. It should be within the same .010 inch from top to bottom and side to side. Mount the dial indicator to an extended arm that places it on the mounting face, and then turn the crankshaft. If you have anything over the .010-inch measurement on either location, then you will need to adjust the bellhousing with offset dowel pins or other methods suggested by the manufacturer.

McLeod Industries

McLeod Industries is one of the major companies in the clutch, flywheel, and bellhousing industry.

Clutches

McLeod Industries offers street and racing clutches in both single- and dual-disc set-ups. It also offers multi-disc clutches for serious racing applications. One of McLeod's most popular heavy-duty clutches for Restomods is the Street Twin clutch set-up. It's available with a steel or a lightweight aluminum flywheel. If you want a clutch that's bulletproof, you can get the oval-track, road-race, or dry-lakes clutches. The non-strapped single clutch set-up holds up to 500 ft-lbs of torque, and the dual-disc model

holds up to 900 ft-lbs of torque. If you are serious about your power, you can step up to the triple-disc set-up, which is rated at 1,500 ft-lbs. McLeod also offers these road-race clutches in a strapped version to limit the chatter. The strapped single- and dual-disk set-ups have the same torque capacity ratings as the non-strapped models, but McLeod doesn't offer a strapped triple disc set-up. The strapped clutches are only available with a lightweight aluminum flywheel.

Bellhousings and Adapters

McLeod makes heavy-duty bellhousings for just about any make and model. For those of you wishing to bolt a T-56 or other Ford, Chevy, or Chrysler manual transmission to your Ford engine, McLeod has come out with the ultimate in bellhousing. It's a Modular, heavy-duty, multi-pattern bellhousing that bolts to most Ford small-block and big-block engines from 1962 on up, including the straight-6, Modular V-8, and V-10 patterns. It also features starter pockets on both sides of the block. Since each transmission has a different length of input shaft, there are adapter rings to space out the transmission-mounting surface. The spacer rings are available in five different thicknesses, ranging from .25 to 1.9 inches.

Tilton Products

Tilton Engineering has a full line of performance clutches, flywheels, and other racing components. If you're racing your Restomod more than you are driving it on the street, you can upgrade to a Tilton Driveline Components OE-diameter flywheel for use with a 7.25-inch-diameter multiple clutch and pressure plate set-up. This set-up reduces reciprocating and overall weight, while allowing you to use a standard bellhousing.

If you are building an Extreme Restomod and want a few extra inches of ground clearance, Tilton Driveline Components has what you need. The Ultimate Low Ground Clearance Driveline Packages replace your standard bellhousing, clutch, pressure plate, throw-out bearing, and starter. The new package has an 8.64-inch-diameter flywheel (compared to the 13.25-inch small-block Ford unit), heavy-duty clutch, custom hydraulic release bearing, special starter, and low-profile custom bellhousing available in steel or magnesium. This kit gives an additional 2.25 inches of ground clearance, while reducing the reciprocating and overall weight.

Automatic Transmissions

There are a few good automatics on the market. I'll be paying special attention to overdrive transmissions in this section, since Restomodding is about driving hard while keeping an eye on street driveability. There are many companies with overdrive transmissions and swap kits. I prefer the products from Windsor Fox Performance Engineering and Baumann Engineering/Baumann Electronic Controls.

In general, when converting from a C4 to an AOD or AOD-E/4R70W, you'll need to install a new block plate designed for the overdrive transmission before installing the flex plate and converter. The C4 block plate will not allow you to mount the starter properly. The C4 dipstick tube won't work either, so make sure you have a new dipstick and tube for the overdrive transmission. Swapping the flexplate is also necessary; however, different engines require different flexplates with different weight. The transmission mount is in a different location, so a custom crossmember is necessary. The overdrive swaps are common, so many companies offer bolt-in crossmembers.

The overdrive transmissions are wider than C4 automatic transmissions, so exhaust pipe and header interference is a common problem. Overdrive transmissions are close to the same case size as the C6, so swapping from a C6 should not pose space constraint problems. If you have full-length headers in your C4-equipped car before the swap, there's a good chance they'll have to be modified. Not many header manufacturers build full-length headers with overdrive transmission size in mind. Ford Powertrain Applications makes headers for some applications with the wider overdrive transmissions.

The McLeod Road Race clutch is for serious high-horsepower applications. This one has the light-weight aluminum flywheel. It is available in double- and triple-disc set-ups. The triple-disc unit is rated up to 1,500 ft-lbs of torque.

AOD

The AOD transmission is a good way to get more drivability out of your Restomod. The overdrive gear allows you to run a lower RPM at freeway speeds for better fuel mileage. The AOD is a less-expensive overdrive upgrade than the AOD-E/4R70W, due to its manually operated TV (throttle valve) cable. The AOD-E/4R70W requires a more expensive computer controller for line pressure and downshifting. With the AOD, downshifting is controlled via a TV cable attached from the transmission to the throttle linkage. The AOD transmissions that work with a TV cable were built from 1986 to 1993. Earlier models had rod-style linkage and are not desirable, unless converted to use a TV cable, which is not easy.

With an AOD, TV cable adjustment is critical. If you don't have it connected and adjusted right, you can destroy your transmission in a matter of minutes. If your TV cable is out of adjustment, your transmission will not shift into gear, or the shift will be sluggish, instead of firm. There are a couple different types of TV cables: the block type and the lift-tab type. Typically, if you purchased an AOD transmission from a company that knows you're doing a swap, instructions will be included for adjusting the type of

cable installed on your transmission. Some Restomodders have found great success with the aftermarket TV cable assembly from Lokar Performance Products.

Some Lincoln AOD transmissions have a specific driveshaft yoke that is no longer in production, so if you pick up a Lincoln unit, make sure you get the output shaft yoke or entire driveshaft out of the same donor car.

AOD Gear Ratios:
First 2.40:1, Second 1.47:1, Third 1.00:1, Fourth .67:1
Horsepower capacity (stock): up to 350 hp
Horsepower capacity (modified): up to 500 hp*
Overall length: 30⅜ inches
Case front to transmission mount distance: 22⁵⁄₁₆ inches

AOD-E/4R70W

The 4R70W (also known as the AOD-EW) is basically an AOD-E with a wide ratio gear set. Both transmissions are electronically controlled. Running one in your non-computer-controlled Restomod will require you to use an electronic transmission controller, available from companies like Baumann Engineering and TCI Automotive. The controller allows you to use a laptop computer to program shift points, line pressure, and torque-converter clutch operation for the best drivability with

your engine set-up and the type of driving you want to do. The electronic controller is the expensive part of upgrading to one of these transmissions. These two transmissions are inherently stronger than the AOD, and worth the added expense if you have a high-output powerplant.

AOD-E Gear Ratios:
First 2.40:1, Second 1.47:1, Third 1.00:1, Fourth .67:1
Horsepower capacity (stock): up to 400 hp
Horsepower capacity (modified): up to 600 hp*
Overall length: 31³⁄₁₆ inches
Case front to transmission mount distance: 23⁵⁄₁₆ inches

4R70W Gear Ratios:
First 2.84:1, Second 1.55:1, Third 1.00:1, Fourth .70:1
Horsepower capacity (stock): up to 400 hp
Horsepower capacity (modified): up to 600 hp*
Overall length: 31³⁄₁₆ inches
Case front to transmission mount distance: 23⁵⁄₁₆ inches

E4OD

The E4OD is known as a large transmission made for heavy trucks. It can be hard to fit the E4OD into the smaller transmission tunnels found in cars, which means you'll probably have to modify

For serious Restomod applications, you can upgrade to a 7.25-inch racing clutch. These dual-disc set-ups are not for everyday street driving. The size of the clutch is reduced so the bellhousing can be smaller.

the tunnel to some degree. However, if you have a 385-series big-block and want to run an automatic overdrive transmission, this is currently your only choice. The E4OD isn't known as a brutally strong transmission in its original form, but the aftermarket has proven to increase its power capacity. Installing an E4OD in your car will be a chore since companies are not producing installation kits for these transmissions. Yet, the hard work will pay off for big-block owners.

Like the AOD-E and 4R70W transmissions, the E4OD is electronically controlled. Running one in your non-computer-controlled Restomod will require you to use an electronic transmission controller, available from companies like Baumann Engineering and TCI Automotive. The controller allows you to use a laptop computer to program shift points, line pressure, and torque converter clutch operation for the best drivability with your engine setup and the type of driving you want to do. The electronic controller is the expensive part of upgrading to one of these transmissions.

E4OD Gear Ratios:
First 2.72:1, Second 1.53:1, Third 1.00:1, Fourth .71:1
Horsepower capacity (stock): up to 400 hp
Horsepower capacity (modified): up to 600 hp*
Overall length: 37½ inches

Case front to transmission mount distance: 29⅜ inches

*NOTE: These horsepower capacities stated are specifications for transmissions modified by Baumann Engineering. The numbers are Bauman's highest-rated transmissions. Other manufacturers offer similar modified transmissions.

Transmission Coolers

All automatic transmissions need a transmission cooler of one form or another. Standard-duty car applications typically require a cooler at least 1.5x7x14 inches in size. If you are going to drive your Restomod like a madman or take it out on a road course on a regular basis, you should upgrade to a larger transmission cooler. The harder you drive your car, the more heat your transmission is going to produce. Each company has a little different way to check for the exact cooler size your car will need. If you contact Setrab (a company that specializes in racing coolers), they will ask you some specific details about your application and suggest a cooler that will best fit your needs.

For more information on cooler types and mounting them, you should check the "Power Steering Coolers" section in Chapter 2.

Rear Ends

Ford 8- and 9-inch rear ends consist of a welded stamped-steel housing. The 9-inch is much stronger than the 8-inch, so it'll be the focus here. The differential and gear set are held inside a cast center section (usually referred to as a "pumpkin") that bolts to the housing. Retaining plates on the ends of the axle housing hold the bearings, which keep the axles in their respective places.

Ford 9-Inch

The Ford 9-inch, besides being easy to service and work with because of its removable carrier, has more gear ratios available than any other rear end on the market. It's also one of the strongest differentials around. The 9-inch is also more common than the 8.8, and though

it is no longer produced by Ford, there are plenty in junkyards and complete center sections, gear sets, differentials, and even complete housings are available through the aftermarket. Companies like CA Chassisworks, Currie Enterprises, and Moser Engineering build complete, new, 9-inch housings that will bolt right into just about any performance car. They come in the correct width and with all the necessary mounting brackets already welded on. Currie and Moser offer housings completely assembled with third members and axles. The availability, plus the brute strength of the 9-inch, makes it the most popular choice for Restomods.

Ford 8.8-Inch

Ford's 8.8-inch rear end is a very popular rear end found in some light trucks and V-8 Mustangs. The 8.8 features an integral carrier, which means you can't remove just the pumpkin. This means that for gear changes, you'll either have to drop the entire rear end, or just do it with the rear end in the car. Many people praise the 8.8 for having the strength of the 9-inch in a lighter, more-efficient design.

Differentials

Having a limited-slip differential of some kind is almost a necessity for a high-performance Restomod. There are two basic types of differentials worth considering for your Restomod: limited-slip and locking. While they operate in different ways, these differentials essentially keep both axles locked together when the car is traveling in a straight line (to varying degrees). The locked axles improve traction.

Limited-Slips

Ford's Equa-Lok and Traction-Lok are examples of limited-slip differentials. They use a system of plate-style clutches to get the power smoothly to the wheels. Limited-slip differentials do a pretty good job of locking the wheels together when the car is going straight, but they also allow the outside wheel to turn faster around corners. Think of them as a more practical, streetable alter-

Automatic overdrive transmissions come in two types. The easiest overdrive to install is the AOD, because the kick-down function is manually operated by a cable. The AOD-E, 4R70W, E4OD, and 4R100 are electronically controlled, and require an expensive stand-alone computer to adapt them to non-computer-controlled vehicles.

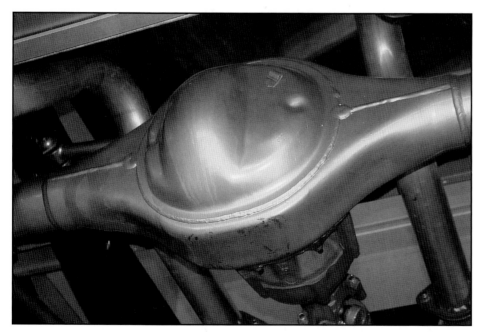

The most common rear axle assembly to bolt into a Restomod is the Ford 9-inch rear end. It's strong, has more gear ratios available than any other rear end, and the housings are being reproduced. Moser is one of the many who can build a complete rear end for any muscle car.

Lockers

If only the most traction available will do, you might want to step up to a locker. A locker gets its name from its ability to fully lock the wheels together when they are turning at the same speed. When a car with a locker goes around the corner, the lock has to unlock before the wheels can turn at different speeds. The transition between locked and unlocked can be a noisy little process, and may be a little unpredictable on the street or a road course. The DAPCO No-Spin, also known as the Detroit Locker, is the most notorious locker and it is available for Ford 8.8-inch and 9-inch rear ends.

Gear Ratios

The gear ratio you choose depends on a number of variables: how much torque your car's engine produces, when your engine produces the most torque, what kind of tranny gearing you have, and how tall your tires are, and more. In general, an overdrive tranny (automatic or manual) will take a lower rear-end gear (higher ratio), from 4.10:1 to 3.70:1. This will give your car good launches, good low-end pickup, and still keep it at reasonable RPM for highway speeds.

If you're using a 4-speed or non-OD automatic transmission with a 1:1 final drive ratio and plan on a lot of highway use, you'll probably want a slightly higher gear (3.50:1 to 3.10:1) to keep the RPM reasonable on the road. A healthy engine with good low-end torque will still let you get off the line okay if you choose this route. On the other hand, if you plan to use the car more on the track or for local cruising, a lower gear will do the job.

Changing or installing gears in a differential is best left to a professional, unless you have the right tools and a decent understanding of the settings necessary to get the job done. The pinion depth needs to be shimmed, bearings on either end of the carrier need to be set with the correct preload, and the proper backlash must be set on the ring and pinion. Limited-slip carriers also need to have their clutches checked and serviced if necessary.

native to a full-on locker. Most limited-slips are a perfect fit for Restomods since they need to accelerate in a straight line and around corners. New, limited slips are available for Ford rear ends from a number of aftermarket suppliers such as Richmond Gear and Auburn, which uses cone-shaped clutches. If you're on a budget, you can also find a Ford limited-slip for your application and rebuild it.

BODY AND ELECTRICAL

Reproduction parts are not all created equal. This '65 Mustang front clip is built from reproduction parts from Scott Drake Enterprises. These are produced from original Ford tooling. Mustangs Plus is just one of many dealers that sell Scott Drake Enterprises parts.

Restomodding is about doing something different, but making body modifications is not required. Yet, sometimes the stock Ford body just won't work with what you want to do with your car. For these situations, some body changes may be in order.

Stock Body

There are a few benefits to using stock body panels. If you have stock front fenders and damage one in an accident, you can simply locate another stock fender, bolt it into place, and add some paint. That is much easier than replacing a front fender customized with fender flare or bodywork. The job becomes a lot bigger when you have to replace a modified part.

Steel body parts are stronger when they are bolted together as the factory intended. For instance, all the shock-tower-equipped cars have bolts across the top edge of the sides of the engine compartment where the fenders attach to the inner fenderwells. I've seen quite a few cars on the road without all these bolts in place. The bolts are very important to the structural integrity of the front sheetmetal. Without them, the strut towers and the inner fenderwells will

start to fatigue. The fenderwells will then eventually crack and cause the shock towers to sag toward each other. The factory export brace helps to support the shock towers, but those fender-to-fenderwell bolts are still very important.

Custom Bodywork

Some Restomod applications require modifying body parts to make your parts fit. Yet, not all barriers can be broken by bolt-on parts. Sometimes you need to modify or fabricate parts to achieve a certain look or goal.

If you want to change your old stock door handles, you could use an old custom trick and shave (remove) the door handles. Then you can use electric solenoids with hidden pushbutton switches to actuate the latches. With new technology, you could even do away with the hidden pushbuttons and use an electronic remote opener on your key chain. Another custom door handle trick is to swap door handles from a newer model car or truck.

Some cars and trucks have fenderwell openings that hang too low or are too small for the size of tire you would like to run. Without flaring the fender openings, you can modify them to look and function better for your application. For instance, if you lower your stance and the fender lip hangs too low for your liking, you can cut the outer lip off and reattach it a couple of inches higher to keep the factory look. This can help you get your tire-to-fender clearance just right.

Modern cars have flush-mounted glass, and older cars use chrome trim to dress up recessed windows. If you want the modern look for your car, you'll need to fabricate a new window channel around the perimeter for the glass to mount to. (Photo Courtesy Dennis Linson)

A finished flush-mounted window has a subtle look. An untrained eye may never notice the difference, but those who know better are drawn right to it. This one has late-model rubber trim around the edges.

This fiberglass Shelby-style front apron is getting an air dam attached to it. Flat, thin fiberglass panels are attached as a foundation for the desired shape. They help give a flat, rigid surface for starting the project.

This is the finished front air dam. Since it's attached to the original Shelby-style piece, it was easier to mount to the body. If you look closely at the front fenders, you may notice they are flared. You can see how this was done later within this chapter.

If you run a large tire in a front-wheel opening that doesn't allow enough sweeping movement for turning and articulation, you might decide you want to widen the front fender opening. You can keep the factory appearance of the wheelwell opening by cutting a couple of inches from the outer lip off the car. Cut the lip in half and reattach it to the fender with a gap between the two sections. If you need more room to turn the tires, make the gap larger. After figuring out how much wider the opening is, fabricate another section to fill that gap. If this isn't the kind of project you're capable of doing well, find a reputable body shop to do it for you.

Sometimes it's hard to find all the trim pieces you need, even at wrecking yards or swap meets. You may want to simply remove the trim for a cleaner look. You can look into having custom trim pieces built at a high cost, or remove the trim and spend countless hours welding in new sections of steel to take its place. Differences in trim can be slight, but removing or replacing some or all of it might be essential in getting the look you want.

Probably the largest job in the history of removing body trim is the job of removing window trim and flush-mounting windows. If it's done right, it looks awesome. It gives your Restomod

the clean appearance seen on new production cars. With the windows flush-mounted and the trim removed, your car will also be more aerodynamic since the air won't catch under all the extra edges. People I have talked to who have accomplished this huge task say they are very happy they did it, but they might not do it again.

Engine Compartment

When you pop the hood on your ride, people see more than just the engine. The shock towers and firewall stand out, especially since they are usually cluttered with electronic ignition components, and other parts people can't seem to find a better place to mount. If you are interested in removing some of the clutter in your engine compartment, you can find hidden or less obvious places to mount your ignition boxes and coils. Wherever you mount these items, make sure you can still access them in a reasonable amount of time when they fail. If and when something fails, you might end up having to spend three hours to replace or troubleshoot something that you hid too well. Remember, don't mount your fuel pressure regulator on your firewall, since some racetracks won't let you race if the regulator is in the path of a scattering flywheel.

If you are interested in smoothing your firewall, there are a few ways to go about it. In the 1970s, guys would take a

The builder of this car knew the front air dam would fold under the car before he reached top speed in his open-road racing class, so he built an aluminum frame behind it to keep it more rigid.

The S7 Saleen was built to give European super cars a run for their money on the street and track. The long, flat panel below the front grill is called a splitter. It helps create downforce, which increases cornering traction.

If you want a front air dam with some classic styling, take a look at the old Trans-Am racers. For instance, the Bud Moore number-16 car has a very functional front air dam.

If you care about quality and the appearance of your engine compartment, U.S. Body Source offers its quality Tech Hood with a smooth gel coat on the top and underside. The appearance of this hood is a far cry from a standard fiberglass hood. (Photo courtesy U.S. Body Source)

large sheet of aluminum and rivet it right to the firewall, with total disregard to how it looked or if it actually sealed engine fumes from getting into the car. These days, builders are taking more pride in their cars, so filled and smoothed firewalls are more common.

The firewall and cowl are high-stress areas, since most unibody cars have fenderwells and export braces connected to them and full-frame cars have frame mounts connected to them. If you are going to smooth your firewall with body filler, be aware that firewalls are spot-welded to the cowl panel and other surrounding panels. If you simply fill the seams up with body filler without performing the following steps, the filler will probably crack. The only way to truly get a clean weld is to remove the spot welds, remove the panels, take all the surfaces down to bare metal, and weld them back up. That is a lot of extra work, but it keeps the weld from being contaminated by paint and 30 years of garbage that seeped between panels.

Fiberglass

Fiberglass is a wonderful material. You can use it to build just about any body or interior dress-up panel. It's easier to work with in small applications than steel, and it weighs much less.

Fiberglass companies are just like any other industry: some have high-quality products, some have low-quality products. For instance, Brand U might have a history of turning out 80 percent of its unlimited line of products with poor quality and defects. The company may advertise in big publications to get a lot of brand recognition. Brand U sells to a lot of guys trying to build their car as cheap and light as possible, so the company may not care too much about the quality. Brand U might have horrible customer service when you call, after receiving your questionable parts, to ask

them about the quality. Then, for instance, there is Brand V. This company has great quality, very few defects, good customer service, but doesn't advertise too much. Be careful when choosing a company for buying your parts. Ask around and get a few opinions before laying down your money for some fiberglass parts. You're better off spending a little extra for a better product because you really do get what you pay for.

A quality fiberglass part will have a good gel coat (without pin holes and air pockets), and it will fit without shaving the edges too much. Most fiberglass is shipped with a matte finish on the external surfaces, so it's fairly hard to tell how smooth or wavy the surface of the gel coat is without putting some glossy paint on it.

A few fiberglass companies offer two different constructions for each one of their products. One is a lightweight version strictly built for saving weight, so they don't have the internal bracing, and they are very light. These parts attach with pins, unlike factory parts. The second type of glass is a heavy-duty street version. It weighs more than the lightweight version, because it has internal bracing and extra layers of fiberglass for strength. The weight savings over steel components is still significant, and you can run them on the street. Some street parts offer attaching points for bolting in as stock sheetmetal, and they even have provisions for mounting factory trim and accessories. Check with the specific company before you purchase.

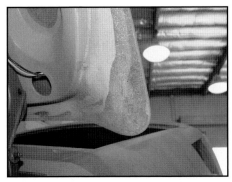

Not all fiberglass parts are created equal. The corner of this fiberglass deck lid had to be completely reshaped to get the gaps to fit. The exterior of this deck lid took over 20 hours of work to get it acceptable for paint.

I've seen people running front and rear fiberglass bumpers on the street. They give the car the appearance of running a legal bumper to keep the local officials happy, unless anyone checks to see if it's metal. These bumpers significantly reduce weight. They were designed for the purpose of reducing weight on drag cars and were never meant to be used on the street. Use them at your own risk.

You should be aware that fiberglass parts save weight, but obviously they are not as strong as the steel parts you replace. In an accident, the steel will have more integrity.

Before you purchase fiberglass parts, talk to the supplier about how you plan on driving the car when it's finished. That way, you will have assistance getting the strength of fiberglass parts you'll need. You typically have to tell a supplier to add extra strength if you want it. If you're going to drive with fiberglass on the street, you are better off getting glass parts that will last.

Lightweight Hoods

A typical lightweight, competition-style fiberglass hood weighs between 12 to 20 lbs. It looks correct on the outside, has little to no internal bracing to add strength, and keeps its original shape. This hood won't have provisions for bolting to your car; it would be a pin-on style, which means you have to attach it to your car with quick-release racing pins.

The street/heavy-duty/bolt-on fiberglass hoods are better for Restomod applications. A bolt-on glass hood weighs between 25 and 50 lbs, depending on the vehicle. Since the stock steel hood weighs between 67 and 110 lbs, the weight savings is significant. Heavy-duty fiberglass hoods have internal bracing to add strength and offer provisions for bolting on the original hood hinges and other parts in their original locations.

One company in particular offers a third level of heavy-duty hoods. U.S. Body Source's Tech Hood line features stronger bracing and a fully finished underside for a better show appearance. If you have ever tried to clean the underside of a fiberglass hood, you would appreciate the clean, smooth finish. This typically adds about 10 lbs compared to standard heavy-duty hoods. Compared to the weight of a metal hood, it is still a good savings.

With a bolt-on hood, you can save approximately 60 lbs. Since the front of the car weighs plenty more than the rear, a 60-lb savings is a huge step in the process of equalizing the front and rear weight distribution for better handling.

Companies like Crites Restoration Products, VFN Fiberglass, and U.S. Body Source offer fiberglass body parts and hoods in numerous configurations. They have a large line of fiberglass hoods for just about every Ford car. Any fiberglass part available through VFN Fiberglass is also available in carbon fiber. Speaking of carbon fiber hoods, if you have a Maverick and want a carbon fiber hood like the one on Derrick Yee's Maverick featured in this book (including the cover), he is offering them for sale at www.maverickman.com

Fiberglass Bodies

Ford and other auto manufacturers have been adding a lot of weight to their cars in the last 20 years with electronics, optional equipment, and safety devices. To offset this weight-gain, they put their cars on strict diets. In search of ways to trim the weight in their cars, they look to plastics in one form or another. The cheapest form is fiberglass. Take a look at the new cars and you will notice a liberal use of fiberglass in trim panels, fenders, and hoods. Some production cars have more than others. You can use this school of thought for putting your older Restomod on a diet. The ultimate diet would be to build the entire body out of fiberglass, much like the Cobra-style kit cars and Chevrolet Corvettes. So far, there are very few companies offering complete fiberglass bodies, including U.S. BodySource, which offers them for early Mustangs. Look to them for a complete shell to build your own featherweight bruiser.

The Promax Corporation is offering what it calls Ultimate Street Cars. Promax has been building serious street and racecars since 1984. Ultimate Street Cars

Promax Corporation is offering fiberglass-bodied versions of muscle cars. This is its version of the 1970 Mustang. Promax changed some of the body lines, modified the wheelbase, flush mounted the windows, and more. It's much lighter than the Mustang and it will never rust. (Photo Courtesy Promax Corporation)

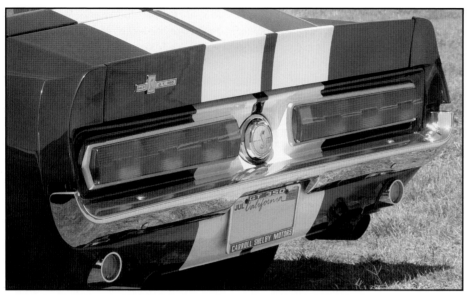

Factory rear spoilers, tail panels, and taillights from Shelby Mustangs are readily available if you want to add them to your standard Mustang.

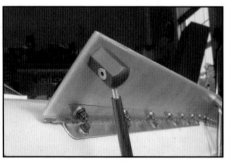

If you are looking for the racing look, you can build your own adjustable rear spoiler. A spoiler like this can actually be adjusted to increase downforce, which can lead to faster lap times at the track due to the added rear traction.

When looking at all the high-dollar front-engine super cars, you'll notice they have vents to allow air to escape from the engine compartment. Air traveling through the radiator can get trapped under the hood, causing high pressure and lift. Mark Deshetler applied this engineering to his Mustang.

Pulling air into the radiator and venting it out the hood is another way to create downforce, while keeping the air from getting trapped in the engine compartment. (Photo Courtesy Preston Peterson)

are turnkey fiberglass versions of a few 1960s cars. When I say "versions," I mean it is the design of a popular car that is built as an altered replica. The first Ultimate Street Car offering was a version of the Chevy Nova. The latest, which is called Vennom, is a version of the 1970 Ford Mustang. When you first look at it, you know it's a 1970 Mustang. Then when you see Ford's version next to it, you realize they aren't the same. The quarter panels flow at a different angle, the nose of the car drops off a little more, the windows are all flush-mounted, the fenderwell openings are different, and more. All the body and floor panels

are made of heavy-duty fiberglass, so they'll never rust. The windows are all made of safety glass. The frames are available with many options, and are available in kit form or prebuilt by Promax. You could adapt a full road racing-suspension with a Modular 4.6-liter and a T-56, or just modify the chassis to accept the 2005 Ford GT running gear. The beauty of all Promax's work is that the Vennom Mustang design was intended to utilize most of the standard Mustang trim pieces. Promax worked with top companies to help make the Vennom-specific parts like high-quality weather striping.

Spoilers, Air Dams, and Body Mods

There are plenty of opinions on air dams, spoilers, and ground-effects packages. Some people think they are ridiculous and are just for looks. On current production cars, they are used more for styling than for function. Coupes and family sedans are available with rear spoilers. If you take a look at all the new spoilers, you will notice a large percentage of them are very flat and neutral.

Rear spoilers and air dams have not always been for looks. In the late 1960s, Shelby started offering spoilers and air dams on the reworked Mustangs. Unlike the versions on most present-day cars, these original spoilers actually worked. They helped create downforce in the front and rear of the car to increase traction and handling at high speeds, especially on the road course. Getting the right size of front air dam and rear spoiler to balance the downforce was important, so testing was necessary to get it right. Too much downforce in the front and not enough in the rear makes for uncontrollable oversteer at high speeds. Too much in the rear and not enough in the front make for understeer conditions at high speed, so a balance is necessary.

Rear spoilers can play a huge part in the traction and downforce applied to the rear tires. Jim Chaparral proved this in the 1960s with the huge wing on the back of his racecar. Less obtrusive spoilers have been played with ever since. On a CMC (Camaro Mustang Challenge) car, a racer decided to install a taller

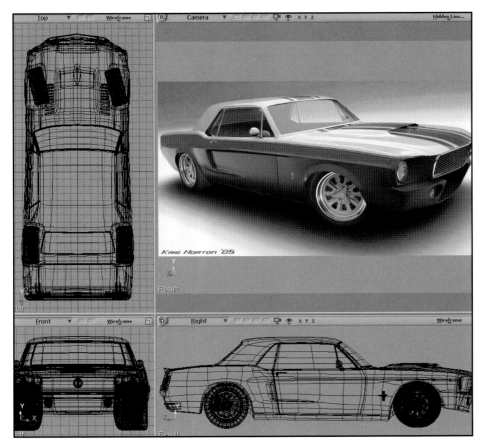

Before spending a ton of time and money on serious modifications, you should contact an artist who can put your ideas down on paper and into a computer. Kris Horton modeled this drawing in 3D on a computer for Robyn Schluter. (Image courtesy Cars-ByKris.com)

Some cars come from the factory with large fenderwells. This '68 Galaxie 500XL doesn't need fender flares unless you want more than 11–½ inches of rubber under the quarter panels.

sheetmetal rear spoiler. It was 6 inches tall and at about a 70-degree angle from the deck lid. He then drove it with and without the spoiler. With the extra downforce created by the spoiler, his track times improved dramatically because he could stay on the throttle entering the corners, which equated to faster exits. You don't have to get too crazy on the street, but an adjustable aluminum rear spoiler might be just the ticket to increasing the fun factor when you hit the road course.

Like Ford engineers, racers have found out through testing that aerodynamics play a part in how well a car handles. Take a look at the F1 cars; they generate so much downforce with the aerodynamics of their cars that at speed, they could be driven upside down on the racetrack. There are a few ways to improve your aerodynamics for Restomod, whether on a road course, at 160 mph in the Pony Express road race, or even on the highway at 65 mph. Air getting under the front of your car creates wind resistance, drag, and sometimes enough lift to hamper steering stability. A good way to limit the air getting under the car is with a front air dam. An air dam with a splitter (a protruding flat front air dam that runs parallel to the ground) increases down force in the front end, which increases tire traction. At high speed (160+ mph), a large front air dam and splitter can create enough downforce to overwork a tire, causing it to heat up and fail. If you are going to try modifying your aerodynamics, do it in moderation.

Every car that has a radiator in the front has to let air into the engine compartment for cooling. Where does that air go after it passes through the radiator? Obviously, some of that air goes into the engine. The rest of the air builds pressure under the hood, before it flows out of the engine compartment down under the car. At high speed, if too much air gets trapped under the hood, it can cause the front end to lift a little. The air that travels under the car also causes drag. If you take a look at all the high-dollar super cars and even some muscle cars, you'll notice engine compartment venting in the side of front fenders.

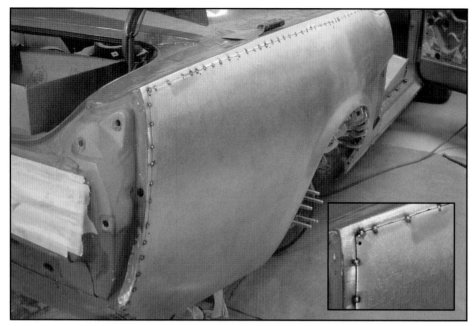

Remove the quarter panel, leaving the edges intact. Do the same with a donor car. Stretch and form both panels. Split them directly over the center of the wheelwell opening, leaving enough material for them to be bulged out, but still meet in the center. Weld both panels in and contour them for an effective but subtle flare.

These vents let air vent out the sides of the car instead of building up under the hood. This also helps keep the air flow through the engine compartment and help the engine run cooler, since the air isn't under there long enough to get heated by exhaust and engine heat. These vents have been referred to as gills (like a fish) or louvers. There are very few people putting these gills on cars that were not factory equipped with them. Front-engine Ferraris, Dodge Vipers, Corvettes, first-generation Trans Ams, and high-dollar racecars have them, so why couldn't you design and install an aesthetically pleasing set of gills on an early Mustang or Cougar?

Some racers simply prop the rear of the hood up with spacers. This allows the air to travel out of the engine compartment between the cowl and the rear of the hood. This seems to be effective and looks good on some cars, but it looks out of place on others. If you have a fiberglass cowl hood without bracing or an air box, the air can escape on its own. But this defeats the purpose of having a cowl hood to get cool air to the carburetor. With the big mouth/grill on early Fords, a lot of air gets forced into the engine compartment. The air pres-

sure under the hood is higher than the air pressure that builds up at the cowl panel. All the hot air from the engine compartment tries to push past the carburetor and out the back of the scoop.

Another way to get air out from under the hood is to vent it directly out the top of the hood. Ford's GT40, the Shelby Series 1, and some CAN AM cars use this design. This would take some serious work, since the top of the radiator would probably need to be tilted forward. Cut a fairly generous hole in the hood, and fabricate ducts to vent all the air from the radiator out the top of the hood.

Aerodynamics

Cars have not always been designed with aerodynamics in mind. In fact, most were designed to be visually appealing. Take a look at 1960s and 1970s cars. Most of them are shaped like bricks. Well, maybe not a brick, but close. Your everyday hot-rodder couldn't care less about how the car cheats the wind. The guys who are finding ways to tune their bodies are the nutty guys running high-speed open-road racing, where you drive a '68 Mustang bodied

car at 220 or even 160 mph. After being a part of these racing events, you will notice people making small modifications here and there to get a few extra miles per hour on the top end.

Fender flares are a good place to start. A fender flare that fits perfectly with the width and offset of your tires and wheels can make a difference in your top speed. The most aerodynamic fit is to have the outside edge of the tire as close to the outside edge of the fender lip as you can get. If the flare sticks out a couple of inches from the tire, it will cause air turbulence around the outside of the car. The fenders can catch a lot of air that could otherwise be flowing around the car.

The grille openings in the front of the car are massive on earlier body styles. The large grille gulps a lot of air that builds up in front of the radiator. The air that gets through the radiator and into the engine compartment gets caught under the hood or travels under the car. This all slows the car down. You can add some gills (vents) in the front fenders to allow trapped air to purge out the side of the car. Take a look at some high-dollar super cars for engine-compartment venting. Mark Deshetler noticed a difference in his Mustang; since he installed gills, his car has less lift at higher speeds. There are some remedies for this explained in the body mods section earlier in this chapter. Restomods could benefit from cheating the air a little bit.

Spoilers and air dams help cheat the wind and create downforce. They are covered earlier in this section. The headlight area is another problem area on the front of most cars. A lot of earlier cars have some sort of pocket around the headlight. Eric Pettersen got an extra 7 mph out of his Mustang on the 145-mph top-end charge just by adding some lexan covers over his headlight buckets. To get that same extra 7 mph, he would need to add about 15 to 20 hp. Imagine the difference in the cost of engine parts to gain 15 hp compared to spending a few bucks on lexan. Take a good look at your car and see if there are any modifications you could make to cheat the wind. Even if you are not

Another flaring technique is moving the outer edge of the fender outward, after slicing it across the top and making a few cuts for street relief. The fender is not sliced all the way to the front or the back. A jack and some wood were used to bulge the fender. (Photo courtesy Total Control Products)

Once the required clearance for the tire is met, a fillet of metal is cut and welded into place. Here is a better picture of the stress-relief cuts. This keeps the fender from warping in the wrong spots and helps with contouring. (Photo courtesy Total Control Products)

This fender-lip-rolling tool is the best thing since Star Wars. It's bolted to the axle, adjusted to the lip of the quarter, rolled back and forth, and then adjusted more. This process is simpler and cleaner than using a baseball bat.

going to drive your car at 220 mph, you could make a difference in your handling and fuel mileage.

Fender Flares

When you mention fender flares, guys associate the term with the 1970s hot-rod vans and bell-bottom jeans. Like bell-bottom jeans, trends come back. What about vans? I digress. Fender flares don't have to be big and gaudy.

Small flares are adequate, subtle, and can look good. Fender flares need to serve one purpose. They need to allow more room for wide tires that don't quite fit in the stock fenderwell. A wider tire will give you more traction, and a wider track width will give you more cornering stability. If you tub your car and put all the rubber between stock fender lips, you are limiting the track width of your car and its stability.

When I refer to flares, I'm not talking about a 7-inch fender flare because you want to put 345/35-17 tires on the back of your '63 Falcon (which barely fits a 235-wide tire). As with everything in life, a little moderation is good. I'm talking about flares that give you about an extra inch of room to stick some wider tires inside the fender lips. Mini tubbing would be the first avenue you may want to pursue on the Falcon. If you want to set yourself apart from other cars and only need an extra inch of clearance, there are different ways you could go about flaring your fenders. Only some of the possible flaring techniques will be covered in this section. Of course, not all cars look great with flares of any type, and some bodies don't lend themselves easily to flaring.

Back in the late 1960s, Trans Am racers were flaring the fenders in a subtle manner. The rules would not allow the cars to have any metal added, removed, or recontoured on the fenders. Teams resorted to heating and stretching the rear fenders within the limits of the rules since they were only bulged, not recontoured. This can be done to Restomods since part of Restomod gets its roots from the historic Trans Am cars. You can perform this extensive modification by removing the skin of the quarter panel around the outer perimeter to keep the perimeter body lines intact. Take another quarter panel from a donor car, then stretch it and shape it. Leaving some overlapping material on both panels over the wheelwell, cut the two panels in half near the centerline of the wheelwell opening. With the panels overlapped over the center of the wheelwell, pull them and stretch them until the bulges are uniform. Then tack-weld it back into place. With the quarter bulged, cut the overlapping material in the center and butt-weld the two halves together. There will be a gap on the inner fenderwell where it meets the outer skin. A panel will need to be fabricated to fill the fenderwell gap, and then tack it into place. The tack welds are followed by a stitch weld and all the finishing bodywork. The finished product is very subtle and nets about an extra inch or two of tire clearance.

The owner of this Mustang trimmed the rear apron to cut down on air that pockets in front of it, decreasing wind resistance. The original wheel lips were also removed for extra tire clearance.

You can flare the fenders without modifying the entire panel in a couple different ways. Some techniques will work better than others for your particular car. Ninety-nine percent of the time, rolling the fender lip or performing any type of fender flaring will damage the paint on the outer surface of the panel. For a small flare in the lip of the fender, you can sometimes do this with body tools if you have extensive experience. I've seen a fender-lip rolling tool utilized for rolling lips and minor flaring. Sometimes it's necessary to make a cut in the inner fenderwell, near the point where it attaches to the outer panel, if hammering the fender does not get you enough space. The cut allows the panel to stretch a little further. Once the flare is made, don't forget to weld up any open surfaces in the fenderwell. Contour the fender lip to your liking, accentuating the original design. If the front and rear fender lips don't match, making them match might be a good idea.

Another style of flare allows you to keep some of the original body lines, but gives a subtle accent. Use your sharp felt-tip marker to lay all your lines out on the fender before you start. Make a cut in the top of the fender about an inch in from the outside edge of the fender. The cut runs almost from the doorjamb on the top of the fender, and nearly all the way to the headlight bezel. Small,

perpendicular cuts are made in the fender to allow it to flare more easily. Some other relief cuts may be necessary to allow the panel to be stretched. Pull the outside panel to give yourself enough flare to clear the tire. There should be a slit open on the top of the fender. Cut a filler strip of sheetmetal to fill the gap. Tack weld every couple inches around the outside of the filler strip.

Rolling the Fender Lip

Instead of adding fender flares, you may only need to gain an extra half-inch of clearance to fit a tight tire in your fenderwell. Sometimes the tire fits in the wheelwell until you pull in and out of a driveway. Then the tires may rub on the inside of the wheelwell or on the outside fender lip. It's also possible that the rear end (rear axle) is not centered in the body. Production car rear axles often lean a half-inch more toward one side than the other, which sometimes causes rubbing. If you need an inch more room on the inner wheelwell, you should get some mini-tubs installed. If you need a quarter-inch in one small spot, you may be able to use an air hammer with a blunt tip to add a little clearance, but this doesn't work on all cars. This section is about getting a little more clearance on the outside of the tire.

Whatever you do, do not cut the fender lip in little sections to bend them

up more easily or cut the fender lip off the wheel opening. You will reduce the strength of the fender and greatly increase the chance of slicing your tires. Nothing hurts more than slicing up a brand new set of tires unless you cut your hand on the fender lip, too.

Compared to the old days of sticking a baseball bat in the fenderwell and rolling the car back and forth, there are better ways to roll the fender lips. There are tools specifically designed for rolling fender lips. Find a good shop that has one or buy one for yourself, and then charge your friends to fix their cars so you can recoup the cost. The tool requires you to remove the tire and bolt the tool base in place of the wheel where it pivots. The tool will crack the paint on the inside of the lip. If you want to take a little extra precaution against the paint peeling all the way to the external edge of the fender lip, carefully use a razor knife to score the paint along the entire radius of the lip. It should be an 1/8-inch in from the outside edge of the lip. Before rolling the lip, keep in mind that the roller could distort or damage the outer fender. You could end up causing yourself some extra paint and bodywork, especially if you try to roll the lip too much or roll it too much all at once.

Sweep the tool back and forth while cranking the handle, until the large roller contacts the fender lip. Sweep it around the arc of the wheelwell. Tighten the roller a little, roll the lip some more, and then repeat until the desired amount of clearance is reached. Adjusting the roller a little at a time ensures you'll stretch the metal a little bit at a time. If you adjust it too much, you'll increase the possibility of distorting the outside edge of the fender. To reduce the possibility of flaking and rusting, treat the bare metal and use a little touch-up paint on the line you scored with the razor knife when you're done.

Safety Upgrades

With all of the lawyers, laws, and safety regulations, we're all driving safer vehicles than ever before. Since Restomods are supposed to embrace new technologies in suspension, brakes, tires, and drivetrain, we should go the next step and embrace technological advances in safety equipment.

Fire Systems

If you're reading this book, there's a good chance you have a lot of time, money, and pride invested in your car. Purchasing a fire extinguisher for placement in your car should be high on your priority list. You can purchase fire extinguishers in hardware stores and speed shops. Make sure you purchase an extinguisher for automotive use, since there are different extinguishing agents available for different types of fires. For your safety, make sure to purchase a DOT-approved extinguisher. To get the best extinguisher and advice, there are companies that exclusively make and sell fire systems. Safecraft Safety Equipment offers many different hand-held extinguishers, mounting brackets, and extinguisher systems specifically designed for cars, motorsports, and just about everything else.

To add some extra protection and insurance against fire (especially if you go to the track a lot), you can install an extinguisher system. Safecraft offers many options in extinguisher systems including 2, 3, 5, 10, and 20-lb Halon bottles. The different systems have 360-degree swiveling push, pull, and pneumatic discharge head options. Installing one of these systems is very easy. Mount the bottle out of the direct sunlight, install the activation cable, and run the discharge tubing and nozzles. Racers typically have discharge nozzles located in the engine compartment, in the passenger compartment near the driver, and around the fuel cell. Call Safecraft for installation suggestions and advice regarding the best extinguishing agents and systems for your application.

Side Mirrors

There are a few reasons to upgrade the side-view mirrors on your car (especially on cars built before the mid-1970s). The newer mirrors are larger for safety purposes, have stronger hinge mechanisms, and are more aerodynamic. For example, the stock side mirrors on a '66 Mustang are small, round units. It's hard to look at them with only a quick

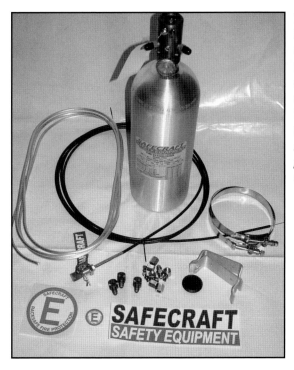

This is a Safecraft Safety Equipment RS extinguishing system with the optional 10-pound bottle. It comes with mounting brackets, T-bar clamps, hardware, pull cable, discharge tubing, and discharge outlets. The 360-degree discharge head has three outlets and provisions for mounting one push knob and two pull cables (separate cables for the driver, navigator, and safety crew).

For safety and styling reasons, you can upgrade your Restomod with side mirrors from a newer car. Dodge Vipers and Chevy Corvettes are good donor cars for this type of upgrade.

glance. The pivot mechanism does not stand up well after a few years of normal driving with stock suspension. Add some stiff springs and shocks into the equation, and they start having a mind of their own. Old chrome mirrors were designed without concern for aerodynamics, but this began to change as early as the late 1970s. Still, even mirrors from the late 1970s don't have the greatest hinge mechanisms. Newer Mustang, Chevrolet C5 Corvette, and Dodge Viper mirrors have a much better design and a larger viewing area. Depending on the body lines of your car, you can find

a decent set of mirrors from a newer donor car that will mount and flow well. For an added bonus, if you found the right donor cars, you can add mirrors with electric movement, heaters, automatic dimmers, or turn signals.

Taillights

Newer taillights are much brighter and easier to see than just about any taillight made before 1995. This is especially true of cars built before 1970. With those, people could barely tell if you had your blinker on or if you were on the brakes. These days, the chrome-plated reflector behind the bulb makes a single bulb look like 35 LED lights. There are also production cars with actual LED brake lights. What's really cool about LED lights is that they generate very little heat and require a very low amount of voltage. A brighter taillight can help save your car from getting rear ended by someone who isn't paying attention.

Taking apart any new production-car light and utilizing the reflectors, bulbs, or LEDs to custom-build some lights for your older car can create some great results. Just keep in mind that light bulbs generate heat, some more than others, and installing one too close to a reflector or lens could cause a fire or at least melt the lens.

MARTIN POND'S 1971 TORINO GT

This Torino sees street time, as well as frequent track time at open-track road-course events. Martin is a member of the Norcal Shelby Club. The red Torino feels right at home with the Cobras and Shelby Mustangs.

There is an old saying that goes something like: "A mechanic's car is the worst kind of car. It gets neglected, and when it gets worked on, the mechanic knows exactly how to just barely keep it running with the least amount of work." While that may be true in most cases, Martin Pond and his 1971 Torino are an exception to the rule. Martin is a mechanic by trade, but in fact being a mechanic is more of a way of life for him. When he isn't performing as the sole mechanic for Tidewater Tire (his auto repair business), or being a husband and a dad, he works on his own car for fun. The drive behind keeping his car in perfect running condition is knowing he will periodically get the chance to race it around local road courses and take it to local car shows.

Martin's brother Randall Pond introduced him to open-track racing, and he's been hooked ever since. So hooked, in fact, that it only took one

month of owning the Torino to have the front and rear suspension upgraded and ready for the track. The front coil springs were swapped for 720-lb springs, the Shelby modification was performed on the upper control arms, a 1.25-inch Mustang front sway bar was installed, a pair of custom high-rate rear leaf springs with repositioned spring eyes was added, and KYB gas adjust shocks were installed on all four corners. Now the Torino GT was ready for some track time.

It didn't take long for other modifications to slowly make their way to the GT. Martin knew he was getting plenty of power out of his 4V 351C, but he also knew the car could use a little diet. He came across a great deal on a 351W crate motor, and he knew swapping the Cleveland for a Windsor with aluminum GT40X heads would shave about 200 lbs from the front end of the car. The old, clunky slipper power-steering pump was

replaced with a composite-case 5.0-liter Mustang pump. The cast-iron water pump was replaced with a 5.0 aluminum unit, and the accessory drive system was converted to a serpentine set-up using all Ford parts. The complete swap took a little off the straight-line performance, but the cornering performance was greatly improved. The weight of the battery was transferred to the rear of the car for further balance.

The transmission stayed a top loader 4-speed unit, but Martin has plans for a stout 6-speed conversion in the future. The clamping force between the billet steel flywheel and Centerforce pressure plate is handled by a Centerforce dual-friction disc. The differential is of 9-inch persuasion. An aluminum third member houses a 3.55:1 gear, Gold Track limited slip, and Daytona pinion retainer to persuade the 31-spline axles.

Braking is handled by stock 11.5-inch front discs and 10x2.5-inch drums in the rear. So far, Martin has found success with this set-up coupled with Bendix brake pads and shoes. Covering the brakes are 16x8-inch Vintage 48 wheels with 4 inches of backspacing. The tires are some great-performing Yokohama AO32 255/50-16s in front and 275/50-16s in the rear.

The interior is mostly stock and in pristine condition. Martin added some AutoMeter gauges so he could keep an eye on the important stuff. For some serious lateral support and safety, he added some Corbeau seats. A Hurst Competition Plus shifter handles gear-changing duties, a full Alpine stereo system adds non-mechanical entertainment, and a Ford Granada Sport model 3-spoke steering wheel fits nicely to round out the interior package.

The 1971 Torino GT body is covered with Vermillion Orange and accented by the black grill with hide-away headlights, shaker hood, chin spoiler, rear spoiler, full-length taillight panel,

The interior is mostly stock, but it has been upgraded with Corbeau seats for comfort, style, and lateral support, all of which is necessary for the type of driving this car sees. The steering wheel is a Granada factory option – it fits perfectly.

Martin's '71 Torino GT has the signature GT rear spoiler, full-length taillight trim, and side trim. The Vintage 48 wheels and stance complete this well-executed Restomod.

and gills on the quarter panels. Most of these were factory options in 1971, but the shaker hood was added before Martin purchased the car. The chin spoiler was added afterward to help with curb appeal and track performance.

Martin wants to thank to his wife Julie and their kids (Martin, Lauren, and Leigh) for their support on his Torino project, Fernando Yanez for giving up spare parts, Skye DeMaria for help with detailed custom touches, Emanuels Mufflers for the great exhaust work, and his brother Randall Pond for getting him involved in open-track racing. Of course, Martin wants to thank Nor Cal Shelby Club for having great track and other auto events for its members.

There are still some modifications on the future upgrade list. The GT is a great all-around package, and it shows that the engineers at Ford designed more than one great body style in 1971. Martin is an impressive mechanic, especially since he still enjoys turning wrenches off the clock. If Martin ever wants to sell his Torino GT, this is one "mechanic's car" you could buy and drive with confidence.

The original 351C has been replaced with a much lighter 351W equipped with GT40X aluminum heads. The shaker air cleaner and hood were installed by a previous owner and look right at home on the engine updated with late-model components.

These are just a few LED taillight kits from The Mustang Shop. These are the easiest LEDs to install. There isn't any splicing necessary; just plug them into the light socket. (Photo courtesy The Mustang Shop)

Well-lit taillights are important on the older Restomods that have extremely small or dim assemblies. Adapting transparent red lenses and internal reflectors from a late-model taillight assembly may be a low-cost upgrade; it'll just take some ingenuity and time.

This LED third brake light assembly came off a 1995 GM SUV. This and other types of third brake lights can be cleanly incorporated into your car and make it more visible to cars behind you.

This Bright Driver headlight kit is a step above standard glass halogen headlights and delivers brighter and safer driving light. These lights are a simple bolt-in upgrade (without modifications), and they are almost a pound lighter than stock lights. They are also made of materials 30 times more rock-resistant than glass, have moisture-proof features, and have available replaceable bulbs. (Photo courtesy Detroit Speed & Engineering)

Lighting cues can be picked up from new cars. This nice split turn signal and driving light combination was worn by the 2005 Mustang Concept show car. This cool idea didn't make it to the production Mustang.

There are a few companies offering LED conversion kits. The Mustang Shop, Mustang Project, and Technostalgia offer complete Mustang LED conversion kits that really work, and they remove the guesswork from converting to LEDs because they use your original lenses and bezels. Mustang Project also offers LED conversions for Gran Torinos. Keep your eyes open for other applications from these companies.

If you want to spend extra time making your own LED brake lights, there are a few companies offering round and oval LED units designed for 18-wheelers. These come as single-function brake lights, taillights, or flashers.

They're also available as multi-function units with turn lights, taillights, and brake lights. For safety's sake, think of ways to convert to LEDs.

If you don't like LED taillights, but want to upgrade to a newer set of taillights, you can always take a look around at other production taillight lenses off new domestic or import cars. Maybe some of them can be adapted or grafted into your tail panel or bumper. With the number of different cars on the market, the possibilities out there are almost endless.

Third Brake Light

In addition to installing safer taillights, take a look at all the new third brake lights on production cars. Most of the coolest units are the slim LED units. Some are for mounting inside the car on the rear deck, or in the headliner, while some are for external mounting on the roofs of SUVs and sunk in the spoilers of sports cars. A few aftermarket companies offer custom third brake lights in plastic and billet housings. A cool way to mount a third brake light would be grafting a thin LED unit into a '69 Mustang spoiler, or installing one in a custom headliner on a '71 Torino. There are many options with the different mounting solutions, shapes, and sizes. Plus, some insurance companies offer discounts on policies if your car is equipped with a third brake light.

Headlights

Stock T3 headlights did their job in the past, but are not as bright or as safe as the newer Halogen units. Halogen lights are direct replacements for original standard bulbs. They plug right into the original socket. If you want brighter high-tech headlights, you can upgrade to a Bright Drivers kit available from Detroit Speed and Engineering (DSE). DSE offers all the late-model features like moisture-proof Gortex one-way valves and replaceable bulbs. The lightweight polycarbonate lens is safer for on-track and everyday driving, and 30 times stronger than stock glass lenses. This kit, unlike others on the market, does not require hooking up relays or modifying the headlight bucket.

To go the extra mile, high-intensity discharge (HID) lights are even brighter, and they are the latest step in high-tech lighting. Sylvania offers HID conversion kits for dual round, quad round, dual rectangular, quad rectangular, and a couple of other headlight combinations/applications. With some electrical wiring skills, one of their kits could be installed in an afternoon. Mounting the HID lights in the stock headlight housings is the easy part. HIDs come with a ballast resistor for each light assembly. You'll need to mount those in close proximity to the lights. Then you'll need to wire in the supplied wire harness and relay.

Wiper Motors

If you want to really update your Restomod, you can drive it anywhere, everywhere, and just about anytime—except when there's snow and salt on the roads. In some parts of the country, you can drive your car everyday, but you'll eventually get stuck driving in the rain. If your car was built before the 1980s, there is a high possibility your car is equipped with one of those annoying windshield wiper systems. You know what I am talking about, the ones with three speeds: off, high, and ludicrous speed. If you're driving in a light rain or mist, you click the knob to the left and then back to off, so the wipers only sweep once. Unfortunately, you are forced to do this ritual every minute or two. Some builders have upgraded to systems from late-model cars equipped with the delay feature. Detroit Speed & Engineering has taken a good look at this problem, and has come up with a system that bolts into the stock location for a clean look. DSE has done the homework so you can reap the benefits of a wiper motor with high, low, and multiple delay speeds, without spending countless hours and amounts of brainpower trying to figure out how to do it yourself.

Some guys don't want a wiper motor mounted on their firewall in the traditional location. For a really clean look, you can cut the wiper flange off the firewall and weld it to the firewall behind the left front fender, and then fill the hole where the wiper was originally. Finally, install a custom extended arm on the mechanism and move the wires. This leaves the firewall with a very clean, uncluttered look.

Charging System

If you add a bunch of electrical components like electric fans, an electric water pump, fuel injection, a stereo system, etc., you'll need to upgrade your charging system by installing a better battery and a higher-output alternator.

The most popular battery on the market is made by Optima. Optima batteries are identified by the color of the top: red, yellow, or blue. The red-top battery is good for typical street car applications where the car is driven almost everyday and doesn't have electric fans, fuel injection, and a big stereo. Yellow-top batteries are best suited for Restomod applications, especially if you don't drive your car for a few weeks at a time and have some power draining accessories. Blue-top batteries are best suited for marine applications.

Optima batteries have a unique Spiralcell technology that provides features standard batteries don't have. The cells have more surface area with closer spacing and the ability to use higher-purity lead. This equals lower resistance, quicker charge acceptance, better shelf life,

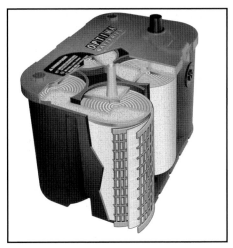

The Optima battery is constructed with the unique Spiralcell technology. The features include more cell surface area, higher purity lead, and immobilized plates that resist damaging vibrations. (Photo courtesy Optima Batteries)

Optima added the group-51 battery to its product line. It was introduced to meet size requirements for sport-compact cars, but it is becoming popular with the domestic crowd because it tips the scales at a svelte 26 lbs. That's 16 lbs lighter than the standard group-34 yellow-top Optima battery. With 500 cold-cranking amps, it exceeds almost any V-8's starting needs. (Photo courtesy Optima Batteries)

and more battery power. The plates are immobilized, which translates to improved vibration resistance. These plates are much better for Restomod cars, since they will last longer under hard driving with stiff suspensions.

Car batteries have two different types of terminals: top posts and side terminals. Optima batteries come in two configurations. They either have just top posts, or top posts and side terminals. Buying a dual-terminal battery will allow for extra connections you may need to make for extra accessories.

Optima Batteries can vent if they're severely overcharged or if the alternator or regulator produced more than 15 volts for extended periods. There are two safety valves that will purge excess pressure and then reseal completely. An alternator overcharge condition is very rare, and you should never experience one. On the other hand, a standard battery outgasses continuously while it charges and is prone to leaking, which causes corrosion around the battery location. Optima batteries do not leak, which helps control corrosion around your battery tray or surrounding area.

Mounting the battery in the trunk is a good way to move 25 to 40 lbs to the rear of the car, which is a great start in a process of balancing the weight ratio between the front and rear. There are a few different ways to mount the battery in the trunk. You can put it in a racing-approved plastic or metal vented battery box, or you can mount it in an open-air battery mount like the ones shown in the Optima battery picture. If you are going to mount a battery in an open-air mount in the trunk, only use a sealed battery, since you don't want poisonous gasses in your trunk.

Basic Electrical and Wiring

As with any other part of Restomod, or any kind of hot rodding for that matter, it's a good idea to do things the right way. The electrical system should not be treated like an afterthought. There are good and bad ways to perform every part of your project. Why do something half-way, when spending a little extra time can produce something so much better? This philosophy is especially true for the electrical system, since problems there can be very frustrating to find.

Cross-Linked Wire

Electrical wires are available in different qualities. There's the normal wire you get at the local hardware store, and

1. This Mark VIII cooling fan installation is in this chapter because of the electrical requirements to power this beast. Its continuous draw is 33 amps, but it uses close to 100 amps at start-up, unless it's controlled by a variable output controller. With the high amp draw, this fan needs at least a 130 amp alternator. The overall dimensions (without the four mounting tabs) are 22x18.5x6.25 inches deep (at the fan motor). Due to its size, most people remove the mounting tabs. This application had plenty of room, so they were left intact.

2. For this application, the fan was the perfect height, but it was a little short on the sides. I would need to fill this space. During the whole install, I kept the cardboard on the face of the radiator to prevent the fins from getting damaged. I also taped the areas I was working with to keep them from getting scratched.

3. I took my measurements to a friend's shop. I used his shear to cut the aluminum and his sheetmetal brake to bend the edges. I added the extra lip on the surface that butts up against the fan to add strength to the panel.

4. The radiator cap was in the way, so I used a set of hand shears to trim the panel and a small file to shape the edge to the correct radius. Riv-nuts were added to the top and bottom panels of the radiator. A single bolt on the top and bottom is plenty to hold the panels in place.

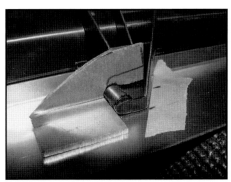

5. The fan shroud has a foot that slides into hooks on the Mark VIII, so I decided to make two hooks out of aluminum that would allow me to easily remove the fan if I ever needed to do so. The passenger side foot rides against the fill panel perfectly. This image shows the hook in an early stage of fabrication.

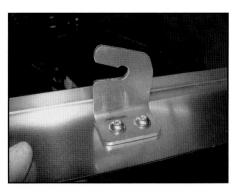

6. The foot on the driver's side was spaced out a little more. The hooks needed to attach to the fill panels, so I installed Riv-nuts in the fill panels and drilled holes in the hooks. For a professional look, I rounded all the edges. This hook is ready for use.

7. This image shows the hook after I had both of them hard-anodized black. The hard-anodizing keeps the aluminum from being damaged by the elements. I took a dozen small parts to the shop and had them all done at the same time.

8. The upper feet on both sides of the fan needed to be bolted into place. Just like the lower feet, the upper feet were not evenly spaced. I used a 1-inch spacer on the passenger side and a 2-inch spacer on the driver's side of the fan. I used Riv-nuts and stainless Allen bolts to mount the fan.

9. The fan installation is complete. It's a snug fit. Undo two bolts, and the Mark VIII fan assembly slides up and out. Perfect! Now for the electrical . . .

there is quality wire. The quality wire is called cross-linked wire. It uses polyethylene insulation to ensure it is durable for an automotive environment. Wire used on a car needs to have good abrasion resistance and the insulation needs to stand up to dirt, oil, and temperatures up to 275 degrees Fahrenheit. Cross-linked wire is resistant to kinks, which is a good thing for wires you pull through panels and around accessories. It would be a big headache to completely wire your project and have a gremlin in your wiring because you kinked a couple of wires during installation. Maybe your fuel injection just won't run right. Later you find out that a kink caused too

much resistance in a wire for your fuel injection, which requires a certain signal, to run correctly. Cross-linked wire is available in bulk from automotive wiring companies.

Wiring Harnesses

Not every project needs to have a completely new wire harness. Some projects need a new fuse panel in addition to the stock panel. Either way, there are a lot of aftermarket wiring companies offering different solutions. Two good companies that come to mind are American Auto Wire and Painless Performance Wiring. They both offer good solutions to just about any custom

wiring job. The better companies offer harnesses that have wires printed with labels, not just a stick-on label that can fall off during installation. The labels are still going to be visible years later to help troubleshoot a problem. If you want a stock wiring harness, American Auto Wire can get you what you need. There are completely detailed wiring schematics available for just about every American automobile, which can be helpful when wiring a car.

Connections

When changing anything or adding components to your electrical system, it's important to make good connec-

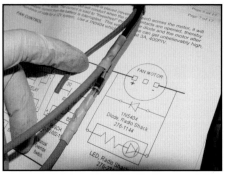

10. I called my local Ford dealership and purchased the correct '97 Mark VIII fan connector. You can use spade connectors, but I wanted a weatherproof connection. There are two different ways to power the Mark VIII fan. There's a hard way and an easy way. I'll cover the hard way first. Do not power this fan without a relay. You'll need more than a standard 40-amp relay, and don't use anything less than 10-gauge wire for the power and ground circuit. Anything less, and you're asking for trouble with burned wires. Get a 75-amp Bosch relay #0-332-002-150 to handle the high-amp draw upon start-up.

11. I enlisted the help of the Internet to learn about the wiring. I found information that I have linked to my website (at www.RaceHome.com/mark8.htm). In short, the information states the fan motor requires a diode hooked between the positive and negative leads to keep your relay from being damaged by voltage produced from the free-wheeling fan when it's turned off.

12. The easy way to hook up the Mark VIII fan is to use this Delta Current Control variable current controller, which was designed specifically for high-amp fans like this set-up. The controller takes the place of the relay and the diode, and hooks up easily with a few wires. It controls the high-amp surge during start-up by slowly ramping up the fan speed, which removes the surging of your vehicle's charging system. This also helps control the cooling system temperature, rather than the normal, but extreme, hot and cold cycling of temperature, which increases engine wear from expansion and contraction variances.

tions. Using crimped hardware-store butt-connectors to splice wires is fine, but splicing using solder and heat-shrink tubing would last longer and be more moisture-resistant. For connecting an accessory in an area that might get any sort of moisture, there are weatherproof electrical connectors available. The best ones on the market are called Weather Pack connectors. The auto manufacturers use them to ensure electrical connections have the best possible connection in extreme environments. Weather Pack connectors have a quick-release male (tower) and female (shroud) connector. Inside the connectors are a male and female terminal. A seal is also installed on the wire to ensure a weather-resistant connection. The nice thing about Weather Pack connectors is the time they can save on wiring, since they're designed to be used without solder. The terminals have a small, cross-hatched pad that the wire is crimped to for a positive lock. Special wire crimpers are needed for assembling Weather Pack connectors.

Electrical Accessories

What size alternator do you think your car should have? I found a good

When upgrading your Restomod to a powerful fan like the Mark VIII fan featured earlier or other power-hungry components, you should upgrade your charging system. Powermaster Motorsports sells alternators and charge wires. A high-amp alternator needs the correct charge wire. (Photo courtesy Powermaster Motorsports)

source of information on how to pick the right starter and an alternator with the proper voltage for your application. Check out the Powermaster Motorsports website. It has a chart and some questions that will point you in the right direction. Alternators come in many different shapes, sizes, and outputs. With the new technology and cramped modern engine compartments, alternator cases and starters are getting smaller,

which also means you can benefit on your older car, too. If you need to make room for your twin turbos, or just shed a few pounds, there are some small alternators and aftermarket brackets available to help.

Interior

There is no limit to what you can do with the interior of a Restomod. Sometimes you only need stock equipment with a few extra gauges, but upgrading to some late-model amenities or going all out with new everything is good, too. Some early factory parts are not as safe as new factory and aftermarket parts, so upgrading could save your life. There are laws and federal mandates that require auto manufacturers to include certain safety features in new cars. They are constantly growing stricter every model year, requiring manufactures to upgrade their safety features.

Seats

The seats in a car are thought of as a comfort item, but they are often overlooked as a safety feature. Low-

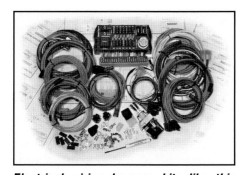

Electrical wiring harness kits like this Power Plus kit are somewhat universal. It comes complete with all the necessary plugs, connectors, wires, rubber boots, and a fuse box. (Photo courtesy American Auto Wire)

Depending on the company, some wiring kits come with easy-to-read pre-labeled wires. They make wiring easier, because you don't have to spend extra hours tracing wires (especially if you're colorblind). (Photo courtesy American Auto Wire)

The Weather Pack terminal utilizes a weatherproof rubber seal (in center of photo) that keeps the elements away from the terminal after plugging it into the connector. The seals come in different sizes for different gauges of wire.

Installing new aftermarket gauges can be a tedious project. The Mustang Shop is manufacturing a gauge chassis that firmly holds Stewart Warner and other aftermarket gauges. It bolts to the original dash cluster and positions the gauges so the original cluster fits perfectly.

back bucket seats work well and go with a stock-type interior. Unfortunately, they are not safe in a rear-impact accident. Imagine you are stopped at a light and someone hits you doing 10 mph or more. Your head will snap back. Without a headrest to limit travel, you run the risk of serious neck injuries. Take a look at brand-new car seats; they all have adjustable headrests for safety reasons.

Seats are also a part of comfort and control. A seat with side bolsters on the back and seat bottom help support your thighs and body from moving side to side as you maneuver your car through corners. You can get seats with this lateral control from late-model factory cars and aftermarket companies. Factory

Seats aren't just for looks; they're for safety too. These Cobra seats give more side support for cornering, and the high-back is safer for your neck than a low-back seat if your car was ever rear-ended. (Photo courtesy Phil Royle)

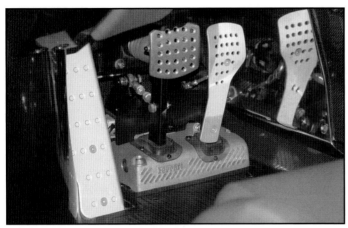

Styling cues can be picked up from looking at other cars. This is the pedal set-up in a Ferrari. Along with the aluminum pedal pads, it's equipped with a big dead pedal. It gives you a place to rest your foot and support your body weight in the twisties.

People who ride with me complain there aren't enough handles to hold. I spied this center console in a Porsche Cayenne. Seems like a perfect place fir a pair of grab handles.

This interior may look familiar to some. It's the Rad Rides by Troy-built EBay Mustang. The custom center console, stereo, and video system are just a few items that were integrated effectively.

seats are built for the average-sized person, so they're not typically as supportive as an aftermarket seat purchased for your size. You can order some aftermarket seats in different widths to fit your rear end better. Since Restomods are meant to be driven, your comfort is important.

If you have a certain type of material you want to upholster your interior and seats with, you can send it to a custom seat manufacturer. Then you can get a set of seats made using your material. Good upholstery shops can reupholster any seat with your choice of fabric, if you have a set of seats you

want to keep. If you don't have a huge cage in your car and you still have a back seat, you can get material to cover your seat and make it match your front seats. Some rear seats out of late-model cars will fit in older cars with very little modification. If you have mini-tubbed your car, you will most likely need to narrow your rear seat or at least modify the seat frame to better fit the larger inner wheelwells.

Center Console

If you're going to drive your car on a regular basis or drive it on long trips,

like on the Hot Rod Power Tour, you'll need some extra amenities. One item to consider is a center console with an armrest, at least two cup holders, and possibly a place to put your cell phone or other electronic devices. Only high-optioned early cars had consoles. Those consoles have a small compartment for vehicle registration and tickets, a little room for a gauge or two, and a place to rest your seat belt buckle when it isn't in use. Modern consoles have extra accessory ports for laptop converters and cell phone chargers, cup holders, CD holders, hidden compartments, and adjustable arm rests. If you do some research and modifications, you can fit a late-model console in your early-model Restomod. Getting a late-model console to fit usually requires modifying the console, mounting the brackets on the floorpan and transmission tunnel, and sometimes modifying the dash.

If you're going to build a console, make it as useful as possible. Integrate some cup holders from a late-model car, truck, or van. Adding at least one cup holder will be very useful. It doesn't get much worse than stopping for a bite to eat and not having a place to set your soda. If there are no cup holders, it usually ends up resting between your legs. If you are unlucky, you will end up wearing the soda or spilling it in your car. I have also heard that some areas of the U.S. have laws against driving with a drink resting between your thighs.

This racing dash is all business. It houses all the accessory switches, fire system activation knob, and a Stack gauge that has an analog tach. Under the tach, there's digital readout that shows multiple gauge functions. It's an all-in-one unit.

The rear seat in this Mustang was deemed useless when the roll cage was installed, so Don Rositch built a sturdy rear package shelf that also holds the speakers. It also has trim sticking up to keep items from sliding off the shelf. (Photo courtesy Mustang Don's)

Pedals

A good set of pedal pads can look racy and actually give your more grip and control with your feet. A stock rubber pedal pad might allow your shoes to get better traction on the pedal, but make sure it is attached well. If a pad were to slide off while driving, it could be dangerous. Once you get used to the feel and size of your pedals, a change could affect your driving and foot positioning.

A dead pedal is very useful for the driver. It gives you a place to support and control your body weight during hard cornering. It also gives you a place to rest your foot, instead of on your brake or clutch pedal. They are starting to become standard equipment on new sports cars. Some cars have their seats so far from the firewall that the passenger can't comfortably reach it with their feet (if at all). This would be a perfect reason to install a dead pedal.

Dashboard and Gauges

Customizing a dashboard is not new to hot-rodding, but the trends have become more elaborate and more detailed than before. A few years ago, guys would just remove the gauge pod, replace it with a little aluminum insert, and squeeze in a few extra gauges. Now builders are going the extra mile to cleanly replace large sections of the dash or replace the entire thing.

Replacing the factory gauges with aftermarket units brings a whole new step to modifying the dash. Most of them have the turn-signal indicators, emergency-brake warning light, and high-beam indicator as an integral part of the gauge face. For safety reasons, you should find the wires connecting to these indicators and wire them into some small LED lights on the new dash, so you'll still have indicators. LEDs are available in different colors and sizes.

The typical street car has a speedometer, tachometer, oil pressure gauge, volt gauge, fuel level gauge, and coolant temperature gauge. That set-up is great until you get out on a road course or go to an open-road racing event. Once you start driving your car harder, you better start monitoring oil temperature and transmission temperature (for automatics). The engine and transmission temps can soar when you're racing. If you don't monitor them, you might have serious failure without realizing there was a problem.

Gauge placement should also be taken into consideration. There may be a better way to organize your gauges. The old trick for racecars is to rotate all the gauges so at average operating speed and conditions, the needles point in the same direction. If all the needles were pointing straight up, the driver knew the car was operating normally. The last thing you want to do is pull your eyes off the road for any length of time at high speeds. For that same reason, placing your gauges up on the dash and closer to eye level is better if you plan on racing your car. Placing gauges on the console was an easy and cheap way for Ford to add factory special-option instruments. Taking your eyes off the road to look down at your console-mounted gauges can be dangerous. The closer you mount your instruments to your line of sight, the safer and more convenient they'll be. The Shelby gauge pod on the top of the 1965 GT350 is a good example of high-mounted gauges.

Air Conditioning

Not every Restomod on the planet needs air conditioning. Some Restomods are set up for more of an all-out performance experience, and some cars are built with a little more comfort in mind. Some cars are equipped with air conditioning from the factory, but some weren't. If you want air conditioning in your car and don't want to use the original factory system, you can install an aftermarket system.

To cut down on noise and heat in the interior of your Restomod, you can install some Dynamat products. Their products also enhance the sound of your stereo. (Photo courtesy Detroit Speed & Engineering)

If you want a high-quality compact bracket assembly, check out the Vintage Air FrontRunner system. The system is well engineered and has all of the best parts. (Photo courtesy Vintage Air)

Hanging the Vintage Air evaporator under the dash can be tricky. You'll need to build a bracket that picks up the mounting points in your dash and on the unit itself. Be sure to leave room for the hoses and ducts on the top.

Air-conditioning systems are comprised of a few key components, the largest of which is the evaporator. It typically fits up under the dashboard. Air is cooled or heated in the evaporator and then blown out of the unit by the integrated blower fan motor. The compressor is driven by the engine crankshaft. It sucks refrigerant from the evaporator and is used to pressurize the refrigerant and pump it through the condenser. The condenser is the large component that resembles a radiator. It's used to dissipate the refrigerant heat generated by the compressor. The refrigerant then flows through the drier, which removes water from the refrigerant. The refrigerant then flows to the evaporator where the process starts all over again.

Vintage Air

The most popular aftermarket air conditioning manufacturer is Vintage Air. Vintage Air sells Sure Fit systems for many older Ford cars and trucks. These kits take the guesswork out of installing aftermarket air conditioning. They come with all the parts you will need for installation, and are tailored for specific applications.

Vintage Air also offers all the parts separately for people who want a custom-fit kit. The kits may fit in custom locations better; perform better because you want a bigger evaporator; and may look better because you can get upgraded controls, fittings, hoses, dash vents,

This is not a system you can order as one part number. Working closely with Kyle Tucker of Detroit Speed & Engineering, I was able to order all the Vintage Air parts to piece together a kit that would be more powerful than Vintage Air's Sure Fit kit. It meant a lot of extra install time, but it was well worth it. The parts necessary for the install were: Gen II Compac evaporator, drier with trinary switch, compressor, bulkhead fitting, condenser, block-off plate (not shown), hose kit, and control panel. The Gen II Series features fully electronic servomotor operation that eliminates reliance on engine vacuum or original control cables. The Gen II also utilizes an adjustable heater control valve to give you that "just right" temperature year-round.

and compressors. Vintage Air offers custom accessory brackets for separate components, or the compact Front Runner accessory drive package.

Installing a Vintage Air Sure Fit kit or a custom-tailored kit is quite an extensive process. The three major installation hurdles are the refrigerant/ air conditioning system, the electrical system (for operating controls, safety system, and thermostatic system), and the engine coolant system (where the heat comes from). Some of the processes for installing a custom-tailored kit are covered in the following series of photographs.

BUYING PARTS AND FINDING INFORMATION

Purchasing Parts

If you're building a Restomod, you're going to need parts. Some parts might be used, but some will need to be new. There are many different sources for parts these days. More manufacturers are making parts than ever before. You can save some money by buying from mail-order warehouses, but you can buy from your local speed shop to support your local economy and get expert advice. Automotive swap meets are a great place to get a good deal on hard-to-find parts. With the Internet growing, options for purchasing what you want or need has increased. Most of the parts you need are available from one or more sources.

If you have a local speed shop, support them. They can't always beat the prices advertised by mail-order companies, but they often have the parts in stock, and they can usually provide you with quality technical advice.

Mail-Order Warehouses

Everyone is familiar with mail-order warehouses. They send you catalogs with ridiculously low prices on all the parts you need for your car. They can offer these low prices because they buy their parts in bulk. They may buy 250 (or more) small-block Ford Edelbrock Performer RPM intake manifolds at one time. The manufacturers cut them deals because of the volume of parts they purchase. Mail-order companies make their money from volume sales and shipping and handling charges. Even when they say shipping is free, they usually hit you with handling charges.

There's a drawback to ordering your parts through mail-order warehouses: They don't offer the customer service that you can get at a local speed shop. Maybe you want a new carburetor, but don't realize you need other parts like return springs, gaskets, carburetor studs, air cleaner studs, hose, fittings, etc. Maybe you don't know the exact size of carburetor you need for your engine. You may need a little tuning help once you receive the carburetor. It might show up damaged from shipping, and you need to return it. If you order from a mail-order ware-

house, these issues are not as easy to deal with as they would be if you paid a little more for the carburetor from your local speed shop.

Speed Shops

Your local speed shop is a great place to buy new parts. If they don't have what you want in stock, they can usually order it for you. The parts may be more expensive than mail-order warehouses, but they offer services mail-order companies cannot. Maybe you aren't sure which part is best for your application. Maybe you want to actually

When you need help finding the parts that are right for you, or some qualified advice, your local speed shop can help. If you have a problem with your purchase, you don't have to deal with shipping it back. Support local businesses.

compare the part to a similar one from a different manufacturer. If you buy a part that turns out to be defective, you can drive back to the speed shop and swap it for a good part. What if you have a question about installing your part? There are always a few employees with the knowledge to assist you. Mail-order warehouses can offer lower prices, but they cannot compete when it comes to customer service. If you spend your money at your local speed shop, you'll be putting money back into your local economy. Some people actually spend hours at the speed shop asking for help, and then they go home and order the

Planning on upgrading to a 4.6-liter engine and overdrive transmission? Some salvage yards like Mustang Parts Specialties in Winder, Georgia are manufacturer-specific and also have engine and transmission combos fresh out of wrecked cars. They typically include computers, harnesses, and sensors. (Photo courtesy The Mustang Shop)

parts from a mail-order warehouse. Sure, they save a few bucks, but they didn't support the shop with the service. Speed shops cannot survive without support from customers. If you have a good local speed shop, support them by buying your parts there. That way they'll still be in business the next time you need a little help with your project.

Swap Meets

There aren't too many places you can get great prices on new and used parts, but a swap meet is one of them. Maybe you're looking for a good deal on a fiberglass hood or some vintage valve covers. Most guys get up extremely early to set out their parts, hoping to get rid of everything. Not all of the parts will sell, but they may be willing to come down on the price so they do not have to pack it all back up.

Wrecking Yards

Maybe your project calls for some stock parts. Maybe you need an interior panel that isn't available from original equipment manufacturers or re-manufacturers. In this case, you may have to check some wrecking yards. The wrecking yard can be a goldmine where you may find everything you need. If nothing at all, it is a good source for simple, small parts like bolts and washers. You may need a complete roof section or a complete firewall and cowl section. These parts are not available from reproduction companies. As time goes on, it is getting harder to find some parts, but if you search yards off the beaten path, you may find what you're looking for.

Some wrecking yards have wrecked cars of all makes and models. Others are specific to antique cars, trucks, or a particular manufacturer. These specialty wrecking or salvage yards help increase your chances of finding the specific part that you're searching for.

Some salvage yards have complete engines out of new Mustangs and Cobras with transmissions and wiring harnesses. Some of these might even have high-performance parts already installed. For instance, a 5.0 might have headers, cam, performance injectors, and ported heads. People have been known to find full-tilt

Some restoration shops have old projects sitting out in the elements waiting for billed labor to be paid. Some of these projects were abandoned by the owners. The shop can put a lien on the title and legally sell it to somebody else. Maybe there's a Restomod sitting at a shop waiting for you.

racing transmissions, engines, and rear axles in wrecking yards. Maybe you'll find a set of re-upholstered sport seats or a new aftermarket shifter. You never know what treasures lurk at your local wrecking yard.

Wrecking yards offer more than just the ability to purchase used parts. They're a great place for getting reference information. Maybe you need to know how a part was installed, which might be necessary because you are doing a custom installation on your project and need to see how a part is factory-installed on a car. You can see how a cup holder or a door panel is installed on a car or truck. A lot can be learned by removing interior panels on a newer car. You will get to see how the factory installs its parts. There are many new engineering ideas waiting on newer-model cars for you to soak up. Attention to these details will give you valuable information that you can use when building your car.

Maybe you need to measure the frame width or the width of a 9-inch rear end for a '76 Lincoln Mark IV. You may be installing suspension for a different vehicle, and you can get measurements from donor cars. Keep your eyes and your mind open to new ideas the next time you stop by a wrecking yard. Bring a pen and some paper to jot down information. You can try bringing a camera, but some wrecking yards don't allow them for insurance reasons. Check with the management.

Keep your eyes on Internet auction sites for car deals. Everything from projects to magazine cars show up on EBay. This beautiful, Popular Hot Rodding-**featured 1969 Boss 302 owned by Rick Flores wasn't on EBay, but cars this nice sell there every day.**

Internet

Before the 1990s, there were fewer places to buy parts for your car. With the Internet growing as it has, your options for purchasing what you want or need have increased. Now, from the comfort of your home, you can access parts manufacturers, warehouses, wrecking yards, distributors, builders, and other automotive-related businesses.

Internet auctions are also a growing source for finding the parts you need or want. With the Internet auctions like EBay, you can buy parts from someone on the opposite coast. It is like having a wrecking yard or speed shop the size of the planet, but accessible from your home. The seller posts his new or used part on the website. You can log in and bid on it. If you are the highest bidder, you win the auction. People sell small parts you would not think twice about throwing into your garbage can. They also sell complete magazine-feature quality Restomods.

Other less formal Internet sites have message boards with good car parts for sale. These message boards are not monitored or controlled by a secondary source to promote honesty. Most of the online buyers and sellers are honest, but you take your chances with any online purchasing, even with monitored sites. High-profile auction websites are not guaranteed either; if a deal seems too good to be true, it might be. There are some real low-down scum who think it's fun to post pictures of a car that does not belong to them, like a '66 Shelby GT-350-S, and then take money for the car without delivering it. Bid with caution.

Purchasing Cars

You may need to start your Restomod project by purchasing a car. There are many items to take into consideration before purchasing a car.

EBay isn't the only place on the Internet to find new and used parts for a bargain. Websites such as www.corral.net and www.pro-touring.com have Classifieds sections on their forums. (Image courtesy www.corral.net)

Unfinished Projects

Check around; you'll find good bargains. I saw an article once that stated over 70 percent of "frame-off" projects are sold before they are finished, or sold multiple times before they're finished. After participating in the automotive hobby for almost 20 years, I believe that figure. There are many reasons big car projects are sold before they are finished. The reasons range from loss of interest, lack of funds, life changes, and changes in overall planning. Most of the reasons can be traced to one problem: the lack of an original plan, or the ability to stick to it. Either way, you can benefit from purchasing a project car that has tons of money and hours poured into it. These cars are usually sold for less than half the money and time invested. This is a good way to save some of your money.

Purchasing an unfinished project car can also be a bad thing. It's possible the builder found a flaw in his plan or found some serious hidden rust or damage. An unfinished project might be slapped together with shoddy bodywork or inferior parts. If the car has a roll cage or heavily fabricated framework, inquire about the type and thickness of the tubing. Bring a tape measure and check some of the measurements for symmetry and straightness. If you don't have experience surveying a car for possible problems, have an experienced person inspect the car before purchasing it.

If you have a good idea of what you are looking for before you start looking, you might not make a bad choice. For instance, if you are making a Restomod, you may want to stay away from some unfinished Pro-Street projects. Some Pro-Streeters are easily converted, but don't forget, they are set up for straight-line racing. It could cost more money than it's worth to get the car modified for street Restomod duties.

Clean Title

Paperwork is one hidden gremlin to watch out for. If you are building a Restomod, you will be driving it on the street, so make sure the title is clear. If the title is not clear, you could spend an eternity at your local department of

TATE WALTHALL'S 1965 MUSTANG

Tate Walthall's '65 Mustang fastback was purchased as an unfinished drag car. Some of those parts were kept, but most were replaced in the pursuit of a car that could drive a straight line and around corners.

This blue 1965 Mustang fastback is getting a second lease on life. When Tate Walthall found the car, it was built for straight-line driving. He wanted a Mustang that would take any line and do it well. He purchased the car and took it directly to Campbell Auto Restoration (CAR) in Campbell, California. He knew the team there was capable of working miracles on specialized cars and had the attention to detail he required.

The 351W was already modified with the necessary parts to suit Tate's needs. It was topped with Dart Pro 1 heads, Edelbrock Victor Jr. intake, and a Holley 650-cfm double-pumper carburetor. The car came equipped with a set of custom headers that were in great shape, so they were spared, but CAR had to modify them to clear the clutch linkage. CAR built a complete exhaust system with a Bassani X-pipe, a pair of DynaFlow bullet mufflers, and a pair of Bassani front-exit mufflers. Some custom oval tubing was used to fabricate some side exit exhaust tips. Overall, the sound of the exhaust is very unique. It actually sounds like an expensive, high-powered European car.

To get the car rolling, the old manual-valve-body-equipped C4 transmission

The healthy 351W was already in place. Tate added A TCP Tower Brace kit to strengthen the front unibody structure. The modified Shelby hood scoop feeds directly into the top of the K&N air filter.

was ditched in favor of a Dodge Viper 6-speed. The 9-inch rear end was already built to handle the power, so that was left alone. Slide-A-Link track bars were installed for traction control. The front suspension was upgraded with Total Control Products' coil-over front suspension and power rack-and-pinion steering.

A hollow track-style front sway bar was adapted to help control body roll. Braking was enhanced with 13-inch Baer brakes on 1970-1973 Mustang spindles and 12-inch Baer brakes in the rear.

Pre-1967 Mustangs don't have much comfortable room for tires wider than 235s in the front and 245s in the

The Dynaflow bullet mufflers, Bassani X-pipe, Bassani front-exit mufflers, and fabricated oval side-exit exhaust tips all work together to give this fastback a distinctive, high-dollar European sound.

rear, but Tate wanted a wider footprint on the road. With the help of CAR, he chose 17x8-inch front and 17x9.5-inch Team III wheels, wrapped with Dunlop SP 8000 245/45ZR17s and 285/40ZR17s. Since the tire and wheel choices were made, and the stock body lines wouldn't accommodate them, some body massaging was in store. The front fenders were meticulously worked with a hammer and dolly for extra tire clearance. The rear quarters were a lot of extra work. They were removed and fabricated from multiple donor quarter panels that were worked with hammers, dollies, and an English wheel. The job netted big gains in tire clearance, but the changes are subtle enough to make seasoned Mustang enthusiasts take a second look to see how the car is able to handle the oversized rubber.

Tate's car had started with a good, solid body when he took possession. It was covered in "Arrest-me Red," but it wasn't Tate's favorite color. With the fenders and quarters already missing their paint and the car disassembled, it only made sense to repaint the entire car to a color Tate really wanted. An R-type front racing apron, Shelby hood, and function-

al side scoops were added, and then the car was ready for paint. Tate picked a custom blue and white from Gasurit. The blue was followed by correctly spaced, variable-width Shelby stripes.

The floorpan had been patched by a previous owner. Unlike most horror stories of shoddy patchwork, somebody had really done a nice job on this Mustang. The strength of the floorpan and body was seriously upgraded with the addition of some integral subframe connectors. CAR didn't cut any corners with this chassis, either. The back of the front frame rail was removed and .120-inch-wall 2x3-inch rectangular tubing was put inside the stock sheetmetal frame rails. The gussets were fabricated to tie the rear unibody frame rails into the subframe connectors. Now the car is solid, and since the subframe connectors tuck up against the floorpan, the ground clearance was not diminished. Further strength was added to the engine compartment with the addition of a TCP Tower Brace Kit.

The interior was completely restored to like-new condition with a few upgrades. Recaro seats were added to give Tate more lateral support when taking the corners. A 4-point custom roll bar and fire extinguisher were added for safety. A full complement of AutoMeter gauges were added so Tate could keep an eye on

This angle gives you a view of the bulged rear quarter and front fender. This was necessary to fit the Team III 17x8 and 17x9.5-inch wheels wrapped with 245/45ZR17 and 285/40ZR17 tires.

everything from the driver's seat. The electrical system was upgraded with a GM 1-wire alternator so the external regulator could be removed from the engine compartment and the typical visible wiring under the hood could be straightened up.

With the help of a great foundation and the hard work of the team at Campbell Auto Restoration, Tate's 1965 Mustang really performs. Now the Mustang can take any line with complete confidence, whether it has an apex or not. Some of the modifications are subtle, but overall, this car really stands out in a crowd.

The Shelby side scoops, hood scoop, and R-type front racing apron really blend well with the bulged fenders and stance.

Here's a pile of paperwork and letters I have left over from the seven-month process I had to endure when I tried to register a car without a "clear" title.

motor vehicles with little headway. Spending long hours and a lot of money on a car that can't be registered for driving on the street would be heartbreaking. Do a little research on the status of a car's title before you fork over your cash.

When I purchased my muscle car from a tow yard, I had big plans. It was a rolling shell. I started pursuing registration right away. When I went down to the Department of Motor Vehicles (DMV), I learned the car had been purchased by seven different parties within a 6-year period. I spent months tracking the previous owners and had many unhappy visits to the DMV. Every time I went to the DMV, I got a different story about what I needed to do. Every teller had their own interpretation of the registration process. After a few visits, I made sure to request the same teller (the one that gave me the path of least resistance). I had to attempt to contact all the previous owners to make sure they wouldn't contest my purchase of the car. I had to send registered letters to each party asking permission to register the car in my name. One of the seven parties was living at the address on the paperwork. The fastest way to get the paperwork straightened out was to come to an agreement that he would refuse my registered letter as if he did not live there. Once I had all the returned registered letters, I went back to DMV. Now I was able to transfer the ownership to my name. Since my car wasn't running, I had to register it as Non-Operational. The process was time-consuming and frustrating. If you're not an easy-going person, don't try this at home. Once the

car was registered in my name, I started laboring on it. The last thing I wanted was to find out the car could not be registered, and have done all that hard work for nothing.

Vehicle Condition

You might think purchasing a rusted hulk of a body would make a good start for a Restomod project, since you won't be ripping up a good car. Some think purchasing a completely restored car with the intent of turning it into a Restomod would be a mistake or downright wrong. Of course I'm not saying to go out and buy an original Shelby GT350 and Restomod it, I'm just saying if you found a restored, bone-stock '65 fastback with a 289, you might have a great candidate for a Restomod. If you spend more money in the beginning for a straight body, you might save time and money in the long run. Body and paint is typically the most expensive parts are of building any hot rod. Restomods are no exception, so buying a car that does not need two new quarter panels and a floorpan is a good investment. You can find rust almost anywhere under a vinyl top, especially at the base of the rear window.

Sometimes sellers are pretty good about making a badly damaged car look very good. A friend once bought a car with the entire trunk area attached with two-by-fours, drywall screws, and a ton of body filler. If she had known to look at the inside of the quarter panels from inside the trunk, she would have seen the

When purchasing a car, look at more than the top surfaces. The person who installed flares on this 1966 Mustang never finished the job. There is a 3-inch gap between the flare and the inner fenderwell.

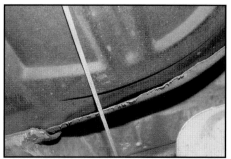

If you're spending a lot of money for a car, you probably want a car that's in good shape or repaired correctly. Arrange a visit to a shop with a hoist before paying good money for a car. If the car owner refuses, there's probably a good reason. These floorpans were not welded or sealed. This gap is just waiting for moisture, so it can rust even further.

horrible work. The trunk section fell off when she was in an accident. The moral of this story is: Check the inside of the body panels. Use a flashlight if necessary. Ask the seller if he or she would mind you taking the car to a shop and putting it up on a lift for further inspection before you purchase it. Check the bottom seam of the quarter panel from behind the rear tire to the tail panel. Check the bottom seam of the tail panel. These areas are often overlooked when a panel is replaced or when rust is repaired. Floor-panel replacement is hard to detect without putting the car up on a rack. Some body shops don't spend a lot of time making floor panels look perfect, since most people won't see them from underneath. Sometimes they leave the old rusty floorpan in place and put the panel right over the top. This allows rust to multiply fast, since moisture gets between panels.

If you're buying a 30-year-old car from just about any state, you should inspect the car for rust damage. Even some California-coast cars have excessive rust from damp coastal weather. When it comes to the structure of cars, there are many problem areas.

Getting Information

Information comes in many forms. It can be technical data. It can be a picture. It can also be advice. There are

When buying a project car, take a good look at all the parts in boxes and bags. This project car sounded like a good deal over the phone. A 1965 Fastback with a new tail panel and quarter panels already installed. (see next picture)

From the outside, the quarter panels looked pretty good. Upon closer inspection through the door jamb, the quarter panel replacement was a hack job. The job was done so badly, the quarters would have to be removed and reinstalled correctly. The cost of doing that would have been more expensive than the asking price of the car.

There are many technical how-to books available from CarTech to assist you on building engines, chassis, and other parts of your car. Even if you don't do your own work, you can educate yourself and tell someone else exactly what you want. Enthusiast magazines can also be a good source of information and inspiration. Most of the time, magazines include a healthy mix technical articles, product installs, and car features. (photo courtesy Travis Thompson)

est trends, while some try to keep more low-buck with cheap ways to modify your car. Cheap is good, but a line needs to be drawn somewhere. An engine rebuilt with 15 dollars and some duct tape will not last you very long. Most hot-rod magazines try to be leading edge, by printing info about current products. Some products aren't even available at the time of print. You may see a new dashboard set-up you think would look good in your car, or you might get to read about the addition of a modern Detroit powerplant between the fenders of a '66 Mustang. Either way, there are many tips, tricks, and modifications waiting to be soaked up on the newsstands.

People

Manufacturers' technical staff, speed shop personnel, friends, family, and other people can be great places to get information. Be careful. Get a second or third opinion before starting a project or buying a part.

Obviously, the manufacturer's technical personnel are the most qualified to give you information on what you need for your application or how to install a part they sell. They know the limitations of their products better than anyone. Be aware that you have to ask them the correct questions to get the correct answers. Some tech personnel want to sell you their parts and might not supply all the information you want. This depends on the company. If you're going to buy a transmission for your Restomod, you need to tell the company you have a 600-hp big-block and spend most of your time on the road course. Before you buy parts, make sure you let them know exactly how and where you plan to drive your car.

Checking with a competing manufacturer is also a good idea. It will give you an idea about what's available and what may work best for you. Do your research before buying parts. Impulse buying doesn't usually pay off.

Speed shops typically have at least one knowledgeable person who can offer great technical advice. Some speed shops are fully staffed with knowledgeable personnel. They can tell you which parts might be best for your application

quite a few sources to find this information. Books, people, and hands-on experience are a few options. There are many other places to get ideas and reference material. Keep your eyes peeled and your mind open.

Books and Magazines

There are many "How-To" books on the market. They have proven to be a good source of information and refer-

ence. I wouldn't have been able to write this book if it weren't for all the information I picked up in books over the years. In most cases, information written in books has been checked and is correct. But as with anything in life, it is a good idea to double (and triple) check information before starting any project.

Performance automotive magazines are also a good place to pick up new ideas. Some magazines try to keep up on the lat-

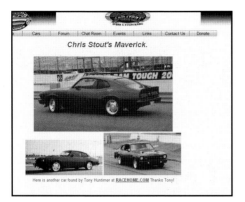

Chris Stout's Maverick.

Here is another car found by Tony Huntimer at RACEHOME.COM Thanks Tony!

There are a lot of websites out there that have good reference material and message boards with builders trading advice and experiences. The owners of the cars posted on this website are friendly and willing to share technical information on how their cars were built. They also have plenty of tips on how to get better performance out of your next upgrade.

based on good and bad experiences they, and their customers, have had.

Friends and family members can be a good source of information, if they know what they're talking about. You will need to make your own decisions on which friends you use as a resource of information. For instance, when I was 18, I had a friend named Chris Fogarty. He had already graduated from a technical school. He constantly distributed qualified advice that proved to be correct. I knew the advice from my goofball 16-year-old friend was not always correct. Even advice from my dad was not as qualified or as good as the advice from Chris. Deciding who to take advice from can be important to your car and even your life.

Internet

The Internet is a great source of information. It can also be a great source of bad information. Getting information from the Internet is much like getting information from your friends. Some websites have message boards and chat rooms. Be careful; a small percentage of people and websites post bad or erroneous information. On the other hand, most websites offer great information and reference material.

I could have spent hours going out to my local wrecking yard to see how the rear frame rail on a Mustang kicks outward. I went to Google.com and typed in a few words. Within 5 minutes I came up with this photo. Mission accomplished. (Photo courtesy Jim Henderson)

Corral.net, Pro-Touring.com, Stangnet.com, and Fordmuscle.com are a few websites in particular that are well put together. The message boards are filled with good information about every aspect of building and driving Restomods and Pro-Touring cars. Knowledgeable people frequent these sites to dispense good information about build-ups. Some of the people have finished a project that you may be starting. They might be able to offer advice on what works and what does not work.

Most of these websites also have good reference material. They have message boards with builders trading advice and experiences. The owners of the cars posted on these websites are friendly and willing to share technical information on how their cars were built, or tips on how to get better performance out of your next upgrade. I have been to a few websites that have some pretty brutal message boards. If you post a question that has been asked before, you'll get some pretty nasty responses. It takes a lot to warm up to that crowd. Not all forums are the same.

The Internet is useful in other ways too. I needed to do a little research on the Internet for some pictures of full-frame cars. I wanted to see how the front suspensions were assembled without going

out to the wrecking yard. You would think there are not very many pictures on the Internet of full-frame cars without their body shells on them. I went to Google.com, and instead of typing full-frame chassis in the search line, I clicked the little words Images above the search box. That takes you to the Google Images section of the search engine. This is very helpful. I picked a full-frame car and typed in Cyclone chassis. That didn't find much, so I tried Galaxie frame, and that gave me a bare Galaxie chassis for the first picture. I decided to find what a '66 Mustang steering box looked like out of the car. I tried Google and didn't have much success, so I went to EBay.com and typed in '65 Mustang steering box. It had some detailed photos of a steering box a guy had for sale. The photos gave me a chance to compare it to the steering box in my friend's Mustang. This works for finding a set of headers that might fit your car. You can search for headers for a 460-powered '66 Mustang. There are images of the clearance between the shock tower and the headers. That way, you can find parts other people have used with success. Doing some investigating can save you heartache and prevent your wallet from getting too empty.

New Car Dealers

Just like the wrecking yard, you can get new ideas on how to install parts and the latest technology by paying attention to the new car models. Maybe you will see a new cup holder or a third brake light that would be perfect for your car. Look under the hood of a new car. You will notice the trend of dress-up covers that hide necessary wires and hoses. Automotive manufacturers have found better ideas for wiring new vehicles. If you take a good look at wiring bulkheads and fuse boxes, you'll notice better components than those used on a technologically challenged 1960s Ford wiring system. Check out the fit and finish of the interior and external panels. Manufacturers have advanced in this area in the last 15 years. Spending a little more time and paying attention to the fit and finish of your Restomod project makes a big difference.

SOURCE GUIDE

Aeromotive, Inc.
5400 Merriam Drive
Merriam, KS 66203
(913) 647-7300
www.aeromotiveinc.com

American Auto Wire
150 Heller Place
#17W Bellmawr
New Jersey 08031-2555
(856) 933-0801
www.americanautowire.com

ARE Racing Engine Systems
8848 Steven Ave
Orangevale, CA 95662
(916) 987-7629
www.drysump.com

Art Morrison Enterprises
5301 8th St E
Fife, WA 98424
(800) 929-7188
www.artmorrison.com

Baer Brakes Inc
3108 W. Thomas Rd, Suite 1201
Phoenix, AZ 85017-5306
(602) 233-1411
www.baer.com

Bonspeed
3544 E. Enterprise Dr.
Anaheim, CA 92807
(714) 666-1999
www.bonspeed.com

Campbell Auto Restoration
260 Cristich Lane, Unit A-1
Campbell, CA 95008
(408) 371-5522

Chris Alston's Chassisworks
8661 Younger Creek Dr
Sacramento, CA 95828
(800) 722-2269
www.cachassisworks.com

Cobra Automotive
37 Warehouse Point Rd.
Wallingford, CT 06492
(203) 284-3863
www.cobraautomotive.com

Cobra Seats
USA Sube' Sports
17161 Palmdale St
Huntington Beach, CA 92647
(714) 847-1501
www.subesports.com

The Corral
www.corral.net

Crites Restoration Products
13155 USR 23
Ashville, OH 43103
(740) 983-4777
www.critesrestoration.com

CTM Engineering
617 West 1900 North
Farmington, UT 84025
(801) 451-5283

D&D Automotive
10 Alta Dr
Whitehall, PA 18502
(610) 432-0041
www.mspmall.com/ddautospec

Delta Current Control
www.dccontrol.com

Detroit Speed & Engineering
185 McKenzie Rd
Mooresville, NC 28115
(704) 662-3272
www.detroitspeed.com

Dyno West
664 D Stockton Ave
San Jose, CA 95126
(408) 298-DYNO
www.dynowest.com

DVS Restorations
910 South Louise Ave
Crawfordsville, IN 47933
(765) 362-1967
www.dvsrestorations.com

Eaton Springs
1555 Michigan Ave
Detroit, MI 48216
(313) 963-3839
www.eatonsprings.com

Esslinger Engineering
1930 Doreen Ave
S. El Monte, CA 91733
(626) 444-4919
www.esslingeracing.com

Fatman Fabrication
8621-C Fairview Rd
Highway218
Charlotte, NC 28227-7619
(704) 545-0369
www.fatmanfab.com

Ford Powertrain Applications
7702 East 96th St
Puyallup, WA 98371
(253) 848-9503
www.fordpowertrain.com

FuelSafe
63257 Nels Anderson Road
Bend, Oregon 97701
(800) 433-6524
www.fuelsafe.com

Ford Racing
www.fordracing.com

Global West
1455 North Linden Ave.
Rialto, CA 92376
(877) 470-2975
www.globalwest.net

Griffin Thermal Products
100 Hurricane Creek Rd
Piedmont, SC 29673
(800) 722-3723
www.griffinrad.com

Griggs Racing Products
29175 Arnold Dr
Sonoma, CA 95476
(707) 939-2244
www.griggsracing.com

Hotrods to Hell, Inc.
100 East Prospect Blvd.
Burbank, CA 91502
(818) 842-4360
www.hotrodstohell.net

Hydratech Braking Systems
26642 Haverhill Dr.
Warren, MI 48091
(586) 427-6970
www.hydroboost.com

Jomar Performance
211 North Cass Ave
Pontiac, MI 48342
(248) 322-3080
www.jomarperformance.com

Jones Racing Products
72 Annawanda Rd
Ottsville, PA 18942
(610) 847-2028
www.jonesracingproducts.com

Keisler Automotive Engineering
2216-B West Gov. John Sevier
Highway
Knoxville, TN 37920
(865) 609-8187
www.keislerauto.com

Koni North America
1961 International Way
Hebron, KY 41048
(859) 586-4100
www.koni.com

KRC Power Sreering
2115 Barrett Park Drive
Kennesaw, GA 30144
(770) 422-5135
www.krcpower.com

Kris Horton
933 West Vicki Ave
Ridgecrest, CA 93555
(760) 481-5542
www.carsbykris.com

Kaufmann Products
7591 Acacia Ave
Garden Grove, CA 92841
(714) 903-9717
www.kaufmannproducts.com

Longacre Racing Products
16892 146th Street S.E.
Monroe, WA 98272
(360) 453-2030
www.longacreracing.com

Meziere Enterprises
220 South Hale Ave
Escondido, CA 92029
(800) 208-1755
www.meziere.com

Martz Chassis
PO Box 538
646 Imlerton Rd
Bedford, PA 15522
(814) 623-9501
www.martzchassis.net

Milodon Inc
20716 Plummer Street
Chatsworth, CA 91311
(818) 407-1211

Mustang Corral
664 Stockton Ave.
Suite M
San Jose, CA 95126
(408) 271-2895

Mustang Don's
www.mustangdon.com

Mustangs Plus
2353 North Wilson Way
Stockton, CA 95205
(800) 999-4289
www.mustangsplus.com

The Mustang Shop
Federal Way, WA 98023
(253) 838-5851
www.themustangshop.com

Optima Batteries
Johnson Controls Inc.
(888) 867-8462
www.optimabatteries.com

Painless Performance Products
9505 Santa Paula Drive
Fort Worth, TX 76116-5929
(800) 423-9696
www.painlesswiring.com

Performance Stainless Steel, Inc.
PO Box 67266
Scotts Valley, CA 95067
(831) 335-7901
www.performancesst.com

Performance Suspension Technology (PST)
Box 396
Montville, NJ 07045
(800) 247-2288
http://www.p-s-t.com

PMM Automotive Services
903 Black Diamond Way
Lodi, CA 95240
(209) 369-2600

Powermaster Motorsports
7501 Strawberry Plains Pike
Knoxville, TN 37924
(800) 862-7223
www.powermastermotor-
sports.com

Price Motorsport Engineering
205 Main St.
Hope, IN 47246
(812) 546-4220
www.pricemotorsport.com

Promax Corporation
207 J.D. Yarnell Ind. Pkwy
P.O. Box 960
Clinton, TN 37717-0960
(865) 457-7605
www.vennom.com

Prothane
3560 Cadillac Ave
Costa Mesa, CA 92626
(714) 979-4990
www.prothane.com

Pro-Touring.com
www.pro-touring.com
www.g-machines.com

RaceHome.com
P.O. Box 8232
San Jose, CA 95155-8232
www.racehome.com

Real Speed Parts
14241 60th St North
Clearwater, FL 33760
(727) 539-7383
www.realspeedparts.com

Rare Parts
621 Wilshire Ave
Stockton, CA 95203
(209) 948-6005
www.rareparts.com

Revelation Racing Supplies
6445 Forestwood Dr West
Lakeland, FL 33811
US (866) 805-1875
www.rrs-online.com

Richmond Gear
1208 Old Norris Rd
Liberty, SC 29657
(864) 843-9231
www.richmondgear.com

Saldana Racing Products
3800 N. State Road 267, Unit B
Brownsburg, IN 46112
(317) 852-4193
www.saldanaracingproducts.com

Safecraft Safety Equipment
5165-C Commercial Circle
Concord, CA 94520
(800) 400-2259
www.safecraft.com

Scott Drake Enterprises
3101 Camino Del Sol
Oxnard, CA 93030
(800) 999-0289
www.scottdrake.com

Setrab Oil Coolers
P.O. Box 419
3958 North SR3
Sunbury, OH 43074
www.setrab.com

Speed Merchant
345 Lincoln Ave
San Jose, CA 95126
(408) 295-0930
www.speedmerchant.com

Speedway Engineering
13040 Bradley Ave
Sylmar, CA 91342
(818) 362-5865
www.1speedway.com

Stambar Stabilizers
5701-A Garst Rd
Modesto, CA 95357
(888) SWAYBAR
www.swaybar.com

Too High PSI
www.toohighpsi.com

Total Control Products
A CA-Chassisworks Brand
8661 Younger Creek Dr
Sacramento, CA 95828
(916) 388-0288
www.totalcontrolproducts.com

U.S. Bodysource
9009 South East C.R. 325
Hampton, FL 32044
(352) 468-2203
www.usbody.com

Vintage Air
18865 Goll St.
San Antonio, TX 78266
(800) 862-6658
www.vintageair.com

Windsor-Fox Performance Eng.
PO Box 2683
Apple Valley, CA 92307
(760) 946-FUEL
www.windsor-fox.com

Wurth-It Designs
3295 San Marco Place
Clifton, CO 81520
(970) 434-7123
www.wurthitdesigns.com

XRP
5630 Imperial Hwy.
South Gate, CA 90280
(562) 861-4765
www.xrp.com

Year One
P. O. Box 521
Braselton, GA 30517
(800) 932-7633
www.yearone.com